UNWILLING JOURNEY

UNWILLING JOURNEY

A Diary from Russia

HELMUT GOLLWITZER

THE MUHLENBERG PRESS
Philadelphia

First published
by Chr. Kaiser Verlag,
Munich 1951, with the title
. . . und führen, wohin du nicht willst
(. . . and carry thee whither thou wouldest not.)
Translated by E. M. Delacour with help
in the early part from Robert Fenn.
First published in English September 1953
Reprinted November 1953
Reprinted March 1954

Made and printed in Great Britain by
William Clowes and Sons, Limited
London and Beccles

CONTENTS

FOREWORD

"HELMUT, you must put that in your book!" That was what my friends always said when anything out of the ordinary happened during our captivity. Some of those happenings I have really written about in this book. Other men experienced a good deal in Russia that was even more extraordinary, and often worse, than what I myself experienced; many were better equipped than I to penetrate into the real life of the Russian people, either because they spoke the language better or because they had more opportunities. So plenty of people could tell you more than I am able to. For that reason I have confined myself to describing my own experiences, and have no intention of trying to compete with those who know Russia so much better than I do. In such an account I shall obviously have to refer continually to what affected me in particular; yet it may, even so, be of value, since my personal experiences during captivity may give you some idea of what so many of our men and women had to endure during those years, and also what conclusions we were able to draw from it all and what helped us most. Even if all the experiences and conditions which I describe were not exactly the same for everyone, yet many a personal experience does apply to a great many people.

It was for this reason that I allowed myself to be persuaded by some of my friends to spend a few weeks of my holiday writing down all that follows. It was done quickly and I had no time to get it into better shape and to polish it. I was faced with the choice of either writing it in later years in a more polished form or of writing it now while it is still fresh in my mind. I felt that I ought to choose the latter course and, for the benefit of a wider public, set down in writing all the stories which I have so far recounted orally, so long as I and others remember all that has happened. This account may perhaps help many people to study these experiences and to draw their own conclusions.

9

Of necessity it has in many places become a political book. Nobody describing their life in the Soviet Union can avoid giving some political judgments. His only choice is between giving a perfunctory or a very detailed explanation, and I have chosen the latter. To many people my judgments may seem too unfavourable, to others not unfavourable enough. The man to whom Communism has never presented any problem will be able to rub his hands in glee and assert that he has been right all along in rejecting it. However, those who cannot so easily reject this disturbing creed and who have pinned their hopes to it because all the injustice and exploitation in this world have become a thorn in their flesh with which they cannot come to terms— these are the people whom, while I was in Russia, I came to regard as the men whose questions I should have to answer when I returned, and to whom I should have to give information about what I had found there. I am sorry enough that this information is as it is.

During all the political struggles going on in Germany at the moment we are hearing everywhere the slanderous nonsense that bourgeois politicians are calling on us to "fight against Marxism", and that by Marxists they mean the Social Democrats; therefore I am forced to point out emphatically that wherever Marxism is mentioned in this book I mean dogmatic Marxism as a politico-philosophical system whose genuine heirs, in spite of all its modifications, are to be found only among the Leninists. Those who, like the Social Democrats, only take over single ideas from the Marxist philosophy, are not real Marxists.

Part II, which is devoted mainly to political discussion, is of course only a fictitious diary, since we were not allowed to bring anything we had written out of the Soviet Union. I have chosen this style in order to show the different stages in the development of my opinions, which, as you will see, were by no means prejudiced at first. I have altered the names of most of the men to whom I talked, in order not to endanger them. All the conversations, however, are based on real ones; those with whom I had them will no doubt be able to recall them.

Of life in Russia I am describing only what I myself was able to observe. In this respect my account seems to me to need filling out, especially as regards the short section about religion and the Church in Russia. Others will no doubt be able to add to it. I will therefore give the titles of some books by people who have a deeper knowledge of Russia, books in which you will find confirmation of my own observations: Ernst Jucker, *Erlebtes Russland* (Verlag Haupt, Berne, 1945—though not up-to-date in every detail); Margarete Buber-Neumann, *In den Gefängnissen Stalins und Hitlers* (Munich, 1949); Karl Esca, *Fünf Jahreszeiten* (Stuttgart, 1951); and K. Ackermann, *Das Land der stummen Millionen* (Tübingen, 1951).

This book may serve to remind us of those thousands who are still held in Soviet camps, contrary to all justice and human rights, and to keep their memory alive and painful to us. May every reader ask himself what he can do for them and their families.

HELMUT GOLLWITZER

Bonn am Rhein
On the 12th anniversary of the
outbreak of war, 1 Sept. 1951

NOTES ON SOME
RUSSIAN NAMES

M.W.D. (N.K.V.D.)—Ministry of the Interior, in its strictest sense the police organisation incorporated in the Ministry under Beria, and having regular troops attached to it, resembling the Gestapo and the S.S. Totenkopf. The P.O.W. administration came under this organisation. When the P.O.W. spoke of the N.K.V.D. he meant mostly the Third or Operational Division, the successor of the G.P.U. and the earlier Chekists.

NATSHALNIK.—Leader, head; now every responsible manager of a factory or of a department in a factory.

O.K.—Unfit for work. (Abbreviation of the Russian for "convalescent group").

PLENNI—Prisoner (VP in Russian letters on the left sleeve = *Voyennoplenni* = P.O.W.).

PRIKAS—Command.

SAKLJUTSHONNYI—Literally: one locked up, therefore a civilian prisoner.

STARSHIJ—President, i.e. responsible spokesman or leader of a group, brigade or camp, etc.

ORDENSBURG—A special school for the education and political training of young Nazis. Most of the "Junkers"—the pupils—later went into the S.S. or other special groups.

I

IN THE
LABOUR
CAMP

I

ARREST

A little greying beard, friendly eyes behind gold-rimmed glasses, trousers carefully creased—the oldish man who stopped me looked so obviously civilian, in spite of his partisan's armlet, that it seemed a pity to quarrel with him. His demand that I should hand over my pistol was more a suggestion than an order. He hastened to add that the streets were everywhere guarded by patrols, who would kill me if they found me in possession of arms. From the houses of the village a few people were looking out. I seemed to be the only German for miles, and it seemed strange, too, that there was no shooting anywhere.

There seemed no alternative: I unbuckled my pistol, feeling annoyed that I had cleaned it so carefully that morning, and handed it over. He lowered the German automatic that he had been pointing threateningly at me—I wondered how he would have handled it if he had really needed to use it—and gave my pistol to a young fellow standing near, who began fingering it proudly, so that I suggested that at least he should point it the other way.

"Has a German ambulance passed this way?" I asked the old man.

"Yes, at least twenty minutes ago, and since then only a few pedestrians."

I asked whether he thought that the war was over now. He said, "Yes, you Germans have had it."

Did he think that the Czechs would fare any better? That depended, he said, on whether they recovered their freedom, and he thought that by no means certain.

"I have always hoped you would," I said.

He shook hands and wished me a safe return home. We parted like old friends.

A safe return could by no means be taken for granted. Half an hour ago we had been driving in a long column through a village that had just been shot up by the S.S., and had pulled up because of some shooting in front. The Czech population had behaved so calmly during our whole retreat, that I was sure that this time also the shooting was due just to nervousness on the part of the country people. As it got more and more furious, however, I jumped out of the lorry and lay down in a ditch beside a fellow who was shooting wildly across the fields. I asked him what he was shooting at. He pointed out a moving figure in the green cornfield and took aim again. I knocked his gun-barrel down. Then the man in the cornfield started to shout and came up cursing. It was a German soldier. Once again the country people had been seeing phantoms. The two wounded men that were brought in were no doubt victims of their own confusion. That did not prevent a subaltern shooting down in a blind rage an old Czech in the next village on his way to church. The old man lay crumpled in the gutter, his prayer-book clasped in his hand, his face in the dust. When the officer tried to climb into our lorry afterwards, our fellows pushed him off. We would have nothing to do with murderers.

Then we had driven on until we found the road blocked in another village. By the roadside stood an abandoned supply-truck being busily looted. I ran across and filled my haversack with tins of jam, and was just stuffing a couple of bottles of brandy into my pockets, when our column suddenly started off, and before I could climb down from the truck with my loot, it had passed by and I was left standing there alone.

Nothing draws people together more than disaster. I could imagine nothing worse than to have to face the future without my comrades. Now they were gone, those splendid fellows, with whom I had shared the field dressing-station and all the adventures of many retreats, and all those precious little personal possessions in haversack and kitbag. They were gone, and there was little likelihood of finding them again. I went on alone, occasionally overtaken by a hurrying German truck; then the road remained empty until I reached this village, where the armed civilian demanded my pistol.

Now I was disarmed—not entirely, of course. I had another pistol in my pocket. It is best to have something of the sort for emergencies. But why should it be? Up till now I had got through this horrible war without using a weapon against anyone, and had I got to make up for it now? Against the partisans? In self-defence? What about self-defence? Does that justify what is otherwise forbidden? Somebody tries to kill me: I get in first and kill him. It is he or I—just like that. Providing, that is, that death is something that must be avoided at all costs. That also justifies what he is trying to do to me, so no sensible man would react otherwise. But the Sermon on the Mount says something quite different, so there is, after all, another way. Perhaps that way might be more sensible, for it promises more in heaven and on earth. Perhaps, I thought, the Russians or the partisans, who are trying to catch you, need someone to sacrifice himself for once, rather than to fight, to suffer injury rather than to injure. Self-defence is solely in one's own interest. It implies an attitude fundamentally different from that of the Sermon on the Mount. Our ethics mostly evade the real issue. They try to justify self-defence. But clearly this is a false, un-Christlike reaction, the reaction of one who is already defeated, who is subject to the situation, not master of it, and who is still afraid. I won't throw the pistol away yet, I thought, while I think this over as I walk along. I will postpone the decision: it is pleasant not to have finally decided, to have the alternatives still open, the good and the evil, the Christian and the un-Christian.

It is the most beautiful Ascension Day of the century. Clean air to breathe in freedom and the sun to greet you with every step. Battlefields have become countryside again. I feel fine. The woods are undamaged; above the grass of the clearings insects are humming. This is what the world looks like in peace time. The war is over; the shame is past. No, not yet completely done with: it will remain long in memory, but those who betrayed us are gone, and we can seek a fresh start. And yet the war is not over for us: my friends and I are still being hunted. The private war of the Schörner army, going on two days after the surrender, was the last crime of these criminally foolish leaders, for which we must now pay the penalty.

While all this is passing through my mind, my resolve to think only of pleasant things breaks down. I find myself wondering again what is going to happen. I do not yet expect to be taken prisoner, but it is already clear to me that whatever may happen, imprisonment or death, is connected with my having allowed myself to be persuaded to put on this hated uniform. I had done so without any qualms of conscience, and not just out of weakness. No clear voice had encouraged me to take any other course. In the general madness there were sensible things I could do. But this uniform had not only been a burden that I did not know how to get rid of with a clear conscience: it had also saved me from a lot of trouble. I had not only suffered through it: I had also profited by it. We had been fed when the civilians starved. We had slept in a warm room while the peasants slept in the stable. Those who refused military service had been flogged and shot, or had died in penal battalions. Nothing like that had ever happened to me. And now all that has to be paid for. That seems to me quite fair. What the uniform had spared me it must now pay back, and it did not seriously occur to me to try to escape this. I could not believe that any merit acquired previously by opposing the Third Reich could now give me any claim to preferential consideration, for I had voluntarily put on Hitler's uniform, and would probably have done so ten times over with a clear conscience. I had lived on it, and must now pay the price. That seems a rather primitive theology, but I often returned to it when in later years rebellious thoughts arose in my mind. There seems to be a certain amount of sense in this balancing of accounts, and after all we do like not only to believe in the reasonableness of our fate, but also to see the sense in it.

10 May 1945 *Afternoon*

We are together again, my friends, my belongings and I, and we are glad beyond belief. Following a series of most improbable accidents, which I could not myself attribute to mere chance, the armoured lorry in which I was sitting got involved in a hopeless tangle of columns in the afternoon, and suddenly we came across an ambulance wagon that looked familiar. There they were—Gustav, the Westphalian hospital orderly, a friend such as only a Westphalian can be; Helmut, the Zwickau comic; Wilhelm, the fat electrician from Swabia; the East-Prussian bricklayer Rudi, who had heard just before the end of the war that his family had escaped safely from Königsberg; and Ludwig the waiter from Tilsit, the incarnation of the prototype of all waiters, not the sort in Paul Fechter's *Herr Ober*, but rather mine host of *Minna von Barnhelm*. We realised, as we embraced, how much we meant to each other of home—the last remnants of home, shelter and security in the great upheaval. We felt the need to celebrate this unexpected reunion, and nothing else would fit the occasion than one of my bottles of looted brandy.

Almost at the same time the rumour began to circulate that the Moldau was already sealed off. The Russians had got there first. Schörner's promise that he would get us across the Moldau to the Ami, after we had been defending for an unreasonable time at his insistence every little river crossing and hill in Slovakia, had proved to be his ultimate folly, and he himself escaped over the mountains into Austria, leaving us to face the consequences. He was arrested there in peasant costume by the Americans and handed over to the Russians, and shortly afterwards, still in the same costume, he passed through the gates of Camp 27/I, near Moscow, that I entered two years later. He was soon afterwards sent to Lubjanka. At the time of his escape there were still hanging on the trees in uniform or in stolen civilian clothes the bodies of those he had executed for attempting to get through independently to the Americans, because they did not trust his promises. We thought of it with contempt and disgust. How meanly this Reich was perishing! How its falsehood was revealed as it collapsed! The hardness that its leaders extolled ("Whatever develops hardness is admirable") had been the hardness of cowards, of place-seekers, of distorted minds. That was proved when its Leader let the

capital be burned for his funeral pyre, while he escaped by
suicide from the ruins, and his trusted Commander-in-Chief
fled disguised as a Tyrolean peasant. They all sought escape
either in death or in an Alpine hut, but none of them died in
the cause for which they had callously sacrificed millions, and
had demanded the uttermost sacrifice from us all. Not one of
those who glorified war and toughness had come and died
fighting with us in the trenches. Some time later, when we heard
that these leaders, with Goering at their head, had let themselves be arrested and be brought before the victors' tribunal,
and that they had defended themselves before this court with
long speeches, explaining and arguing, fighting for their lives,
instead of dying in proud silence, we at first refused to believe
it. How hard it is to accept unpleasant facts! How much we
hope for a pleasant disillusionment.

The comedians, who had conjured up great historic examples
in order to contrast Teutonic defiance of fate with the bowed
knees of the Christians, were now a pitiable rabble. And it was
better so. They had themselves prevented their notoriety
developing into a myth in after years. If our people were not
utterly demoralised, if they had not lost all sense of values, and
were not a hopeless prey to the gloomiest morbidity, then it
could never happen that these wretches, who were willing to
survive their shame, could be transfigured or could ever again
find a following. The shame of having followed such leaders
must surely lead to a critical examination of their words by
which we had been seduced.

The feeling of disgust that arose in me was, I knew, un-
christian. In God's sight perhaps the baseness of these dodder-
ing leaders looked different. He does not see only what the eye
sees: He sees the heart. Perhaps He saw many of these men
standing, not before a human tribunal, but before the judgment-
seat of God. It is a judgment-seat that reveals the truth. Now
they see themselves in their reality, deposed from their arrogant
position, shorn of their pretended strength. It might even be
that what seems to us base cowardice was in reality the penitent
self-abasement of those who see their ruin as a judgment of
God.

In these days my mind was obsessed with the idea of the German collapse as a gracious divine judgment. It was a question that affected us all, and I tried to bring it up in all my conversation with my friends. The 73rd Psalm had never been so clearly fulfilled. Could a generation, a nation, that had been through this experience, ever again be deceived by heroic rhetoric, by the claim to everlasting power? It was power more than anything else that had dazzled the German people. It was impossible to imagine that it would not last for ever—and it had vanished over night. Now every opportunist party membership, every perversion of justice, was having its revenge. In the last few years two sentences out of the Bible had proved their truth as a guide to wisdom in human affairs: "Whatsoever a man soweth, that shall he also reap. For he that soweth to his flesh shall of the flesh reap corruption" (Gal. vi. 7); and, "For with the same measure that ye mete withal it shall be measured to you again" (Luke vi. 38). Now the Germans were being measured with the measure that they had applied to the Jews. Would they see the connection? Was there ever given such a clear example of the often quoted Divine Providence? The reality of God, who is not mocked, must surely inspire the nations with fear, unless they were stricken with blindness. They had experienced a sign from God.

The Moldau sealed off—that meant at least being taken prisoner. We were on a broad arterial road leading westwards with no side turnings. The Czech peasants told us that there was a Czech control point in the next village, where a preliminary disarming was carried out, and in the next village after that a Russian control point where a final search for arms was made. And then? "Then," they said, "they will send you home. Everyone is going home. Stalin says so." To us that was like honey. But why not? What would they want with so many of us, anyway? Was there not going to be peace at last? Did not everyone want that?

Meanwhile our fear of the Russians was forgotten. We heard how correctly they were behaving, no ill-treatment, no shooting. For long enough the Russian bogey had frightened so many into choosing death rather than the prison-camp. It was not only the effect of Goebbels' propaganda. Time and again people had arrived at our dressing-station after fighting their way through to us, and had described to us the most horrible incidents. When we were in the Vistula I had bandaged a man with a bullet lodged in his head. He had been stood in a tank-trap with the survivors of his company and shot down by a Russian commissar. And I remembered the naked bodies by the Donetz, bodies of German soldiers that the Russians had driven into the river in the middle of winter. And I remembered also that Russian hospital on the Donetz, from which after the capture of the town a German officer had turned out the comfortable German prisoners to make room for Russian wounded. Fear of the Russians was partly the fear of oriental cruelty and partly fear of well-deserved vengeance. It was surprising how quickly it was forgotten. We went on towards the next village fearing no harm.

The Czech control had been perfunctory and correct. Our over-filled ambulance had been let off particularly lightly. In order to arouse sympathy we had previously put enormous bandages on the slightly wounded cases, and had tied on to them hospital labels with terrifying details of their wounds. At the entrance to the next village we were stopped by Russian soldiers. They were just starting to empty the lorry, with a good deal of shouting, when a lieutenant came along. He had a broad Mongolian face—he must have been a Siberian—and such kindly eyes. I began to like him at once. He showed friendly sympathy, when he saw our wounded. With a soft, gentle voice he asked for our weapons, did not make us get out, and at my request referred us to the major in command for a safe-conduct through the country beyond. The major was no less pleasant, a big stout fellow, who said laughingly, yes, of course we were all going home, "*Wsjä domoi*, all going home. War over, *wojna kaputt*." How often were we to hear these words. I began to get indignant: I did not want to go on without the pass.

It is true that in the market-place we saw the peasants lined up in long rows being searched for weapons and watches, but apparently they wanted nothing from us. The major consoled me. In a minute, he said, he would make out our safe-conduct, as soon as he had time. Another major came along: he might well have been in the S.S. He was faultlessly turned out, slim, with hard eyes. He took a fancy to our second ambulance van, in which we had our luggage and surgical equipment. He told us to empty it, put the equipment in the road, and wait. I showed them both the case of surgical instruments and told them how many thousand roubles it was worth. At that moment a Russian lorry came driving straight at us. I called out to the officers to stop it, but they just jumped to one side and laughingly watched the heavy lorry drive right over our stuff, leaving crushed boxes behind it. When they saw my rage at the destruction of such valuable material, they only laughed the more. It was Russian property now, they said, so it did not matter to me anyway. It did matter to me!

Slowly we learned the first lesson in dealing with the Soviet people—the worthlessness of their promises. It began to dawn on us that any sort of safe-conduct was just a pipe-dream, that a written document was meaningless, and that we were in imminent danger of being robbed of everything, and that it would be best to get away as soon as possible. The major was busy. We told the other Russians, who tried to stop us, something about a *Prekas*, a permit, from the major and drove off in the burning heat out of the village on to a fine, broad main road.

By the side of the road disarmed German soldiers of all types were trudging along, silently, slowly, in little groups. Nobody knew whether to be sad or glad. The war was over—that was a good thing, anyway. That it would end like this had been clear for a long time, so it came as no sort of shock to us, but what now? The Russians called out to us as they passed on the other side: "*Domoi*, comrade, all *domoi*, home! *Wojna kaputt*, war over!" and all with much good-humoured laughter. It was a complete army that was going past us towards the North, mechanised or horse-drawn—nobody on foot. A model army, that was the general impression, strong and well fed, the horses were well cared for, no lack of petrol, and what was strange to us, the many girls in uniform, with rank-badges

25

and weapons, radiant youth and in the best of good spirits, with music and singing. Their proud consciousness of victory expressed itself sometimes in clenched fists and curses, or in most cases in an inquisitive stare and encouraging shouts, without any trace of vindictive hostility.

So these were the "last reserves of Stalin, scraped together in the remote villages, the children and old men," as we had heard during the last two years, as we went from one retreat to another, the final call-up of the Russians. That was all we had to defeat in order to achieve final victory! Our captain, an S.A. doctor from Munich, had assured us of this in endless variations. Probably he had himself been stupid enough to believe it, or German enough to believe what the high-ups wanted him to believe. Now perhaps he was driving along this road somewhere. I wondered whether he was hiding his head in shame. How could he help being ashamed at the sight of these deluded Germans stumbling along on the right, while on the left this model army rumbled by? I saw him a few days later in the assembly camp. Like many of his sort he was full of excuses, protesting, ingratiating. No, he said, they had not really been in favour of this policy of deception: they had seen this coming for a long time, but had always tried to do their best for their men!

11 *May* 1945

An African climate! At night teeth chattering with cold, by day melting in the burning heat of the sun. The main road to Tabor wound through the hilly countryside south of Prague like an endless red-hot wire. And we had been trudging along it for a long time, because our last ambulance had caught the eye of a Russian captain. ("Gestern noch auf stolzen Rossen"— yesterday on our proud steeds). We had been forced to transfer the wounded to a lorry, but for the rest of us there was nothing but loathsome foot-slogging. With the greatest difficulty I had managed to extract from the amiable captain a slip of paper with some illegible Russian words confirming the confiscation of the ambulance. This I was later able to use successfully as a

Soviet *laissez-passer* with some Czech partisans, who could not read it either. We had nothing else but the heavy remnants of our kit. We jettisoned as much as we could. I was particularly sorry to have to throw away *Der grüne Heinrich*, the first volume of Thomas Mann's Joseph-Trilogy, and *Abu Telfan*. This latter I had just begun to read, and how often later on in the isolated concentration camp in the forest I comforted myself with the memory of Leonhard Hagebucher. He had endured ten years amongst the fellaheen near the source of the Nile, and had fared far worse than we. Should I not then put up with a few months? As First Formers we had learned "solamen miseris socios habuisse malorum", but it was not only for a few months: it lasted almost five years.

Yesterday evening we made an attempt to break through to the Moldau, and then gave it up for fear of roving bands of Cossacks. We did not know what to do. Should we turn off along the road to Tabor, where the Americans were said to be? Perhaps the Russians were there after all. Every Czech said something different. In our present unstable state of mind every word easily cheers us up or casts us down. The gloomy prophecies of a pessimist are enough to make us imagine ourselves prisoners for years. Someone reports that it is dangerous for anyone above the rank of lieutenant, so we get rid of our shoulder badges. After an hour or so I am so annoyed about it that I put mine back again, and wonder why it is that these badges, which have completely and finally lost their significance, seem suddenly to have acquired for me an exaggerated importance.

And so we trudged along the red-hot road. What a road! I shall never forget it. I often wonder what became of all those who were then united in a common bond of misery, those thousands of troops, in long columns or in little groups, the wounded lying by the road-side, thrown off some lorry, with plaster bandages, covered with dust and gasping with thirst and pain; the grandmother with the child, whose last few possessions were tumbling out of a burst bag ("Where shall I put them? The child must have something to eat after all. Give me a rucksack for Christ's sake"); the desperate mother, whose

27

daughter had started off in a car, goodness knows where; the South-German peasants trekking with worn-out horses ("They have gassed all the gipsies, so now we have to turn gipsy"); the road-side ditches full of steel helmets and equipment of all sorts, and bits of furniture and splints and flour-sacks, from which the contents have leaked out: jetsam of defeat, thrown away in the misery of general ruin. And above us the sun, the sun! God! Could it not be more merciful, where there was no water?

A Red Army troop surround us. They take a fancy to Rudi's boots, and he has to exchange them. That is understandable, because their footwear is miserable, and now Rudi has to pay the penalty for his ingrained East Prussian sense of duty that made him polish his boots so brilliantly this morning. For that he now has to shuffle along in a pair of old worn-out "dice-boxes". I suppose I must have shown my disapproval of this exchange, for the leader of the Russians suddenly drew his pistol with a shout and aimed it at me. I stared into the muzzle, and it somehow seemed a pity to have to be killed, now that the war was over. But that sort of thing was still going on, although the war was supposed to be over. "Potschemu? Why?" I asked, and laughed. "You can shoot me, of course, but you won't."

"How do you know what I will do, you Fascist?" he shouted, but all the same he put his pistol back into the holster and rode off muttering to himself.

That was only the beginning. In the very next village, in front of the church, from the towers of which the white and yellow Papal flag, the blue, white and red Czech flag and the red Soviet flag were waving in the breeze, two Red Army soldiers looking round cautiously first, because looting was officially forbidden, picked out Rudi and me at pistol point. Nothing could be done about it, and the others hurried on, when they saw us being marched off into the woods.

Anyone wishing to get an idea of the German people after the surrender, the beaten nation that was a nation no longer, a nation at which the rest of the world pointed the finger of scorn—all that focused into one unforgettable picture, typical

of all the rest—should have seen me as I walked into
Tabor.

In the last rays of the setting sun, there was no other German
soldier in sight. Those that had not been collected in the
assembly camps had crawled into shelter somewhere or other
for the night. The inhabitants of this smart and quite undamaged town were promenading in the streets past the gaily
decorated houses, fraternising with the men of the Red Army,
joking, singing, celebrating peace and freedom. Suddenly they
stop laughing, the girls cling to the arm of their boy-friends,
the children start to follow and are sharply called back by their
mothers. The shadow of war, of the war just finished, or of one
to come, seems to fall across the peaceful rejoicing of this
holiday evening. A single German soldier is coming along,
wearily dragging his feet, in a torn and dusty uniform, his face
covered with a crust of grime and sweat, limping, for on one
foot he has a flapping shoe much too big for him and on the
other nothing but a torn sock. He stares indifferently straight
before him, or up at the houses, or at the people, as if he is
unaware of his peculiar appearance or as if it has become
incredibly unimportant. Behind him he is pulling a little hand-
cart such as luggage is taken to the station in, or vegetables
fetched from the greengrocers. On it, back to back, facing
behind and before like the Hapsburg double eagle, sit two old
people, a man and a woman. She is dressed as a peasant, he as
a townsman. Both are only half conscious, swaying from side
to side, with eyes shut, gasping, and every now and then
collapsing in a heap. Then the soldier stops and sits them up
again back to back. Once the old man falls off in the dust:
once the old woman gives a deep groan. If the barracks are
much farther, it is doubtful if he will get them there alive.

And all you who see this, you on the pavements and at the
windows, why do you say nothing? Are you choked by pity
wrung from you by the sight of the defeated enemy before
you remember your hate and scorn? Or is it that you get a peep
into the future, the future of your beautiful town here, so near
to the frontier, where the armies of the two remaining world-
powers stand face to face, and are already growling at each

other like two monsters over a carcase that they have slain?
These miserable three—they are the people, the nation, that
has known better days. Their infant lullaby said nothing at all
about being carried alone on a hand-cart to die, as a nag that
can no longer walk is carried to the knacker's yard. All these
three, whether they liked it or not, belonged to the Herrenvolk,
the Master-race, whom only yesterday you were cursing. Now
the Herrenvolk are finally finished. There is no roof over their
heads. The children who should care for their old age—where
are they, alive or dead? None of this was sung to these three in
their cradles. This old peasant-woman was firmly settled on
the farm of her ancestors. What had she to fear? And this old
man was enjoying the evening of his life in respect and
prosperity. Where would you others be if you were Germans?
Where will you Czechs be tomorrow?

Those two Red soldiers had robbed me of my top-boots and
of practically everything else. The shoes I had found underneath the cart belonging to a party of refugees that had been
stopped and sent away with nothing more than they could
carry, leaving the cart to be plundered by the inhabitants of
surrounding Czech villages. The old man had been wished on
me by an Ack-Ack soldier and an Air Force woman at the
entrance to Tabor, just after he had collapsed in a marching
column. I had brought him back to consciousness and then
rang up the casualty station, which refused any sort of help. I
stood wondering what to do, surrounded by an inquisitive
crowd, and finally sat down beside the groaning old man,
intending to spend the night on the pavement, when a Czech
policeman offered to get me a hand-cart. I accepted joyfully, so
he brought it along—with an old dying peasant-woman on it.
I loaded them both on to the cart, which was much too small,
so that they were always in danger of falling off, and so we set
off. And if perhaps they realised what all this really meant, that
here a nation was reaping as it had sown, and everything that
belonged to it must reap with it, I thought that maybe they
would look to their own sowing and their own harvest. How
precarious is the present moment!

By evening things may be quite different
From what they were, when day began.

These lines from an old song kept passing through my mind
as we went on—a reminder of Him who today lifts up and
tomorrow brings down—on through the town to the barracks,
at the entrance of which my load of misery was taken from me.

The gate was shut behind me. Russian officers and sentries
were standing about, as they were to stand between me and
the world outside for five long years. I went in believing that
it was the first step towards demobilisation and home. When
the gates closed, I knew that I was a prisoner, and that the
bitter cup must be drunk to the dregs.

A few minutes after I got in I found my lost friends again.
In the crowd they might easily have remained lost for ever. We
took it as an indication that all these situations were intended
to teach us to see what all these many happy coincidences, on
which so much depended, really were—not just chance
happenings, but the dispensations of a benevolent guiding
hand. We stuck together like burrs. It was some days before I
pulled myself together and had a look at the hospital, that was
set up in one of the barrack buildings, and was overcrowded
with sick and wounded. The surgeon in charge, to whom I
offered the services of our medical unit, shrugged his shoulders
regretfully. "If you had reported a day or two earlier," he said,
"I should have been glad to get a complete unit, especially one
so good as you describe. I have now collected one myself, and
I cannot turn the men away. I could, however, find room for
you personally." I refused the doctor's invitation, because it
would have separated me from my friends. The misfortunes
that resulted from my mistake were greater than we then
suspected. A few weeks later the patients together with most
of the hospital personnel were sent home. My decision was in
no way a question of principle. Separation from comrades, who
represented both family and country, was a disaster that out-
weighed everything else that the hospital had to offer in the
way of better living conditions. It just was not to be. In the
event, instead of a quick return home it was years in prison

31

that were ordained for us. Our efficient Helmut from Zwickau was to die in Russia, Rudi and Wilhelm—I don't know what became of them. Gustav and I, by devious ways and in the manifold mercy of God, were to see our homeland again. Such was our destiny.

Within a few days more than forty thousand German soldiers collected here, because there was nowhere else they could go, and because they all hoped to be released here and sent home. The barracks with all its courtyards and garages soon proved too small to accommodate them; the camp soon extended far out over the fields and meadows behind, and it was days before it was enclosed in barbed wire and guarded by sentries. The men tried to protect themselves from the heat of the sun and the cold at night by digging holes or improvising huts made of planks, old targets or bits of derelict cars. At first there was nothing else to eat but what each one had brought with him, and that did not last most of them very long. Friendly generosity could not be stretched beyond one's own little group. The Russians seemed to be making no arrangements for feeding us, and so, as the hope of release faded our conviction grew that they were going to let us starve to death. As we were lying on the hard flag-stones of the courtyard my neighbour told me in a whisper that in a camp for Russian prisoners that he was guarding at the beginning of the Eastern campaign, starving Russians used to cut pieces of flesh from the bodies of their comrades who had died, before they were taken away. "Hunger makes men worse than animals, worse than animals," he kept repeating. "We shall all become animals, even that fat sergeant over there, but I don't envy him. The officers too over there in the barracks, the good-time boys, they will all become animals."

A text-calendar of the Moravian Brethren proved of wonderful power at this time. On the 9th of May, when all effective organisation broke down, and the retreat became a headlong flight towards the Moldau, the text was the summons and response: "The Lord called Samuel, and he answered: Lo, here am I" (1 Sam. iii. 4). Throughout all our subsequent

experiences this answer was to seem significant. The prayer of
Teresa of Avila: "I am Thine. What is Thy will for me?", that
had been with me all through the war, now acquired a new and
deeper meaning. On the 10th of May I received further illumina-
tion: "And I will put my spirit within you, and will make of
you such people as walk in my statutes, and ye shall keep my
judgments, and do them" (Ezek. xxxvi. 26). God knows how
far short we came of being "such people", but the promise
had been given, which made sense of whatever might happen.
Everything that happened was to help make me one of "such
people". Every attempt to understand the working of fate
broke down on the inscrutability of the divine ordering of
history, but for me personally it was quite clear. Everything
that should be ordered or permitted for me was part of the
purpose of God to make me one of "such people".

Up till now "walking in His statutes" had not succeeded very
well, but now God was going to help me. It was therefore my
concern to allow myself to be helped by whatever might happen. The words "such people" rang in my ears throughout all
the years and made sense of everything that at first seemed
meaningless. The text for the 11th of May confirmed that:
"The Lord hath given me my petition which I asked of him"
(1 Sam. i. 27). Gustav made a face when I read it out to him in
answer to his question: "What's the text today?" We were
stiff with cold, conscious of every bone in our body; we were
prisoners and hungry. All our prayers seemed unanswered.
But perhaps the little scrap of Christian faith that had grown
into my life, with all the prayers and Communion Services
and self-discipline, had been nothing else but one single
supplication—make me one of "such people". And "now"—a
wonderful "now", right in the middle of the first realisation
that I was a prisoner of war—"now" the answer to this prayer
was assured. And so on May 12th my ear was tuned to hear
besides the curses and orders around me, besides the death
rattle of a mortally wounded nation and the cry of the tortured
world, something quite different: "From the uttermost part of
the earth we heard songs of praise, even glory to the righteous"
(Is. xxiv. 16). The judgment in which we stood that let us lie

here starving on the pavement without hope of escape, was a sign of His long-scorned and presumptuously doubted justice, but only a token, not the whole of His justice. His whole justice is a righteousness that can be welcomed with songs of praise in the midst of judgment, a righteousness that does not cast out, but saves.

The text for May 13th showed me my unrighteousness. "And he (the righteous) shall be like a tree planted by the rivers of water, that bringeth forth his fruit in his season; his leaf also shall not wither; and whatsoever he doeth shall prosper" (Ps. 1. 3). And then, as we were travelling along towards Russia, and the guards told us in a matter-of-fact Russian way that we should never come back, but would have to work to the end of our days rebuilding Russia, all of which seemed to us by no means improbable, and when the life before us seemed without any prospect of "bringing forth fruit", this text seemed to me to shine forth like the morning star in the night sky. Once, when I was feeling particularly depressed, I tried to recall all the verses in the Bible about "fruit", and built of them a ladder, whose steps led upwards from the gloomy abyss into the light, and I realised that in Siberia or wherever else it might be, there would be "fruit" that no one could prevent me "bringing forth". "He that abideth in me and I in him, the same bringeth forth much fruit" (John xv. 5). The indicative, "bringeth"! No other power can prevent it, it is automatic! Life in Siberia cannot then be fruitless or meaningless. There also there will be people, and with them tasks to perform, and therefore fruit to bring forth, and meaning to life. There was no cause for despair, however sorely the heart might grieve for homeland and loved ones. The loss of them could not make life meaningless. Everything depended on whether or not its roots reached down to the right "rivers of water". And these rivers would not fail, they would be flowing there too, they were God Himself present in His word, that was speaking to us now so powerfully. Never failing, inexhaustible, living water! Refreshed by that one could endure hunger, even starvation. I found myself during these days possessed by an inward conviction, which supported me and prevented me from becoming an animal; it gave me strength not to think of myself alone, to share the little that I had without reckoning how long it would last me. Even starvation could only lead to eternal life. And often, when we were faced with the likelihood of that, I felt the wonderful power of this conviction. Those were times of the most intimate prayer, not for bread but for grace to be ready for sacrifice if He so willed. What seemed at first to be divine anger, was drenched with grace—as the text for May 14th, with its all-embracing promise expressed it: "In a little wrath I hid my face from thee for a moment; but with everlasting kindness will I have mercy on thee, saith the Lord thy Redeemer" (Isa. liv. 8).

19 May 1945

None of us who were in Tabor camp will forget Whit Saturday 1945. In the morning we were ordered to parade with all our kit. We were taken out into the fields beside the camp, trampling down the young corn, and were drawn up in long rows. Then, after an interminable wait in the scorching sun, some Russian officers arrived, including a general, and with them some men whose emaciated faces and marks of punishment told of recent imprisonment in a concentration camp. Slowly they walked along the rows, looking long and carefully at each man. They were looking for their former torturers, who might be concealed among us. The German soldiers grew apprehensive. "Perhaps they will confuse some of us with the men they want. People often look so alike. Who knows whether their memories are exact? Punishing a few innocent men would be nothing to them." And they added contemptuously, "What jailbirds! They have forgotten how to shave!" They did not know that in a few months they would look just the same! Whether the search was successful, I was unable to discover. When it was over the ten thousand lay down and waited. Since we had been in the army we had got used to waiting, and thought very little of it. But now the sky grew black, a few drops of rain fell and then suddenly down came the worst hailstorm I had ever seen. We could not protect ourselves: only a few of us had overcoats or groundsheets. Hailstones as big as pigeon's eggs came hurtling down. We put our rucksacks over our heads, put our hands beneath our bodies and huddled close together. The minutes dragged by. Now that the world had forsaken us it seemed as if the heavens themselves had joined in by shooting at us. With certain aim and with whistling force the ice-bullets struck our bodies like stones. When that was over, pouring rain soaked the earth and us. It did not occur to the Russians to let us go back into the barracks. Gradually the rumour went round about what they were going to do, and for the first time we heard the word which was to occupy so significant a place in the prisoners' vocabulary: "Filzung" (frisking), i.e. "kit inspection", meaning the removal not only of all weapons, which is usual everywhere, but also of any articles of value, all clothing not included in the camp equipment, all photographs in which there was a uniformed figure, all printed matter and all those trifling personal treasures, if they just happen to catch the eye of the inspecting officer or seem at all questionable.

This time it was carried out not only by Russians but also by a group of old prisoners (i.e. German soldiers who had been prisoners for a long time). Meeting them caused us considerable surprise. It was not surprising that they, as tried and experienced veterans, treated us like unsuspecting novices. What to us was a new experience was the way they tackled their task without any comradely leniency, doing the Russians' job with zest against us their German comrades, and incidently enriching themselves considerably with our property. We realised how brittle comradeship, morality and character soon become.

Not till years later, when I had been with larger groups of old prisoners, was I able to understand what I had so much resented this first time. I got to know men, who had been taken prisoner as long ago as the first few months of the Russian campaign, and who until their release in 1949 had been working ten hours a day in quarries and mines for years without a break and under the horrible conditions of the Russian war years, men who had seen thousands of their comrades die at their side, and who had only been able to keep themselves alive by fighting bitterly for their share of what was going.

36

Human kindness had not been completely killed in them, but driven into a remote corner of their hearts and hidden behind a wall of suspicion, bitterness and indifference. Only towards their closest friends had any feeling of sympathy survived, and the gentler emotions had vanished with all regard for the many conventional rules of attitude and behaviour that smooth the social life of a civilised community. But if you gained the friendship of one of them, then he was staunch. Any attempt to form judgments about the modern Russians should bear in mind that on a much larger scale they have been through the same harsh school of hardness and bitterness as these old prisoners. Only so is it possible to understand them and to appreciate what humanity they have retained.

While the "frisking" was going on by the main gate we sat and waited till our turn should come. At nightfall thousands who had not yet been searched still remained sitting there. The almost incessant rain, and being soaked to the skin, produced a feeling of misery, for which on similar occasions during the war there had been remedies, from the brandy flask to the consolation that the discomfort would not last long. Now the men were a prey to inward misery even more than outward. I crouched there beside Gustav and tried the remedy for such situations that so far had never failed. We talked about beautiful and far-off things: he told me about his children and the music they played at home; I told him about my last holiday in Switzerland, about the mountains and about Champex, and, in talking of the past, the present disappeared. Towards morning someone nearby collapsed with ague and cramp. I carried him into the barracks and got past the guard, and in the dawnlight of the early Whit Sunday morning I read the text: "I will not make an end of thee: but I will correct thee in measure and will not leave thee altogether unpunished" (Jer. xxx. 11).

Whitsun services were held. There were some German chaplains amongst us who had with some difficulty obtained permission to hold them. Of all the ten thousand only a few hundred of both confessions attended, not only because it was badly advertised, although the big cross that had been prepared for it was set up in the centre of the camp. Why did they not

come? Because they expected nothing from it. Only bread and
soup would have enticed them out of their holes. When men
are alone and have only themselves to care for, when they are
not encouraged by their wives, when the struggle for existence
is not combined with responsibility for a family, they have a
remarkable capacity for avoiding all serious questions and
drifting along on the surface. Unless some definite stimulus,
perhaps the sound of church bells, the singing of a chorale, or
meeting some strong personality, stirs their emotions and
starts them off, they turn over on the other side and go to
sleep again rather than walk ten yards. Without the expectation
of something important, something immediately connected
with their everyday life, they are at the mercy of indolence and
the ingrained popular rationalism with its negative metaphysics,
that is the philosophy of nine of our men out of every ten. As
the war went on I became much less hostile to church parades
than I used to be. The soldier is the typical mass-man. He does
not stay away because he disapproves on principle, but because
he has no initiative, because he only does what he is told to do.
The Roman Catholic Church, in its insistence on church
attendance as a definite rule, has understood better than the
Protestant Churches that the laziness of the average man needs
a little helping push. By leaving everything to voluntary
choice, we leave a man a prey to his own indolence, and so he
misses the effective help that the church service could give him.
On this occasion a great many of them missed it. For a long
time afterwards the thrilling text of the joyous sermon remained
in our minds: "The Kingdom of God is peace and joy in the
Holy Ghost."

The spectre of starvation had been just another product of
our fear of the Russians. What actually happened was something
quite different: the whole camp was reorganised, and divided
into regiments, battalions and companies. For each battalion a
cooking stove was constructed of petrol tins, the potato stocks
of the district were confiscated, the bakers of Tabor, the
population of which was rather less than that of our camp,
were made to bake only for the camp, and sell the townspeople

flour. We were informed that we should receive the same rations as the Red Army, and within a fortnight everything was working so splendidly that we were being fed far better than anything we were to experience throughout our years of captivity. A German staff-lieutenant said to me: "I think in the German Army they would have taken four weeks to organise that." Our health was looked after in much the same way, decontamination stations were set up, the German doctors and ambulance men were attached to each company and provided with some equipment, and medical parades were held. Our heads were shaved too, which we found humiliating, until we were gradually convinced by the shorn heads of the Red Army men that it was the usual thing there, because of lice. The mind was catered for also. A department of culture was organised with musicians, actors and intellectuals. Plans were drawn up for a sort of camp school, in which I was to look after Philosophy and Literature. A Soviet cultural liaison officer made an impressive speech in fluent German about the anti-cultural attitude of the Hitler regime, and the cultural revival of the German people, and the necessary purification of the German language from Nazi barbarisms. He recalled the spirit of Goethe, Lessing and Heine. Our hearts swelled. The vision of a new land opened before us; we saw ourselves playing our part in a new cultural development free from the poison of propaganda. Every assistance was promised by the Russians with the greatest friendliness. Politics were scarcely mentioned; the only signs of political propaganda were the political news on the newly installed camp radio, a few copies of the paper *Free Germany*, that were hung up and eagerly read, and a lecture from a member of the National Committee on "Free Germany". The Russian officers told us with a smile that the constant battering of Nazi propaganda made it unnecessary to do more: the Germans could now see for themselves the high cultural and material standard of the Soviet people. As a matter of fact we had not so far seen much to convince us of this; even here some horrible stories reached us from the women's section of the refugee camp. Only after a father had cut his two daughters' throats and then his own, were the outrages of the

Russian soldiers stopped. In contrast the impression made by this other more cultivated type of Russian, and our humane treatment, was all the stronger. Those outrages had confirmed the propaganda about "sub-human Bolsheviks"; these new impressions contradicted that and made us think. Thus a psychological factor was established, that might have marked consequences, not only for the individual, but for the whole mass of prisoners of war. Furthermore, the behaviour of the guards was a model of correctness; in the camp itself there were fewer to be seen, and we still lived in hope of being sent home, when the immediate post-war problems had been cleared up. That was what the general in charge of the camp told our German officers more or less on his word of honour. "Why you keep asking me? I not lie? I officer of the Red Army. I tell you: you all go home soon."

20 *June* 1945

"Human material", that is what we had been during the war, although the use of the words had been discouraged because of its revealing inhumanity. As "human freight" we had been travelling towards Russia for several days. With us went long lines of cattle, lowing with thirst, horses and sheep. The only difference between us and them, the last remnant of human dignity, was that we were more strictly guarded, and the gaps in our trucks more carefully boarded up. To find a comparison for this load of dejection and silent fear, empty stoicism and shocked despair, which was on its way to Russia, one would have to go back to ancient Greece and Rome, to the sullen misery and hopelessness of the columns of conquered peoples being driven away into slavery. The only certainty in our minds was that we were leaving behind us ruin and desolation. We had no idea whether our home was still there, whether our relatives, from whom we had not heard for months, were still alive, or whether we should ever again hear news of them, let alone see them. What was Germany? What was the State? What was the "Reich"?—all these spellbinding words of the quasi-magicians, from Möller van den Bruck down to the court poets of the Third Reich? The Reich was a lie, in so far as it pretended to be more than just these men, who were being taken as freight into slavery. It pretended to be the supreme power, that would give meaning to their lives, when all the time it had no meaning itself apart from them, and only in so far as it served them, instead of swallowing them like an insatiable Moloch. All this talk of "higher purposes", Germany as an "idea", the "Myth of the Reich", the State as a super-individual, in which small and limited individuals find fulfil-ment, according to Schleiermacher and Hegel—all that is a lie, just as describing men as "masses" is a lie. This idealism is just as wrong about man as is the naturalism which regards him simply as a speck of dust in the mass, capable of being reproduced at any time by nature, the loss of which is felt and mourned by himself alone. Both of these turn men into "material" or "freight". All these men who were rushing northwards beneath the Ukrainian sun, packed a hundred at a time in each truck, had been made drunk and misled by this lie, which had promised them fulfilment in the supra-individual State. They had all participated in this lie, when earlier on they had themselves seen long columns of Russian prisoners being herded like cattle, and had forgotten the individual in the mass. Now they were themselves specks of dust in a similar mass. Now they could see that the mass that forgets the individual is a lie. The truth was that this mass was nothing but individuals, each with his love of life and fear of life, his desires, his love, his guilt, each faced with the questions: Whence? and Whither? and, when he found no simple answer, pushing them aside. The truth was that the State and the Reich could not answer these questions, and that they lied when, with the promise of fulfil-ment, they had demanded from him faith and utter devotion. Now State and Reich had collapsed, and all these men bore witness, by the simple fact of going on living, that they had not given themselves up for lost, that they still saw some meaning in life—but what sort of meaning? If you ask them, they will bring out a few photographs and tell you about the people at home, who are waiting for them. The great ideas have vanished; the important things in life have shrunk into the little circle where love is. The young schoolmaster, who was lying beside me, put into words what many of them had discovered: "At school I used to set the older boys an essay to write on 'What is happiness?' I have only just discovered the right answer myself. Happiness is being with the few people whom one loves, and by whom one is loved in return. It is the same with you and me, and all of us here, and that Saxon over there by the door, who does the bargaining with the civilians for the whole truckful of us. But does happiness depend on actually being together? That is a nice point. But it is essential that I have somebody whom I love and who loves me. That is what gives meaning to my life and is therefore the ground of my happiness; without that I may have the wealth of Pierpont Morgan or the power of Stalin, my life is poor and meaningless."

And so this became clear: that the meaning of life was not to be found in the super-individual, where I am denigrated to just "material", but only in the "individual", in "I and thou", in personal love. But the mass disappears where love is. Love takes no count of large numbers: it sees the individual, and takes him seriously in just those things that are lost in the mass, but which remain for him as real as himself, his fear, his hunger, his longing, his guilt, his soul. Why did they bring out their photographs? Because nothing made them so happy as these. Here is a person to whom I matter, and who is concerned about me. Without somebody to whom I matter, to whom "I" am "thou", for whose sake the rest of the world is nothing, there is no happiness, and no meaning to life.

Young Hans, lieutenant in the Kossack-Division, do you remember our conversation in 1948 at Holzberg? Before you lay your surrender to Jugoslavia. What did the future hold for you? The crippling of this poor, gay young life. Who cared? Who even took notice of it? That was what you were asking, for the world went on turning, not caring if the Jugoslavs smashed your skull, or let you succumb slowly in slavery. One day the earth of the grave will dry the tears of your mother in Swabia, and the world will go on turning.

"God knows it," I said.

"I cannot believe it. He is too great. He doesn't bother about individuals."

"Don't ask whether He does. Ask first of all what it would mean if He did?"

"It would mean that besides me and my mother there was somebody who cared about me."

"What does that mean, 'cared about'?"

"Well it means that He worried about me like my mother does now, but God does not need to worry, that is human language."

"Stick to the point, we must be clear about this. Why does your mother worry about you?"

"Because she loves me, because I matter to her."

"Hans, you blind man, that is the simplest and most beautiful definition of Love that you gave so casually. If someone loves me then I matter to them. I am as important to them as they are to themselves, or as I am to myself."

"Yes, that is why one feels so desperate in our situation. You have the feeling that you are important to yourself and perhaps to your mother, or some other woman, but that is all, and to everyone else you do not matter in the least."

"That is the demarcation line between despair and meaningfulness. The love of God is the meaning of your life, and cannot be destroyed even in the Jugoslav concentration camp. It amounts to just this: I am as important to God as I am to myself, and as He is to Himself. Draw a cross on your camp bed, and repeat that sentence three times whenever you look at it. And take my Bible today and read it, and insert that sentence whenever the Love of God is mentioned. Then you will understand what the Gospel is, and the joy that overcomes the world."

What was peculiar about these conversations during the journey and during our period as prisoners was that they took place in the vivid circumstances of immediate need, and that the message applied equally to giver and receiver. For we were all up against the same thing in different form and degree. We were all victims at the disposal of a power to which we were of no account, which did not "love" us, to which we were replaceable specks of dust. But this position of being exposed

43

to victimisation was the appearance and not the truth of our lives: the fact that we were not specks of dust to God but that we were as important to Him as He is to Himself—that is what the Gospel told us, that is what we went on telling each other, and that was now to prove itself true.

There were practically no political discussions. Did Germany still exist? In Tabor we had read Stalin's speech, with the famous sentence: "Hitlers come and go, but the German people, the German nation remains." That had given us hope. But for most of us the world had shrunk to our personal fate. The life of the German soldier had been too hard during the war. He had developed a complete technique of using his time, enjoying every little bit of happiness or of relief, deferring problems till the morning and enjoying the present. *On s'arrangera*—that is a marvellous defence in life, in any difficulty to forget tomorrow and think only of today and the immediate things, a roof over one's head, some tobacco for one's pipe, a crust of bread in one's pocket, an undisturbed snooze in a corner and dreams—with such things one can live. The business man from an office in Prague had the misfortune, as it turned out, always to be graded C3, and only succeeded in getting into uniform five days before being taken prisoner. He found everything difficult, civilian needs and habits were a continual torment to him. I was very sorry for him, and glad to have had four years of preparatory training in the army for life as a prisoner.

I told him, "You are just RU."

"What does that mean?" he asked.

"Oh, during these last few years we have learned to divide people up into RT's, whose who are able to stand the retreat, and RU's, those who are not. During the retreat you could soon see whether a man was able to tackle each new situation or not. The RU's wilted like cowslips, if you did not keep an eye on them."

"And what are you? Are you RT?"

"Oh, definitely."

"Then let me stay with you."

"We'll see what can be done."

44

Then there was the young major, with whom I walked up and down during one of the longer stops, when we were able to get a breath of air. He could not live without Germany, he said. He was not a Nazi, or at least not more so than most, with reservations about the Party, vague remnants of Christian conservatism, a broad humanity, and faith in the Führer, which only began to waver when he discovered that Hitler was personally responsible for the liquidation of the Jews. That was a severe shock to him. Since then he had dreaded the end of the regime, and now that it had come he could not understand why they all wanted to go on living. I asked him why he did not commit suicide. "Cowardice," he said, "when I wake up in the morning I spit at myself." Or was it, I suggested, the thought of God? "I don't believe in God any more. The collapse of Germany makes nonsense of everything."

The same despair was expressed to me in similar words in the spring of 1943. We were sitting in a little town on the Donetz, a little circle of friends, who had for a long time been closely associated with the Church struggle. I had just come from the West, and had been giving my analysis of the political and military situation. There was a young lieutenant there with several decorations, a first-rate leader with long experience of work with students in the Confessional Church. Whenever I saw his frank, shining eyes beneath his mop of fair hair, I thought what a shameful sacrifice of the youth of our nation all this was. He suddenly burst out, almost as if someone had struck him, "If Germany does not win, the world has lost all meaning for me." To which his best friend beside him replied gloomily and poignantly, "If Hitler wins, then the world will have lost its meaning!" They looked at each other horrified and bewildered. Youth of a totalitarian state, robbed of its good conscience!

In June 1945 at Tabor, then, we were marched off and loaded into trucks. We travelled hour after hour through Austria, Hungary and Rumania, as far as Ramnicul Sarat, familiar to me from the days of the Rumanian retreat. Here we were separated from the officers and transferred to wide-gauge Russian goods-wagons, and taken on through the Ukraine as far as Briansk. Why did we not try to escape? At Korneuberg near Vienna we halted for a whole day. I knew the district well, and had friends there. The opportunity was favourable, but they threatened us that for every one that escaped ten men from the same truck would be shot, and we were frightened fools enough to believe it. Some actually did escape during the journey, but apart from a few beatings, and the annoyance of a few minor punishments inflicted on the men in the same truck, nothing happened: of course not, but we were not to understand why until later, when it was too late. The Russian guards had indeed no interest in diminishing our numbers: on the contrary they wanted to increase them in order to arrive with a full complement of men and, far from shooting any of us, they went out hunting, when several transport trains stopped at the same station together and the men were crowding round the water-taps fetching water, and stole from some other train. These unfortunate wretches, scantily clad on account of the heat, had to sit with us and bemoan the loss of their kit and their friends. Even they were better off, however, than the odd Hungarian and Rumanian civilians that were occasionally picked up off the roads to swell our numbers, when no prisoner transport came along.

The unloading at Beschiza near Briansk, the first few days in the half-finished stone huts of that camp (No. 7251/10), the biting wind of that unfriendly summer, the interest in finding out the customs of the camp and the habits of the Russians— all this and more besides, some better and some worse, many others have experienced. One important incident of this short period is however worth recording—the further individual inspections, and in this connection can be related what might be called the *Ballad of my Bible*.

Introduction. Any idea that in the course of these searches the Russians took special care to remove any religious books and papers is just as mistaken as most other impressions of the Soviet Union. There seems to have been some official instruction issued from higher up to let all religious objects, books, etc., alone, and the fact that this order was to a considerable extent obeyed, although it could easily have been ignored, shows that it coincided with the views of the Russian people. Of course it did happen that they took Bibles away, and the complaints made about this to the camp commandant were sometimes dismissed with a surly or scornful "No", but that was not the general rule. It was much more likely that in these searches the Bible or the hymn-book would be handed back with a pitying remark, "Oh, you still believe in God," or with a sort of timid shyness. There was never anything to fear through confessing that one was a Christian. It would have been considerably more risky in one of Hitler's concentration camps.

First Section. Three army huts: In the first we waited to be searched; in the second the inspection took place, and from there we were passed on into the third. It was all well designed to prevent smuggling, but so carelessly carried out, in the usual Russian way, that we were able to meet outside the huts, and those not yet searched were able to pass to those already searched any things that they did not want to be discovered. Here and there in the half-light figures could be seen sitting down with assumed carelessness and scrabbling apparently absent-mindedly in the earth, secretly burying things that they knew the Russians would covet, from shaving tackle to an army compass, in the hope of being able to dig them up again later. I, too, had concealed one or two things in this way, but books might, I thought, be too easily damaged by burying, and so I asked one of those who had already been searched, a lawyer from my former division, whether he would mind them for me, particularly the Bible, which I prized more than all the rest. It was a little "mustard-seed" Bible, a present from some friends who had emigrated, and I had carried it with me for years. He said he would gladly take charge of the books. "But the Bible, no!" he said. "I mean, you should carry the Bible openly. That cannot possibly be taken from you." I looked at him with astonishment. For the first time I realised that an angel can look like a little lawyer from Crossen an der Oder, for it was surely the voice of an angel speaking to me.

"Thank you," I said. "You need say no more. I know now what I have to do."

47

In the inspection room there were a number of tables, with a Red Army man at each, and everywhere junk-heaps of confiscated things. Presently my Red Army man came to the books at the bottom of my rucksack. "Ah! Fascist literature!" he said. Fortunately a Russian lieutenant happened to be standing near. He was interested in books, and turned the pages. It was an anthology of the lyric poetry of all nations, which had been published before 1933. He found a picture of Goethe and looked at it with great respect, then Heine, whom he recognised at once. "Oh, here is Geinrich Geine—a great poet!" Then he came across Pushkin and his delight was boundless. He began to recite some lines of Pushkin, and asked me whether I could repeat a poem of Heine. Of course I could think of nothing but "Leise zieht durch mein Gemüt", which I recited with a good deal of unction. He found it in the book and spelled it out as I repeated it, and suddenly we were oblivious to all else, on a little island of poetry in the middle of a sea of junk. Meanwhile the Red Army man rolled himself a cigarette, but at last he began to get bored, and interrupted our little idyll by handing over another book. At once suspicion checked our budding friendship. How is it that a Fascist soldier has no Fascist books with him? Fascist books, of course, are poison, and must be confiscated and destroyed at sight. He was finally convinced by the date of publication that an eighty-year-old "Siebenkäs" edition was scarcely likely to be infected by Fascism. And then he found the Bible and was about to throw it on to the junk-heap with a contemptuous gesture, "Why a Bible?" I looked on in silent surprise, sure that he would not really be able to do it, and just as his arm was raised to throw, he changed his mind and started to turn the pages over. Inside it he found a little Roman Catholic picture of the Sacred Heart of Jesus, put there in gratitude by a little Polish girl whom I had rescued from a burning house. He noticed it and asked if it was a Catholic Bible. I said, "No, it is a Lutheran one."

"Are you a Lutheran?"

"Yes."

"Why then have you got this Catholic picture in it?"

I told him about its origin, and asked him how he came to

be so well informed about the different confessions. He said shortly that there were different religions in Russia also, but what he could not understand was why I, who was obviously a cultured man, who read Goethe, "Geinrich Geine" and Pushkin, should also read the Bible. My Russian was scarcely sufficient to explain to him that it was the really cultured people who were able to reconcile the two things. Shaking his head over this dialectic, which was clearly too difficult for him, he gave me back the Bible, waved the Red Army man aside, and let me go through. Outside I passed a whole heap of useless junk that was being burned. On it I saw the remains of an old Silesian hymn-book. I took it with me, and felt myself the richest man in the world.

Second Section. Two hundred of us, including my group, had been sent away, first by train, and then by two days of marching in charge of a lieutenant, who was a bundle of nerves. At first he adopted a ferocious attitude, and talked about nothing but executions, and then began to develop into a human being. We arrived at a half-finished camp in the forest, and were welcomed by a hundred old prisoners. At first we were kept three weeks in quarantine, for that was the rule. All new prisoners had to have three weeks' complete rest and feeding up in order to recover. Pleasant weeks of sunshine and conversation and making new friends. But almost at once the spectre of the searching began to haunt us. We heard that here it was even more unreasonable than elsewhere, and so we had once again to start looking for hiding-places. There was nowhere in the huts themselves, for they were also searched. If we gave our things to the old prisoners, it was by no means certain that we should get them back, so, as we could leave the huts at night, we looked about at dusk for places to bury them. It seemed safest underneath the huts, which stood on posts, and so I buried my bread-satchel with letters and books, and in a specially selected spot the copy of Dante's *Divina Commedia*, which I had recently acquired, and the Bible. My faith had weakened somewhat, and I thought, on purely rational grounds: "You got away with it once, but what guarantee is there that you will do so a second time? Do what common sense and prudence suggest." I did so, and was immediately punished. The searching was delayed, and we were beginning to think that it was not going to happen at all, so after a day or two we dug up some of our things. My satchel, Dante and the Bible were gone. The old prisoners, who were allowed to move about the camp freely, even at night, or the Rumanian *konvois*, the Soviet word for troops escorting prisoners of war, must have stolen them. Paper was in great demand, not for writing on, not for reading or any other ordinary purpose, but for the first and noblest use of paper in Russia, for which it was providentially invented centuries ago by the Chinese—for rolling cigarettes! Dante had rather too stiff paper for that, but the India paper of the Bible was just ideal. I appealed to the leader of the old prisoners. He was quite decent and promised to do his best. Actually he brought back the satchel next day with very little missing, but none of his men had Dante or the Bible: he could assure us of that. That was my punishment, and I had only myself to blame for my loss. My immediate companions were almost as shocked as I was. They knew what it meant to me, and probably hoped for some little comfort for themselves from the presence of a Bible. Now the coming days, the most difficult in all our lives, must be faced without it, or at least without being able to open it and read it and discover new truths in it. The Word of God would of course remain with us without it. Had it not spoken to me through the words of the Bible for many years? It would be there inside me without the printed text. Wherever I was I carried on a kind of Bible study. In order to retain in my memory what I already knew, and in order to be able to call it to mind quickly, I tried to recollect and memorise the contents of the Bible from the first chapter of Genesis onwards, and was distressed to find so many gaps in my knowledge, and was glad, too, of what I could remember. But I could still not completely realise that I should now be entirely deprived of the written word. Those who despise it have no idea what it means to be without it. I remembered that day during my first arrest in 1937 in the cell in the Alexanderplatz police-station. After a few days this little Bible was handed to me with my washing, and as I held it in my hand, it seemed as if the prison walls were down, leaving me free and happy. I thought that it could now go on as long as it liked, for months or years: I had occupation and company enough in the Bible, as much as in the free world outside. And now it had gone without hope of recovery, and I was foolish enough to say to Gustav: "Gone is gone, and even God Himself cannot give it back to me, for only the Rumanians could have taken it, and they will certainly have torn it to bits and smoked it." But next evening, following a vague hunch, I crawled underneath the hut once more and hunted about. I found a spot with newly turned up earth, scraped it away, and pulled out my Bible! Dante, so unsuitable for smoking, was nowhere to be found, but the Bible was lying in a quite different place from where I had buried it. It had obviously been re-buried for some reason or other by that unknown Rumanian. So my period of captivity began with this assurance: "I will never leave thee, nor forsake thee", and as a sign this little black book of infinite blessing remained with me unchallenged in all the searchings, until I returned home.

Third Section. December 1949. Swerdlovsk station in the Urals. Our four years' dream was about to be fulfilled. The transport was to take us back home. Stephan tugged at my sleeve: "Come here," he said, "I want you to meet a remarkably fine man, Dr. S." I was glad to do so, for I had heard a great deal about him, and we had often been close together without actually meeting. He was the brother of a fellow-worker in Dahlem, who had been killed. He had won a great reputation in the prison-camps, running Bible-classes and even a church choir, and had, as a doctor, stood up for the German soldiers so vigorously that he had become a nuisance to the Russians and they had set him to work. He had just arrived from a neighbouring camp to travel home with us. We shook hands cordially, with a familiarity almost unknown in civilian life, and his first words revealed his chief anxiety: "In your prayers, please ask that the Russians at Brest may leave me my Bible and my music. I mean the motets that I have written during these years. You can imagine what that would mean to me." At Brest. That meant at the Russian-Polish frontier, where, as we knew, the most ruthless examinations of all took place, before we left Russian territory. Every scrap of written or printed paper was confiscated, even religious writings. Everything was examined to see whether any secret notes were hidden. Even the cigarettes were examined, in case notes were concealed in the wrappings. The bottoms of our home-made wooden chests were pierced, the seams of all garments scrutinised. The panic fear of spies, which was part of a system based on the belief that its very existence depended on keeping its life hidden from the eyes of the wicked world, had gone to fantastic lengths. I shared Dr. S.'s anxiety. Only those who have experienced such fears know how they can obtrude themselves even into the joy of returning home. Every time we met during those two weeks' journey Dr. S. spoke of his anxiety, and he so impressed me with it that I made a little bargain with Heaven. As it was clearly so much more important to S. to get his things through the frontier examination than it was to me to keep mine, I was prepared to sacrifice my Bible. I would forget my wish to bring it through and reconcile myself to its loss without regret, if only he could be allowed to keep his things. At Brest we had to wait a whole day before we got off the train and passed through the examination, and we discovered that the narrow-gauge train for Frankfurt a. d. Oder was standing waiting on a line near by, and that it was possible after the search to cross over from the new train to the old one and fetch any stuff we had hidden there to save it from confiscation. Unfortunately this way was not possible for me, because I had to carry my Bible openly, and because I had secretly offered it as a sacrifice. So it happened in my case according to my expectations. There was a long army hut with tables on both sides and an army security man at each. We paraded naked in front of them with our kit and were subjected to the most rigorous search. Bible, hymn-book, prayer-book, and a little Turkish Koran, printed by the German military authorities for the Turkish volunteer battalions, and so small that it could only be read with a magnifying-glass, all these found their way on to the junk-heap. The interpreter, to whom I spoke about it, shrugged his shoulders sympathetically. It would be quite useless, he said, to appeal to higher authority. The order to confiscate all written and printed matter was strict and admitted no exception. So I passed through with the sad conviction that Dr. S. also, who had been sent through a neighbouring hut, must have lost everything. I found him in the new train over on the narrow-gauge track, and said: "Well, there was nothing we could do about it, was there? Smuggling would have been too risky anyway. An officer in our group, who had some letters hidden in the double bottom of his case, was arrested at once and sent back to Russia. It is better to get home without a Bible than not at all."

"What do you mean?" he said, "I got everything through." I gaped. "How could that happen?"

He told me that he had spread all his things out in front of the security man, and when the man was going to take them away, he had appealed first to an interpreter, and then to a woman commissar, who happened to be passing. She listened to him, but refused regretfully to interfere. Suddenly, when all seemed lost, she turned back and said that he could lay the matter before a higher commissar in the room "behind the door over there". And so he gathered together all his things without any protest from the security man, went out at the door indicated, saw the commissar's office on the left, and straight ahead the way out from the hut to the train. Of course he went out that way, and here he was with all his precious possessions. I almost threw my arms about his neck. I was poorer by one Bible, but richer by one "sign".

Another thing about these searchings. To many of us they were one of the features of life in a prison camp to which we could never get accustomed. The harder we strove to maintain some little area of normal human living amidst the forced labour and communal life, by accumulating a few precious personal possessions like old photographs and letters that had somehow survived, or a few books, a notebook containing poems and jottings, or a Bible, the greater was our fear of the next search, when all these things would be at the mercy of the caprice of some silly or spiteful inquisitor, unless some timely opportunity occurred to bury them, which was seldom easy. This searching is the most unpleasant reminder that the prisoner is still a human being who has nothing that he can really call his own, no sphere of privacy, where he can do as he likes and which he can use as he wishes, and access to which he can control. Prisoners of war are examined everywhere. The special character of these Soviet searches arises from the nature of Communist-totalitarianism. Any private life is robbery against the community. Since a man is only a function of society, the isolation of a sphere of private life would imply a denial on the part of the individual of the interests of the community. Instead he must live completely under the control of the organs of society, which means in practice under the eyes of the totalitarian leaders and their secret police. Those cross-examinations by the security police and the confessions that the Party member sometimes is forced to make, are really the same sort of searching, but of the mind and heart, in which everything has to be displayed openly to the inquisitors and nothing may be kept back. Any tendency to revolt against this is attributed to bourgeois prejudice which has not yet been eradicated with sufficient determination. Nevertheless I should have very much liked to see how Dr. Karl Marx, born in Trier, and living in London as a scholar, with no definite occupation, would have boiled with rage, if he had been himself subjected all his life long to this sort of inquisition. In his earlier writings anything private is regarded as the greatest evil, the development of a sphere of private interests is man's "original sin", the Rights of Man of the French Revolution, with their defence of private life against the encroachments of society and of the government, were nothing but the idealistic disguise of the subtle egoism of the bourgeoisie, which will permit no interference with its business affairs. There is a lot more that might be said about that, but during these searches only one thing interested me, whether Marx, in his individualistic bohemian existence, had by any chance imagined this other side of the picture; whether he had any idea that the Communism which he expected would not function without these practices; whether he would not have been the first to prefer the hangman's rope or a rifle bullet to such a life. Who is to protect the world from Public Danger Number One—the intellectuals who propound their theories, and vilify existing conditions, and mesmerise the masses with utopias, and who airily remove the moral safeguards against the wielders of power, without considering the cost and disadvantages, and without being willing to bear the cost themselves? They did everything possible to encourage the anti-bourgeois romanticism of Left and Right, they lauded the totalitarian society or the totalitarian state, and looked with shocked naïvely childish amazement when the loosened monolith of power fell not only on others, not only on the bourgeoisie, but also on themselves, and crushed their life out. How many examples could be cited of such Fascist or Communist intellectuals! Thus, intoxicated by the desire to be freed by collectivism from the burden of individuality, they did not see that this collectivism is in reality the total power of other men over us. They did not ask what is indeed the most important question for us today, what can rescue my humanity from this power, supervision and planning, to which I am subjected, and by which I am reduced to an ant-like function of collective society? The last time I was searched I was able to conceal a letter from a fellow-worker in Dahlem, which she wrote to me after a long imprisonment in a concentration camp in Ravensbrück. She wrote that amongst the most important lessons for her in these days was the acquisition of "possessions that cannot be taken away". The more we have of these, the less power all searchings have over us.

2

LABOUR CAMP
1945-47

THAT forest camp, to which we had been brought for our first spell of labour, lay in the vast forest that extends between Briansk and the Desna. It had been laid out in a big square a few hundred yards from an isolated village which had been completely destroyed by partisan fighting. The inhabitants had crawled away into holes and caves. It was surrounded by a wooden fence protected by barbed wire. We had built some extensions, so that when we left it, it included four big dormitory huts, a workshop, a carpenters' shop, a forge and a kitchen hut. The troops called it *"Ramasukha—annihilation camp"*. This was somewhat exaggerated, because the number who died was, thank God, less than it might have been under the circumstances, and yet it was not without some justification, because, apart from a few privileged people, most of us were reduced to physical exhaustion during this period, and many had their health ruined for the rest of their lives. The fact that the camp lay within the area of the great drought that visited large parts of European Russia in the summer of 1946 made our situation considerably worse.

The camp was managed by a Russian staff of about eight officers under a major, with some non-commissioned personnel —the usual extravagant assignment of the security authorities for at the most 350 prisoners. On the German side were a camp C.O., with two captains and two sergeant-majors. We never attained the object of the P.O.W. camps, namely to make enough profit out of the labour of the prisoners not only to support the prisoners and the Russian personnel, but also to

56

swell the funds of the security authority. Forestry work, which was our main occupation, is too badly paid in the Soviet system, and only a very limited output could be exacted from the exhausted men. And so, shortly before Christmas 1946, the camp was dispersed, because it did not pay, and its workers were distributed amongst other camps in the district. In this way I arrived at a factory camp at Beschitza which had been set up when the locomotive factory there had been rebuilt. This was the biggest factory of the kind in the Soviet Union, and had been completely destroyed during the war. After I had been put to a variety of jobs, in the saw-mill, as a locksmith, or making railway lines or digging, my physical condition became so bad that I was transferred to the section for those unfit for work. Here I enjoyed for a short time a period of *dolce far niente* before I was moved to the Krasnogorsk camp near Moscow, which will be described in the second part of this book.

When we first arrived at the forest camp, it was just a wide space not yet completely cleared of roots, on which there were two half-finished army huts. When we left it, it was a complete camp, laid out with flower beds, birchwood seats and tables, so that it looked like a garden restaurant. And it must be remembered that only a very small proportion of the available labour could be withdrawn from productive work and used for work in the camp, so that most of it had to be done in spare time and with some help from those unfit for work, the so-called "O.K." people. Work took most of our time. We had to listen to lectures in which every sentence contained the word "work", "Rabota, rabota", like the droning of a Tibetan prayer-wheel. It is certainly not true that in the Soviet Union there is a fanatical devotion to work, a disease to which the German is more susceptible than the Russian, but there is certainly a work-fetishism, which has taken the place of the property-fetishism of the capitalist countries. Work is a god, from whom one expects everything, and whom everyone must worship, but whom one also tries to cheat and deceive, like other gods. You preach about it to others, but you hope to wax fat on the offerings that you exhort others to make, and you try to reduce your own obligations to the ritual performance of ceremonial—the appearance of work. It is a religion, with its priests, who grow fat on the sacrifices, and in which its adherents are fleeced, as in other religions. This time it was to us German prisoners of war that the religion of work was preached. We should not have been Germans had this seed not fallen on fruitful ground, in spite of hunger, constant deception over wages and in spite of the apathy of the slave. It is astonishing what these three hundred prisoners alone achieved in two years in that camp under the harshest living conditions. This district had been fought over by the partisans, the villages had been burned down several times, and the population had crawled away to hide in holes in the ground. After two years the village had been rebuilt and a long motor-road made of tree-trunks leading into the forest for the lorries that carried the logs. Many thousands of cubic metres of wood had been cut down, carted away and cut up in the saw-mill, a performance that can only be explained by a combination of two factors, the work morale that against all reason had asserted itself again and again, and the Soviet methods of forced labour. They know how to get work out of a man even against his will. The idea is never to let a man have enough to eat, and at the same time to hold out to him the prospect of getting enough. In addition, every effort is made to drive a wedge into the group solidarity of fellow-sufferers by a system of individual stimuli, so that even the weakest, no longer able to rely on his companion, gets the last ounce out of himself.

A hundred men go out into the forest to fell trees. They are divided into groups of four men each, and each group has so many square metres allotted to it to clear. And here is the first hazard: the area may be boggy or dry; it may be full of young saplings, that make a lot of work and yield little timber, or there may be a few big healthy trees yielding highly paid timber in amongst a lot of valueless poplars or more valuable oaks. Two men saw, one carts the branches away, one, the weakest, burns up the small branches, and at the end all help together to stack the fire-wood. Amongst the hundred there will be forest workers, farmers, artisans, bank clerks, school teachers, musicians and others. The wages of each group are calculated separately, and the group lives according to the percentage that it earns. If this keeps below 100 per cent. then a reduction is made in their daily 600 grammes of bread. If it continues above 100 per cent, then they get at least the normal food allowance, with which they still remain hungry. If they average above 110 per cent, they have the prospect of being satisfied, even well satisfied. What wonder, with so attractive a goal, that those with the best chance of reaching it should join together. In this way were formed shock groups of farmers and foresters, and such-like brawny fellows—and the devil take the hindmost. Finally, there were a few groups of hairdressers and office clerks, who had never used a saw and had no idea how to wield an axe. How could they be expected ever to do this sort of work? The Russian boss, however, saw his chance. He would give the shock groups the best squares of forest, the best tools, and the most favourable rates. He would use their example to break the morale of the others. "These can do it, so you must also be able to." By thus playing off one against the other he would get the last ounce out of them all. Some would be bursting with strength and others would get steadily weaker. But in the evening in the hut Max, Carl and Paul, the best group, sat while the others scraped the last pieces of potato skin out of the empty jam tins, and then they started on a real meal: extra bread and porridge, and a piece of ham. The others watched hollow-eyed and pulled the blankets over their heads.

"Are these three going to have any to spare?"

"I say, do you know how many cubic metres we have done today? Don't you think our knees are wobbly too? Are we to do less, so that we also become O.K. (unfit for work)? We want to go home healthy, after all. Everyone must look after himself."

Yes, each looked after himself, and a year ago they were all lying together in the trenches, they shared the last scrap of bread, and carried their wounded comrades to the rear under fire. Over the door of the hut hangs a notice in big letters, "Socialism is the way to Peace and Freedom".

The organisation was such that the security authority, which was behind the P.O.W. organisation, let the prisoners out to individual "firms", i.e. concerns, in our case the great Forest combine, which was concerned with the exploitation of the surrounding forests, and in which the entire population was employed. In return this combine had to supply the camp with building materials and food, reckoned in proportion to our output. Thus our food supplies varied according to our output, and we had to aim at so increasing the output that supplementary food could be allocated to us, and in addition the entire camp organisation, with all its personnel and material costs could show a profit for the security authority. That depended, of course, not only on our output, but just as much on the government-controlled wood prices and the labour norms. The norm is the standard output of a workman. Up to 100 per cent. of this standard he receives a fixed minimum wage. For those over 100 per cent. output the wages rise steeply as "progressive performance wages". The wage obtainable is moreover dependent on many factors on which the worker has no influence; how high Government prices are in his particular job, whether his actual working conditions are favourable or not, for the norm is, of course, calculated under specially favourable conditions, how his physical reserves of strength are, and, last but not least, how much he is in favour with his boss, who estimates the results and records the percentages. Thus a subjective element is by no means to be excluded, for it can be often of considerable consequence which working conditions, as laid down in the norm book, are regarded as obtaining in any given case and which not, for example whether, in excavating, the ground can be reckoned as frozen, stony or sandy, and how the weather conditions or unforeseen obstacles are reckoned. The norm book is the most important book in all Soviet literature, and contains an impressive scheme of differentiated calculations for all work output according to changing conditions. In Western countries when such matters are in dispute the trade union or industrial council or some other institution looks after the interest of the worker. The Soviet worker has nobody, for his union will never go against the interests of the State as represented by the management of the industry. The P.O.W. had at least his camp commandant, who had a personal interest that the camp should earn a maximum income. Thus it happened sometimes that we were unemployed all day in the camp because the commandant and the firm could not agree about the rates. But if the firm was cunning and got in with the commandant by means of all sorts of under-the-counter supplies, then we were without protection and were fleeced accordingly.

In the autumn of 1945 the first consequences of this overwork began to show themselves. In the Sunday Turkish bath you saw Buchenwald skeletons. Oedema appeared, a condition not unknown to us, but soon to become a familiar sight. It was particularly alarming to me to see so many faces begin to change, especially the younger ones. From being frank, smooth boys' faces, out of which naïve and untroubled eyes looked out, without suspecting, in spite of the war, what the world and people were really like, they became drawn and haggard masks with an expression changing from fear to insolence, from mistrust to greed, which their own mothers would not have recognised. The death-rate that winter was nevertheless not so appalling as we had expected. When the camp was closed in the winter of 1946 there were in the little cemetery in the forest about thirty-five graves, only about 10 per cent. of the total strength, in our bad living conditions a much more favourable number than in many other camps.

The most alarming thing about each death was the indifference of the others. It seemed as if they not only had to ration their physical strength with the utmost economy but also their feelings. They got as far as a brief regret, no longer took part spontaneously in the interment, and after two days the dead man was forgotten. I buried almost all the thirty-five. When one of them died it was usually from exhaustion, without any sort of resistance to death. He lay naked on a stretcher in an empty hut. With one or two people detailed for the job, who had previously dug a six-foot grave in the frozen earth with a good deal of cursing, I fetched him, covered the frozen emaciated body with a few pine branches, and the sad little procession went almost unnoticed through the camp into the forest. There

I spoke a few words at the graveside, and the words of the
Bible were like a shining light. We said the Lord's Prayer
together, and then I got down into the grave, the naked body
was handed down to me and I bedded him in the alien earth.
The earth fell on the branches that covered him, and then we
stumbled dumbly back into the camp. In the summer of 1946
the order came that each prisoner was to be buried dressed in
clean white under-clothing. We could hardly believe it at first:
it seemed as if we were once more recognised as human beings.

As I am writing this here at home the figures of these buried
men pass before my mind's eye as they often do in sleepless
nights. I can see you, young Günther Becher of Dortmund,
whose parents I have not so far been able to find. You came
marching into the forest camp with brisk elastic steps: then your
lungs in your under-nourished body were not able to resist the
germs. While you were struggling in vain against a rapidly
developing tuberculosis, the only thing that worried you at
first was whether it would come out that you were not an
infantryman but an S.S.-man, but during the last few weeks you
worried much more whether the Jesus Christ who was still
unknown to you was real, and again and again you sent for me
to discuss this with you. I had to promise you a real catechism
class for the time when you recovered. Now you have found
a better one in heaven, after we carried you out as one of the
first. A few graves farther on lies young Helmut from East
Pomerania, who was killed by a falling tree, the big Hamburg
butcher with the dropsical heart, the smart subaltern from
Prignitz, who was loading tree trunks when the rope broke and
the heavy pine logs crushed his chest—the young ones and the
old ones, with limbs so swollen with dropsy that, after death,
the water flowed from the burst skin like ichor; young Alfred
W. from Berlin, who came to us so care-free and charming, but
in whom suddenly something seemed to snap so that he sank
lower and lower, neglected himself, incurred floggings and
imprisonments for more and more thefts, and withdrew more
and more into himself, so that it was no longer posssible to
make contact with him. He went steadily to the bad and seemed

already half rotten when his poor tortured life ended. Then there was the old factory worker from Augsburg, who did not come home one night, and whom we later found, on the site where we had been working, frozen to death by the burnt-out fire, and next to him Augen K. from the Grenzmark, who could never resist anything eatable, and one evening on the way home stopped to collect a few mushrooms that he noticed. He ate them raw and a commando sent out to look for him found his emaciated body dying. The horse on which they brought him home fell and crushed the last embers of life out of him. And, finally, there was Albert S. who during the great drought disregarded the warnings of the collective farmers, who were concerned about their own lives in the winter and said they would shoot anyone who trespassed on their private fields. He crept away from his group one night-shift into a turnip field, the farmer on watch fired a charge of small shot into his stomach at short range and then in senseless rage slashed the dying man's face to ribbons with his knife. How each one of these deaths might have moved us, accustomed though we were to death, but each of us was so preoccupied with his own hunger and exhaustion that in most cases only a passing feeling of sadness stirred the heart of most of us. For none of us wished to have to die here in a foreign land. To die here would put the final seal on the senselessness of life: only returning home could give it meaning. Only he who knew something of another and eternal homeland could contemplate without despair the prospect of being buried out there beneath a cross of birch-wood.

The German camp leader was one of the old prisoners, a young man from the district of Warthegau, with the nationalist outlook of the frontier German. He had a gift for leadership but lacked moral background. He made the most of his privileges without consideration for anyone else and showed a cynical contempt for his fellow men. In his milder moments he was approachable enough. His first greeting to us was: "You know what spit and polish is. You thought it was now over and done with. Make no mistake about it, here you will find it to the nth degree," and that's how it was. A dug-out was quickly turned into a prison, and every other word of the major who commanded the camp was "bolsche disciplina"—more discipline. He was a fat red-faced man, who could never decide between cruelty and kindness. Of course we could not do without discipline. A man loses half his virtue as a prisoner, so how can he be treated as a responsible individual? But how could discipline be rightly applied so long as the Russians continued to regard us as a dangerous gang of Fascists, and as long as the German camp officers were a selection of "ne'er-do-wells" appointed by the Russians according to their pliability and political affinity?

It was some months before their arbitrary floggings were forbidden, and over and over again their punishments were quite outrageous. A twenty-year-old youth, who had helped himself to something while working as a builder, was rescued by us after two days in a prison dug-out in the depth of winter. His face was grey and disfigured and he thought he was left there to die. Another one was captured trying to escape. The camp commander paraded the entire camp, and ordered us to flog him because, as a result of his action, the whole camp would be deprived of certain privileges. With teeth clenched with horror the troops had to watch some of their number beat the poor chap with fists and boots, before he was thrown into the prison like a limp and empty sack. Thefts were certainly a serious problem. It was difficult to put a stop to them without flogging, and what we had to do was to try to see that the flogging was carried out immediately on the discovery of the thief in order to avoid horrible and sadistic scenes. A train driver who made out that he was a former Rhenish Communist was particularly prominent on these occasions. He had adopted the title "the executioner of Ramasukha", and it was he who with a few companions carried out the sentences. Once the whole camp was disturbed by thefts of food and money for several weeks without the culprit being discovered. At last he was unmasked quite by chance. He was a rough powerful fellow and an excellent workman, who had no need to steal. Although he was convicted he still protested his innocence. He was put in prison and still persisted in his denial. Then one night "the executioner" tackled him. The poor chap was handed over to the hospital more like a boneless bundle than a man. For a few weeks he wandered about the camp broken and half demented, and then he was transferred to another camp, where I met him again later. He was still a wreck and so he has probably remained for the rest of his life.

Since I have mentioned the hospital some account of it may give a more cheerful ending to this tale of woe. In spite of the lack of medicines and bandages, in spite of dishonest Russian nurses, who stole from what little there was, it represented the last remnant of humanity in the camp, and that was entirely due to the two men who ran it. There was the young Russian doctor, a cultivated Jew, small and thin and with sad eyes. He was too timid to take the risk of energetic action on our behalf, and was himself involved with the agents of the Security Police. I felt sorry for him. However, he tried to do his best for us. The other man was my Westphalian friend Gustav, the one man in the camp who was completely untouched by gossip, envy and suspicion, and to whom many of them owed their lives. Once when we were celebrating his birthday he admitted with tears in his eyes that life had never seemed so good to him before. The hospital with its white beds was decorated with pine branches, a birthday table was arranged with all sorts of presents on it from rations of tobacco to clay figures modelled and baked in the camp. Poems were recited, speeches made, and Mozart's Cradle Song was played on the accordion. It was all very friendly and moving.

When the quarantine period in the forest camp was over and we had already been working for a week or two, the camp leader came to me one evening and said:

"Helmut, you will not go to work tomorrow. You have got to take over No. 1 Company as sergeant."

"I? Sergeant in charge of No. 1? Not on any account. I'm not anxious to commit suicide. I value my life too much."

"But look, old man, that whole mob is becoming completely

out of touch with us. In the winter many of us will die. We must do our best to get them back."

"In the winter? We want to be home by then, not here. I am going to work. I don't want to be a boss."

But I allowed myself to be persuaded and accepted the position. If I had known how a job like that separates you from your fellows, and how difficult personal contact is when you do not share their burdens, then I should not have taken it on and I should have later refused any other official position in the prison camps. But perhaps it was as well that I did not know this and did not refuse, because I was able to be useful to many of them. I knew that it would be a difficult task, full of unpleasant situations. No. 1 Company was a company of old prisoners who had nearly all been taken prisoner in the last winter of the war. The rigours of life in prison camps had made of them a band of brigands in which murder and violence prevailed. They lived like wild animals, blows and curses were their language, and the new prisoners, who still retained many of the trimmings of western civilisation, looked at them askance. And so I faced the parade of these half-defiant, half-curious faces and remembering a well-tried pedagogic rule, that you should begin with terror and end with kindness but not the other way round, I greeted them with a murderous speech, in which I threatened them with frightful things for any breach of discipline. They received this in sullen silence and the only reaction was a whispered aside, "And he's supposed to be a parson."

That was, in fact, the problem. With all that I demanded of them, with all that I handed out by way of punishment, I could not tell them how sorry I was for them and that I was desperately concerned about their welfare. Most of them gradually discovered this and the fact that one of them, who once attacked me and broke a tooth on my fist, later attached himself to me like a faithful squire, was just as cheering as was the present of mushrooms that one of the most incorrigible thieves, Eugen, brought to me out of the forest, after I had roared at him and put him on a special sawing fatigue.

As sergeant I was responsible for the life of the company

66

inside the camp, but fortunately not for the work outside, so that I avoided the direct suspicion of being a stooge of the Russians. I was, of course, released from all labour and realised all the time what a great improvement in living conditions that represented, although I had no other advantages and no more food than the others, which, however, they never believed. I had plenty to do, of course, for the sergeant was a sort of maid-of-all-work, both the mother and the servant of the company. He had not only to get provisions for the company from the camp quarter-master and look after their clothing, but also to clean the huts while the others were at work, fetch fuel, and cart the lunch out to the forest workers. When the company returned to camp in the evening he had to allocate jobs to them without any regard to their weariness, some to saw wood, others to dig graves, another for work in the camp, another to load lorries, another for sentry duty at night, all of which evoked loud protests. Often there were logs to be loaded after normal working hours, for which the extra pay usually remained in the pockets of the camp officers. The men gathered round my table watching jealously as I distributed bread, tobacco and sugar. This I had to do without scales, and the result was suspicious comparisons and furious protests, if anyone thought he had received too little. After that came the torn stockings, ragged shirts and the holes in the shoes, an everlasting worry, because of the importance of clothing for their work. They were exposed all the time to the winter weather and had long distances to march to the places where they worked. The tailors and cobblers never caught up with their repairs, and there were no replacements available. It was a reflection on the sergeant if one of the men was not allowed by the doctor to march out because of defective clothing. And at last, when the tumult had subsided and everybody was in bed, someone would call out: "Sergeant, tell us a bedtime story."

It had become an established custom. In order not to begin with terror alone, I had from the beginning given the men a short talk before they went to sleep, talking over the events of the day, telling them the political news, as far as it penetrated to us, and discussing the latest number of the camp newspaper which always reached us several weeks late. Occasionally I introduced a story, and so it was they discovered how nice story-telling is. I would sit on a camp-bed in the evening and ask:

"What would you like today—an adventure story or a love story?" and I would tell them whichever they chose. All the world's literature from the Trojan War to Kaspar Hauser was brought in. Edgar Wallace was just as welcome as *Peter Voss the Million Pound Robber*. Fidelity to the original did not matter very much. When I could not remember the end of Gotthelf's *Black Spider*, I made it up. Claudel would certainly not have recognised his *Annonce faite à Marie*. Penzoldt's *Etienne and Luise* was elaborated but produced a deep impression and Eckstein's *Visit to the Prison*, somewhat modernised, proved one of my greatest successes. All this sounds perhaps much easier than it actually was, but it is only necessary to try to repeat a well-known story or classical drama to discover with shame how defective the memory is. We once tried for days to recall Keller's *Kleider machen Leute* and even the film fans failed. And so my repertoire became exhausted and I had to fall back on ballads. I made a full evening's programme out of *The Cranes of Ibykus* and built up a series of revenge stories lasting several evenings and finishing with Jack London, *Orestes* and the *Feet in the Fire*. This last never failed in its dramatic effect in spite of its length. In the end I was driven to make up stories myself, without any scruples about plagiarism, though, of course, I did not disclose their authorship, for a prophet is without honour in his own country. Once when I announced that I was going to tell them a fairy-tale there was a protest that they were not children, but when I had finished telling them the story of *Faithful Johannes* they admitted that they never knew that fairy-tales could be so beautiful. The most vivid effect, however, was produced by Bergengruen's *Spanish Rosebush*, which was asked for over and over again. As the story-telling went on I watched to see how many of them kept awake, and when I finished usually only a few had listened all through, and all round me the others were snoring like pigs. But it was most gratifying to me to hear them asking each other next morning how the story finished after they had dropped off to sleep the night before. It was amusing to discover how much they had understood and what to them had seemed important. When the camp was closed and we had to be separated, I realised from their expression of thanks for this story-telling, which often came most warmly from the most unexpected quarters, how good it had been for these deprived men to be transported for a while into another world at bedtime. I ought to have done this more regularly in spite of my own weariness, particularly since the story-telling gave me the opportunity of speaking indirectly and sometimes directly about the Gospel, after the rowdy Communist Action group on New Year's Eve had led to the prohibition of the services that I had hitherto held every Sunday.

When the hut was cleaned in the morning (and it was most important that it should still be wet when the commandant came round), then I went across to the combine's stables, harnessed a horse to the cart or sledge, fetched from the kitchen the stout barrel containing soup for lunch, and drove out to the forest brigade, often driving many kilometers along roads that were not roads at all. These were the pleasantest hours of those days, alone, unguarded, in open unspoilt country with the call of the woodpecker amongst the trees and the cry of the kite above me. I had a comforting illusion of freedom, although never so complete that the weight was ever quite lifted from the heart, or the enjoyment of nature unspoiled. There were, of course, accidents enough. The roads were hardly passable in rainy weather, sometimes the cart collapsed in the mud, or on hot days the horse would bolt, maddened by the flies that settled on him like a second skin, and dash the Russian farm-cart against the trees and upset the tubs. I sometimes stood in despair with tears of rage in my eyes, thinking of my comrades who had already been waiting eagerly a long time for their food. Nor was it very safe, for in the period after the war, brigandage had spread everywhere in Russia and particularly in these poorer wooded districts, so that we heard of fresh incidents every day, and even prisoners were sometimes attacked. But I had no such adventures and usually enjoyed quiet and pleasant hours, in which I let my thoughts roam as they would or prepared my evening story or learned by heart a little more of my hymn-book. These quiet forest roads are so well described in Turgenev's *Sportsman's Sketches*. Sometimes narrow, sometimes broad, they wind as they wish through clearings and marshy grassland along the beds of streams, and through bogs. If you were very fortunate you would catch sight of a little herd of deer, or a hare loping away, for game is very scarce in this district. Under the leaden midday sky in summer you can hear the voices of the women reapers. They sing traditional songs rather like the South German *Schnada-hüpfl*, with peculiar four-line verses. New ones are always being invented, and they would be a mine of interest for students of folklore. They are all about people and contemporary events, in this case mostly about return from the war. In the loud shrill way that Russian peasant women sing, the verses follow one another in endless succession. I was surprised that these women sing at all, for their wages are only 2 roubles a day, with 10 roubles for the overseer. The vegetable soup from the communal kitchens, that I sometimes took out to them, contained a little more fat, but was not thicker than ours. It cost 1.80 roubles, so that not all of them could buy it. But after all they have a cow and a goat and a garden at home, and were not dependent as we were on the communal kitchen. It was not very much that they were able to add to their diet in this way, but nevertheless they were great strapping creatures bursting with strength. In a neighbouring wood is a women's brigade engaged in loading logs on to motor-lorries, heavy muscular work. They seem to think nothing of it, and our troops are careful not to start a quarrel with them. Whatever happens to them, they sing. But a few days ago in the camp we heard something startlingly unusual. At first it did not dawn on us what it was. One of our men, up on the top of a hut mending the roof, was whistling a popular song. So heavy was the pressure on the spirit that in the first two years you scarcely ever heard anyone singing or whistling at his work. Later on, when we got enough to eat, it was different, and during the last year of our captivity I remember standing on the roof of a

building in the Urals, and from the sheer joy of living, singing
yodelling songs into the forest at the top of my voice, so that
the pine trees, that had never heard anything like it before,
shook their heads in surprise.

At home in Germany the world is never silent. The ear is
always aware of sounds: only in the high Alps can one escape
them. But here in the winter forest it is really quiet—not
deathly quiet, for the wind is moving in the branches, and
everything seems to be breathing, but inaudibly. I tie the nag to
a tree, throw him some hay, and go stamping far into the forest
across to the old oak tree in the clearing, where in summer I
saw the raven sitting—Woden's bird.

But the heart leaps with delight when in the spring the cart
turns into the wood of young birch trees. Never before has it
seen a green so silky, so light, so delicate, so silvery. Only he
who has seen a birch tree at home can appreciate its true beauty
when the world around, even the air itself, is filled with this
green. A feeling of joy steals through his heart, drinking in the
intimate bliss of this matchless colour.

And what clouds in that rainy summer of 1945! Even the
sky of Lake Constance cannot offer anything like the variety
and majesty of the pictures they make. They pile up in overwhelming colours; the wind, for ever changing its direction,
drives them on from all sides, and we sit on the grass amazed,
and watch the ever-changing patterns as though they were a
thrilling drama. When the wind blows them towards the west,
Bruno the Rhinelander, this loyal helper and travelling poet,
rich in country lore, in sayings and legends with which he
entertains me in the evenings, asks: "What was that poem
about the sailors of the sky?"

> *Scurrying clouds, Sailors of the sky!*
> *O could we but follow as you hasten by!*
> *Carry greetings, my friends, to the land of my birth,*
> *For I am a captive, a prisoner, bound,*
> *And, alas, have no other messenger found.*
> *Proudly you sail through the air so free,*
> *For slaves of the Russians you cannot be.*

Those among us who, thanks to inner reserves or their more privileged positions of sergeant, camp orderly or book-keeper, could keep their heads above water in the general atmosphere of gloom, took every opportunity of conjuring up magic hours when they could once more act like human beings, forgetful of self and of everything. We had to fall back on memories and on our ability to do things ourselves. There were no books to speak of. Fortunately I never knew beforehand that I was to spend two years of my life practically without books. How they would have helped us then, and what a good influence they would have had, above all during the long weeks which many would have to spend in the hospital. My volume of Reuter, and the "*Siebenkäs*", the pocket edition of Steban Zweig's selection of Goethe's poems, a volume of C. F. Meyer's short stories, and the Bible—that made up our whole collection. How could we enlarge it? We took bundles of thick cigarette paper with which we had once been issued, and wrote down all that we could. Kurt made up short stories, for which Alfred provided the illustrations, Carl-Heinz wrote satirical and lyrical poems about birds and Indians, I dug up from my memory whole anthologies of poems, fables and anecdotes, and the tailors sewed them together into small booklets.

The importance of poetry in the life of the camp deserves some mention. In every camp there were to be found a few people who had made up such anthologies for themselves; they were passed from one to the other, there were lively exchanges, and whoever added something new enjoyed great esteem. For lack of other reading material many a man grasped at such collections—a man who had never had anything to do with poetry before would discover for the first time that poems are something with which a sober-minded grown-up need not be ashamed to occupy himself. In this connection it was strange to note—and it had the validity of a Gallup-poll—how Rilke enjoyed an unrivalled popularity among our generation. Not without reason of course, as I had to admit after listening carefully to the best of his poems. "Liebeslied", the first verses of the *Book of Hours*, "The Panther" and "Autumn Day" were to be found in almost every collection, whereas Stefan George had receded into the darkness of oblivion and was remembered only by the pure lyricism of the "Year of the Soul". His challenging "programme" verse seems tedious and shallow to people who already have had so much demanded of them. Little more than calm respect greeted my experiments of reading poems from *The Seventh Ring* or *The Star of the Covenant* (*Stern des Bundes*). What, however, could have moved a not unknown German author, living in the Soviet Union since 1933, to present one of my friends, a young Austrian S.S. officer, who had been adjutant to Kaltenbrunner, with a copy of the *Star of the Covenant* and to write a nostalgic dedication in it? Was he reminded of Maximin by the fresh youthfulness of the Austrian or of his own past, so full of youthfulness?

Carl-Heinz, I must not forget to mention you! Your intellectual profile had impressed me first on the transport train, and again when you were lying naked in the grass reading the New Testament while we were all waiting to be de-loused. Then began our friendship, which made life so much easier. It did not grow just because you were the only intellectual in the camp besides me. I lent you my Bible—it was a discovery for you—and in those years you read it through twice. For weeks our conversation centred round it, you pressed me for historical and theological information and would not have been a poet had not the impression it made been converted into poetry. While I only knew your charming satirical animal-poems, I liked your writing but did not take it very seriously. But then, in November 1945, when hunger was gnawing at us all, you returned from the forest with the poem about the bull-finch, and I was amazed to see that there are people who can forget hunger and misery for the shining blue and red of a bird's feathers. In January 1946 because of your strength of character you got on the wrong side of the Russians and were transferred to one of the worst brigades. The sudden burden of life, the apparently hopeless prospect of returning home, released some creative urge within you, and day after day you returned, as though unaccustomed work had no effect on you, with a poem, some of them masterly, and not one lacking mention of one of your beloved birds. Often we sat up late at night and

73

went over them, disagreed over single words, and you took no
offence at my suggestions. But when you brought the first
verses of the great ballad of the "White Horse of the Prairies"
I could hardly wait for each evening's instalment.

This round-up was a great success,
Your eyes are shining with pride!
I long to tell the tale, I confess,
Of the white horse of the prairie.

In the crowded corral they stamp and rear,
The finest ones you ever saw.
The fence is high and strong. This black horse here
Is one in a thousand—and yet

Since that white stallion first caught my eye
The mustang lures me no more.
Twice he slipped through my fingers and passed me by,
And then—but that was long ago!

You see, I can still remember it! When you read the whole
poem through to us for the first time, we felt as though we had
been present at an important first-night performance, and when
after Easter we stripped off our thick winter clothes, and our
bodies—long muffled up—once more saw the light of day, we
realised that we had experienced a victory of spirit over matter.
You had grown as thin as a lath, yet in the bright light of your
genius we suspected nothing, and it was just in time that they
labelled you O.K. and transferred you at last to a better camp,
otherwise you would never have seen your home again.

The first variety concert which we organised during that
time of famine in the late autumn of 1945 was a roaring success.
The Russians, whom we had invited, sat amazed, and I thought
of the feeling of triumph with which the concentration camp
prisoners proved their superiority to the unintellectual S.S.
guards with Wolfgang Langhoff's "Moorsoldaten" at just such
a variety concert. Sketches, songs, poems and acrobatic tricks,
string trios and a gypsy-band with home-made instruments
transformed the barracks. Thus we tried, without any assistance,
to produce for ourselves the sort of musical and theatrical

performances which were provided in larger camps. A varied New Year's programme such as I saw later in our main camp, or the performance of Konstantin Simonov's anti-American propaganda play, *The Russian Question*, which I saw in the Moscow Camp, could have been shown in every European city.

The evenings which we enjoyed most, however, were those which we spent in the little tailor's hut. We wanted to prevent the dulling of our minds, and assembled there to discuss pre-arranged subjects. Alfred, the worthy sergeant-major from Upper Silesia, told us for two consecutive evenings about the confectionery trade, so that our mouths watered; Kurt gave talks on architecture, the other Kurt told us about Greece, and I gave a whole evening's recital of poems about autumn, from Goethe to R. A. Schröder, and another evening I read them tragic "fate" poetry. We had still other plans when suddenly an "anti-Fascist club" was formed—mostly made up of "Pirun-nies", i.e. a rowdy group from Upper Silesia, who boasted of their alleged Communist past, but who in fact did nothing but profit by the ease with which, from their knowledge of Polish, they could talk a sort of Russian and because of their lack of moral restraint—and they upset everything "in order to curb Fascist tendencies". That event was typical. Our life in Russia would have been much easier if we had had the freedom to develop intellectual interests in the camp. It was not only the few intellectuals who felt this spiritual as well as physical hunger. Many would not have felt that these last years were wasted if they had been able to increase their knowledge and be stimulated spiritually through books, courses, lectures and discussions, such as existed in the camps of the Western countries. The Russians did soon try to start "the work of culture", many camp commandants supported it eagerly, and displayed the "culture club" to every camp inspector like a sign-board advertising their good camps. But by reason of their own intellectual deficiency they thought that beyond films, the theatre and music nothing more was necessary, and had no conception of the intellectual qualities of the Germans. The greatest obstacle was however the unquenchable fear of Fascist tendencies—with all the exaggeration that the word "Fascist" underwent in the mind of the orthodox Communist: it comprises "idealist philosophy", "un-political objectivity" and "religious obligation", and it rejects everything that is not impregnated with Communist propaganda. That led to a detailed censoring of all programmes. At an Austrian evening a national song called "The Church Tower" had to be renamed "The Watch Tower"—a title senseless to us but full of meaning for the Russians. When the folk-song "Kein Feuer, keine Kohle" (No fire, no coal) appeared on the programme after a lecture, it had to be cut out, for the political officer saw in it a complaint against the inadequate heating in the barracks and cried, "Feuer menocha, Kohle menocha" (Plenty of fire, plenty of coal). Above all, however, any efforts at a general system of education were stifled, even when the most trusted members of the club took responsibility for it. Whether it were literature, history, science, or training for the professions—they trusted us in none of these spheres. Only gradually did it become clear to me that they imposed upon the camp merely those principles which had for a long time governed their own intellectual lives.

So we had to carry on these studies unobtrusively and within a small group, and in spite of the limitations we enjoyed them thoroughly. In that forest camp we would sit, on the long winter evenings round the fire in the tailor's hut, discussing and narrating; it was most enjoyable, however, when Carl-Heinz, his head full of ornithology, told us fairy-tales from the world's literature—and Karl May recounted a story about Winnetou (I could not then feel any scorn for this "dead-end kid" whose exploits live despite the scorn of each new rising generation!). Later in Beschiza we arranged a course on the history of philosophy from the pre-Socratic philosophers up to Kant, and not until we reached the camp for important people, 27/II (see Part II), was the weekly programme full, and it was often difficult to choose between an account of the Cordillera Expeditions, an introduction to higher mathematics or a course on the history of architecture. In 1949—the Goethe centenary year—I had to pay my tribute by giving lectures on Faust for several weeks running. These I did with three different groups, graded according to the audience, and I myself got quite a lot out of them.

It is from the Jewish-Christian heritage that Sunday has come to be a day of rest, a day which is now important because it gives man the opportunity of forgetting the cares of this life and prevents him from being exploited by the ruling powers.

What happens on Sunday is a clear indication of how far a man has lost himself as an individual and as a social being. Whoever has observed in the West how senselessly people of every level of society, week in and week out, bring discredit on their Sunday, can see in the fate of Sunday in the U.S.S.R. merely the facsimile of its fate in the West. Since in the West it has lost its positive sense of peace and devotion to God and hearing His Word, so in the Soviet system, reflecting the spirit of the West, it is merely a *Wychadnoi*—a work-free day in the negative sense of the word. It is well known that before the last war in the U.S.S.R. the five-day week had already been introduced in many business concerns; thus Sunday had lost something of its essence of being a communal holiday for the whole of the population: there was no longer a communal holiday even for the members of one family. Because of the war, the six-day week came into operation again, in order to increase production. So in the Russian towns there is once again a greater emphasis on Sunday; the majority of the people wear better clothes and wander about the streets with no occupation. The negative character of this "work-free" day has persisted, however, as has the fact that only part of the population can enjoy a day of rest at the same time. The country therefore never wears the "Sunday look" that is so enjoyable and uplifting at home, as we realised nostalgically only when in captivity. The farmers use the day to work their private plots of land, the factories work at half strength, heavy industries continue with a full complement of workers, the factory hooters still send their shrieks through the air. "Russia, the land without bells, the land without Sunday," said the troops scornfully when they wished to express the whole difference between life in the U.S.S.R. and life at home.

77

On the orders of the Soviet Government, the P.O.W.s themselves had three free days a month, after the transfer to a peace-time economy. These days could have served at least to change us from working animals into men again. But they were often spoiled, and many men had lost the capacity for using them. During the first years the *wychadnoi* became the day when productive work ceased, but not all work. The camp had to be enlarged, cleaned, above all beautified with flower beds, sports ground and all kinds of things, so that the commandant could be proud of it, when the frequent inspectors came round; the Russian camp officers wanted their fields dug and all kinds of housework done, they wanted to earn a few roubles privately by lending the prisoners out to their friends for private work, or else the prisoners engaged themselves to do that so as to eat their fill. The German camp leaders could have ensured a good Sunday for many, by better organisation, but were often too unsympathetic, too harsh and unfeeling to set themselves to do it, and to recognise the necessity of filling the Sundays of their exhausted countrymen with human interests. So the prisoner was usually robbed of this day. Driven first from cleaning the barracks, to changing clothes, from there to planting vegetables in the commandant's garden, then to medical inspection and finally to repairing the camp fence, he would sink down on his wooden bed in the evening and be thankful that he had got to the end of the worst day of the week and could look forward to his usual regular work on Monday. If for once on a Sunday they had peace and quiet, then its lack of work was a joy only to those who could fill the time with their own interests. For many, this being left to themselves was a heavy burden. For hours they would lie silent on their bunks and stare at the ceiling covered with the bloodstains of squashed bugs. Thoughts and conversations turned on the homeland. When I saw them lying and chatting like that, I asked myself whether ever before in the history of man one knew, as one knew of these hundred-thousands of German prisoners, that the only subject of thought and conversation, the only question that always moved them, was home and returning home.

Our homeland lay behind us, shrouded in darkness, the hope

lay before us but was uncertain and incalculable. The news that reached us in the first months was only scrappy. There was the newspaper *Free Germany* that arrived at the forest camp weeks late, afterwards exchanged for *News for German P.O.W.s in the U.S.S.R.* and then appearing once a month, and later once a fortnight. It was edited by the Russians, brought little news of Germany and from the first described conditions in Western Germany only in negative terms, in East Germany only positively.

We devoured these papers, tried to read between the lines, and to augment them with what we managed to decipher in the Russian newspapers. Most of the members of our little group in the forest camp believed that we had been "written off", were forgotten and would remain "missing". Many of them had read Kröger's novel *The Forgotten Village*—a story of German P.O.W.s held for a long long time in Siberia after the First World War—and drew from it dismal parallels of our destiny. So there was no little excitement when in November 1945 postcards arrived for the first time through the Red Cross and we could write home. "They only want to find out if we gave our correct names and addresses!" "They only want to lead us to write things for which they could arrest us and never let us return home." This distrust seemed foolish and I put in a good word for the Russians. Laughing scornfully, an old prisoner lectured me: "You don't know them as I do! I believe anything of the Russians except good, and then only the very worst!" It turned out that these words were as false as any generalisation which the prisoners liked to make about the Russians. Anyway, they all wrote—and it was worth it.

In the spring the first replies from home arrived and by the autumn we had nearly all received letters, all of which, except mine, brought pleasant and encouraging news into our small camp. They were passed on from one person to another, were discussed countless times down to every comma, and served to help us to construct for ourselves, like a mosaic, a picture of the conditions at home. This picture was, of course, much more favourable than was really the case. But at least we knew who was still alive, where they were and how they were surviving.

And we knew that we were not forgotten and ignored, but that we were "registered"—"registered with the International Red Cross" as some put it solemnly, as though they personally were under the protection of a power which was mightier and more reliable than either Stalin or God. Those who have known themselves and witnessed in others the inspiration which this receiving of letters brought with it, have learned two unforgettable things; that one can never write too many letters to prisoners, because often more is revealed than one intends, and that one cannot express oneself too concretely. Our relations and friends showed both these faults. I determined that in the terrible event of yet another war I would set myself up as a "letter-writer for P.O.W.s", in order to make up for the deficiencies of the relatives. The spirit of the prisoner is continually coming up against the wall which separates him from his homeland, and needs plenty to occupy him, and since his thoughts are always on his home, he needs to know what conditions are prevailing there. Everything interests him, because everything serves to make up his mosaic. So that one must not limit oneself to general assurances of well-being but must write about practical things, above all about such things as could lead him to draw conclusions about the general conditions of life at home. A daughter working in a factory has received a rise in wages resulting from a strike, a son has bought himself a motor-bike, a neighbour has once again got a horse in the stable; these were the items of news that went round the camp and provided subjects for much conversation. If a man's wife wrote to say that during the days when one could no longer trust one's neighbour she had found God again and now said her prayers with the children every evening, then for her prisoner-husband would begin a new understanding, which meant that these years had not been wasted for him. Thoughts continually turned not only to past home-life but also to the future return home. The hope of this return could not be driven out of our hearts, even when reason could hardly agree. When a man sat staring in front of him with lost gaze it was a safe bet that he was dreaming of the moment of home-coming. We went to sleep picturing this hour, we dreamed of it, and often while eating our morning soup in the half-light of the cook-house, one man would begin to tell of his dream, his face still alight, until the others joined in. If a conversation started with the words "What's the news?", then only one item of news was meant, namely the latest rumour, a new date for the next transport lorries, fresh indications of a general liberation, new reports about the civil population which concerned us. These rumours had already begun to fly around the camp at Tabor, alternatively positive and negative, spreading with astonishing speed, and of course, always distinguished by absolute reliability. In August 1945, a few weeks after our arrival in the forest camp, and then again in April 1946, they became so numerous and were accompanied by so many indications, that it was quite ridiculous to believe them. Such exaltation was usually followed by deep depression when the imagined zero hour had passed without incident. If, after such a swing from hope to despair, we did not wish to suffer mental instability such as occurs after leaping too hurriedly from a cold bath to a hot bath, we had to develop our own technique for preserving our sense of balance. Many became thorough pessimists because of this, and declared that they would believe nothing more until they could themselves turn the handle of their own front doors. Yet they could not quite bring themselves to turn away when the next "parole" from a reliable source was passed round. My technique was to believe nothing but always to listen willingly and allow my hopes to rise. When asked if I believed the rumour I would reply, "I don't *believe* anything but what is in the Bible, but I *hope* that there might be something in it." It was a well-proven technique, disappointment did not worry me too much, and I still had something to look forward to.

The Russians themselves were frequently the instigators of these rumours—the officers as well as the civilians. Gradually we came to realise that in the spring the officers and commissars started a flood of hopeful rumours, either directly in highly confidential whispers to the German servants and by indiscretions that appeared to slip out by accident, or indirectly through the Russian overseers at work. It was the easiest means of avoiding attempts at escape in the summer. For they could now be sure that everyone carrying around such thoughts in his head, said to himself, or had said to him by a companion, "What! Escape? Now that we have been here as long as anyone! We'll be home before you. This summer all camps are to be closed, in our factories the Russians are already forming civilian groups who are to take over our work, and staff officers are looking for new posts because they are being de-mobbed!"

This was one of the few times when we could at least see a good reason for the false promises given by the Russians. In the majority of cases, we were at a loss to know why the truth was not told. Do you remember my account of how, when we had our weapons taken from us, the Russian major promised me a pass so that I could reach the Americans in freedom? There was no obvious reason why he did not refuse my plea point-blank since he had not the slightest intention of fulfilling it—but he promised all the same. That was our first encounter with the Russian conception of truth. Briefly it can be described as a great reluctance ever to say "No". Their *njet* (no), it is true, has become proverbial throughout the world. But this is possibly more of a Soviet than a Russian characteristic. (At this point I am in danger of talking nonsense about that much-discussed "Russian". He is a vague phantom, of philosophical and political literature, who is so useful that one can use him as a peg on which to hang all the difficulties which people of Western countries get into the farther east they move. This "Russian" is of course not only a literary legend, though it is true that people in Russia, as anywhere else, are different and cannot be given definite labels; bearing all this in mind I presume to speak of "the" Russian.) He hates nothing more than giving a categorical refusal, especially when he is moved by pity, which is often the case. It seems to him unjust to disappoint a suffering person and he will consider any lie justified to avoid doing so. When it is not a case of pity then it is at least a convenient way of preventing further importunate requests. At that time, we did not yet know this, and believed "yes" to mean "yes", and "no" to mean "no". As Germans of the Third Reich we were used to being told lies, on the wireless, in the press, in the speeches of the N.S.F.O. (National-Socialist Official Leaders), but were not accustomed to lies to our very faces, to which we learned to grow accustomed only by long and bitter experience. Several weeks later, we were travelling eastwards in the transport train to Russia going through Vienna to Budapest, almost dying with thirst in the heat of the overcrowded closed wagons. Our German transport-doctor warned the Russian major who was in command that there would be a high death-rate if the doors were not opened and some exercise allowed during the longer halts. His promises gave us new hope. In a few hours we would reach a large lake, would stop there for two days and would be able to drink and bathe to our heart's content. This encouraging rumour swept through the wagons like a refreshing breeze. Even I—I admit it freely—passed it on, although I knew the district but knew nothing of the lake. Perhaps the major knew better. "There must be something in it!" This fateful sentence was at the root of countless disappointments.

However strange it may seem, we were, in spite of having been dominated by Hitler for twelve years, still too accustomed to straightforwardness. There is an old saying that a lie always serves the truth, and thus forms part of the truth. We learned that this is not true in all parts of the world, but that there is a kind of lie which forgoes serving the truth and has no longer any connection with reality. To think this is less painful than to experience it. To experience it is to feel as though for a moment the ground had fallen away under one's feet. "It is not possible", one says to oneself, "he gave us such a positive assurance and looked at me with such a candid expression; surely he does not wish us harm—it is just not possible!" Because we did not think it possible, for years we allowed ourselves to be led on a piece of string; many men, like me for example, could not force themselves to suspend belief in a Russian assurance or promise until it had come true. That lake never appeared; for two days we travelled on, till a long halt gave us some relief. The major had kept us quiet and had refreshed us by a promise, no less than the many civilians who from the first moment that we entered Russia called out to us "Skoroi domoi!" (Home soon!) They said they had read it in the paper, heard it on the wireless or at the last Party Rally. Periodically, these waves of promises swept through the camp and many would weaken and declare, "Up till now I have believed nothing; but there must be something in it, for I have never heard it so widely broadcast before." However, there was nothing in it after all. It was either due to calculation or kindliness, or was perhaps done to quieten their own consciences which felt these prisoners to be a burden so many years after the end of the war; at any rate a little easy consolation was so much pleasanter, and we were always thankful to fall in with it, all except those who believed that there was not an atom of truth in what the Russians said.

I do not know if this habit of sitting lightly to the truth, which has always been attributed to the Eastern and Asiatic races, also belonged to the Russians in olden times. In the memoirs of Maxim Gorki there is to be found this statement, "A Russian who neither lies nor steals in not a Russian", and in the copies which were in our camp libraries attention was usually drawn to this sentence by heavy exclamation marks in the margin, added by those prisoners who read them. There is probably some connection between this and present conditions in the U.S.S.R. For decades this nation had been consoled in times of greatest need with the promise of future prosperity, which never came true. They were fed on promises—why then should they not feed them to us too? They were not allowed to doubt those made to them—why should they not be offended when one of us expressed his disbelief rather forcefully? They themselves had to say daily what they did not think, feign love for Stalin which they did not feel; facts were always firmly denied which they could see with their own eyes, and realities were affirmed, even when they felt in their bones the unreality. How then could they expect us to lay stress on words and connect reality with their garbled version of the truth?

The first thing that struck us when we arrived at the forest camp and saw the old prisoners working, whom we regarded with curiosity, was their slow dragging gait—the "Plenni tempo". It had a physical as well as a psychological cause; physical because their dwindling strength forced them to ration their efforts carefully; psychological because it is the expression of a man who has found in indifference the formula of the exhausting conditions of his world. He expects nothing from his environment, what he does no longer interests him, nothing can shake him any more. He prefers the even uniformity of his days, changes—even a move from one bed to another—upset him, yet he becomes acclimatised to them at once and to such an extent that his workmates of the previous day are already strangers to him; it is all the same to him, what he does and with whom he works, everything is one to him, for he has become a slave. After a few weeks, we too had adopted the Plenni tempo.

Thus it became most important not to become a slave but to remain human, or at least to become only partly a slave and to preserve a sphere of humanity from which humanising influences could flow into that sphere in which we were slaves, and in particular into our working lives. The problem varied for each individual; one who belonged to the bourgeoisie of the camp, such as a driver, tailor, cobbler, cook, group leader or skilled worker—or even to the camp aristocracy such as a company leader, chef or club president—did not throw himself down on his bunk at night, worn out and famished, and did not sleep in the large dormitories, but in a smaller room which he could furnish to his own taste; he could arrange and plan his work and take an interest in doing it well, had free time and physical reserves of energy; in short, he could order his life to suit himself, and was treated as an individual by other people. There were some who spent all these years in a position of prominence, and knew little of the real rigours of captivity. The accounts of those who belonged to this exalted class are necessarily different from those of the crowd.

The "camp proletariat" had even greater problems to face in their efforts to remain human. But even here there were important distinctions. One who belonged to the "culture group", i.e. to the group who catered for the musical and theatrical entertainment of the camp, stood on an island of humanity on which he could develop his own initiative—the most important fundamental activity of man! Wherever this right to be a human being has been contested, there has begun the descent to the sub-human level—alike in the barracks as in the State. Such a man had the right to "say something different for a change". For those among us who were Christians there was the Bible-study circle, or at least brotherly companionship with one or two others, or, failing that, the inner island of companionship with Christ, the evening reading of the Bible, turning up texts every morning—those of the Moravian Brethren or ones chosen at random—prayer, or repeating verses of hymns or of the Bible while at work. All this gave an opportunity to lead a human life, here I was addressed as a person about my behaviour and my decisions, here indifference was conquered, here there was always something to think about, to answer, to consider, to experience amid the uneventfulness of the every-day life in camp. The great majority of prisoners, however, grew dull and listless. There was a change for the better in the years after the currency reform in Russia which took place in December 1947, when our standard of living rose together with that of the native population. This return to "humanness" in our countrymen, and the revival of the "initiative to order one's own life", revealed itself in a manner which could only astonish one who was lost in false idealism about man; namely that women (with an emphasis on the most vulgar obscenities which left nothing unsaid) became "topic No. 1" of conversation, as they had been during the time of actual fighting. On the other hand during the years of under-nourishment, conversations on that subject were all that they should be; if anyone dared to make any obscene remarks they were ignored and "topic No. 1" was exclusively food—what we had just consumed or what was to be expected in the evening —recipes and kitchen gossip. With this return to "humanness" it was obvious, too, that the readiness to engage in serious conversation and in deeper thought had been less impeded by that listlessness than it was now by this newly awakened interest in distractions, women and experiences.

The lack of interest of slaves is connected with the fact that their existence has an eschatological significance. In my own experience that existence grew to have an extraordinary likeness to the Christian life as expressed in the expectation of the Second Coming of Christ held by the first Christians. The prisoner was not without any expectations in his life, he was in no wise condemned to hopeless slavery, indeed he expected a great deal and was the personification of expectancy; he expected everything from the future and not from the present, from a definite future time, a "day" which was for him in biblical language "the day of the Lord"; the day which made life in the present worth while (that is why there are surprisingly few cases of suicide in the camps) and which gave meaning to life. The mere mention of this day made faces light up; the high-spot of that day, the reception at home, was painted in all its details in the imagination a thousand times before going to sleep and during working hours. This day was the subject of everlasting and unavoidable question in every conversation and at every meeting; "What's the news? Have you heard what X said?" and so on. One could understand what the Bible meant by believing in a day in the distant future. For this thought alone brought us joy and life. This went so far that now and again we heard one man reproving another who had praised the soup at the midday-meal: "The soup is never good in prison!" Joylessness was a characteristic of the present to an extent almost unknown in civilian life. For however glum a free life may seem, there are always some little pleasures which add excitement to it; a cheerful evening, an illustrated magazine, a tasty dish, a small gift, a walk, a celebration, an embrace, all the unobtrusive little everyday pleasures, which few people lack and which we ungratefully take for granted, not to speak of the daily joys of family life, when this is a happy one. All these afford constant excitement and new and surprising emotions, which are almost completely lacking in the life of a prisoner, so that many men lost the ability to find pleasure in little things.

The present had lost its value. Only the eschatological relationship between the prisoner and time gave the present any value. "One day less," sighed everyone on going to bed, and the consoling thought: "One day nearer the end of our captivity!" made up for the inactivity and waiting. The Plenni tempo witnessed to the fact that here were men for whom life meant only the passing of time and not the using of time to its best advantage. Life in the present had value only so far as it gained meaning from its eschatological purpose, towards which it moved. In itself, apart from that purpose, life was meaningless, and only a few were tempted to deceive themselves about it, and to be content with a short-sighted policy of making the best of what was temporary. The Zeppelin-builder, who was loading logs beside me, would have been able to secure a pleasant job at once if he had not kept his trade a secret, though he would have delayed his return home by revealing it. Instead of this he toiled away at his work in the forest, grew weak, and as early as 1947 was sent home as unfit. On top of that, this life was meaningless because everything was done only in the interest of a foreign power; the more we slaved, the greater its profit. It would not have been in the Russians' interest to set us free, and they exploited us as much as possible. It was to their advantage when we worked conscientiously, carefully and eagerly. They promised again and again that by working hard and carrying out our duty we should bring about our release earlier, but finally we realised with bitterness—and here is an obvious parallel to the problem of the reformatory value of good works—that our labours and our good works only delayed our release. Not until we were "free", released from the domination of this foreign power could there be any sense in labour or good works again.

For that reason, "home" became the equivalent of Paradise. Everything was beautiful in our memories and our hopes. We rarely heard about unhappy marriages, and saw only the tenderest husbands and most loving fathers. Bad news from our homes in the post-war world did not worry us. "People at home are better off than the Russians are here, and *I* will manage somehow, don't you worry!" and besides, "Bread soup at home in freedom is better than a roast joint here!" The present could not deceive us; we regarded it as a mess of

pottage over which our birthright had precedence. Life meant
to be free, to be able to live and order our own life, not a life
empty of purpose but full of meaning, to be united with those
we loved—and what we knew here was not life.

Those who understood this comparison could see therein
the workings of our human life: if this life is bound up with
Christ, then to Him is attributed the power to release us from
the domination of a foreign, slave-making power, and to ensure
our arrival in our eternal home. The fleeting and transitory
nature of our mortal life can no longer make us sad, death and
the end of the world are no more to be feared, because our
longing reaches out beyond what is temporal. The present has
meaning for us only when looked at from the point of view of
the promised future, and this meaning is so assured that it
cannot be moved by any bitterness of our present circumstances. But rather this bitterness serves to make incontro-
vertibly important for me the promise of future release.
"Grant that Heaven may sweeter seem, and earth more bitter
yet, And amid the tumult of this world, eternity be set." Lines
from hymns of this sort, which in modern times have been
reviled as "escapist", took on a new significance, and one
could oneself learn to understand afresh the ancient Christian
Weltverachtung aus Hoffnung, the scorn of the world which is
bred by hope, which had become part of a more secular
Christianity.

The world is a prison, belief in Christ means the knowledge
of future release and homecoming; this hope which gives
meaning to life is lacking in those without faith. Life seems to
come from nothing and lead to nothing. Therefore it must
come to terms with imprisonment; it must seek to win a meaning from the present, which the present, however, cannot give.
Because it lacks a purpose it must take life as it comes; it does
not long for a shorter road, but for as long a journey as
possible; it does not look forward to the end of the road with
hope but with fear. It must be content to be given temporary
transitory meanings and must shut its eyes to their worthlessness so soon revealed, since (as St. Augustine said once) it is
only the eternal that can give meaning to the temporal. A man

without Christian hope must be satisfied with what freedom he can achieve under the slavery of a foreign power, and the hope of the other essential freedom is for him an illusion far removed from reality. That means nothing less than that he must be satisfied with an existence that never attains real humanity. That is the resignation out of which Pascal tries to shake us. A life without faith means a life of resignation which must continually soothe the pain of going without, and must deny and conceal itself. It is a life which has to find consolation for itself in transitory things in which there is no real consolation.

A man living without faith behaves as foolishly as a P.O.W. who no longer sees the present in relation to returning home. Many a man did this; he made friends with the power whose slave he was, put himself at its disposal as its tool, enjoyed small privileges which it offered and became the slave-driver of his companions; consequently, the return home which brought joy and freedom to his companions meant for him the terror of a trial, where he had to give an account of his misdeeds during his imprisonment. Many a man, in order to avoid this trial, got out of returning home, bound himself to the Russians completely, and now, as an official in the Eastern Zone, has exchanged one captivity for another—in every case, however, he has sold his birthright for the mess of pottage of small privileges.

These comparisons were continually revealing new parallels, which we often thought out for ourselves in our friendly discussion groups. Thus the difference between our life of Christian hopefulness and a life lacking in faith and hope was parallel with the difference between our own imprisonment and that of our comrades condemned to twenty-five years' imprisonment; the happy ending which always lay before our eyes was sooner or later our return, which would make it worth while having endured the hard road for so long. The latter, however, could no longer count on returning home and had to come to terms with the fact that this present vegetating was their only life, and that beyond it there was no other free life at home. And yet—and here is the weak point in the argument—only in their first deep depression did the hope of return

A CATHOLIC WOODCARVER

seem completely cut off; then hope, which is as natural to us as breathing, raised its head once more above all the depressing arguments of reason, and it still bears them up today. The fact that we could find joy even in simple pleasures, and derive our happiness from ordinary things and not only from what was inspiring according to our eschatological beliefs, was closely connected with the Christian faith and thus strengthened our powers of resistance even in the most difficult circumstances.

At this point I must write something in memory of Andreas Doll, who was one of my dearest friends during captivity. "Joy out of Gratitude" are words that ought to be written on his tombstone, if we could set one up over that distant grave near the forest camp, which we could at that time only decorate with a cross of birchwood. He was a Roman Catholic woodcarver from the northern part of the Black Forest, and he afforded me great pleasure with his broad South German dialect, when we marched towards the new camp side by side. Then he became my brother in Christ, one whose death at Easter 1946 left me very lonely. He was full of a quiet joyful piety. You could tell by looking into his eyes that he began the day by making the sign of the cross and by saying the words, "In the name of the Father, and of the Son and of the Holy Ghost! O Holy Trinity, to Thee be this day dedicated!" All the practices peculiar to the Roman Catholic faith served to lead him to Christ and not away from Him. Thus there was never anything to come between us. Every morning before marching out he would get a text from me "to have something to pray about", and in the evening he would sit with me under the big oak tree behind the barracks and listen to my stories or describe his past or his future life, his favourite picture being of how, on the day after our return home, I would be at church service, and he, making a detour on his homeward journey, would be in the pilgrim's church at Altötting. And at midday, when I took food out to the brigades working in the forest, curses of disappointment at the pig-swill dished out were hurled at me from all sides. He, who was a very valuable member of the brigade because of his professional experience,

91

would accompany me a little way and would say with that convincing simplicity so characteristic of him, "Let us thank God anyway for sending us so tasty a soup." When, after a long illness, he died of pneumonia, even the young Russian doctor, who had spared no effort to help him, stood sorrowing by his bed; I could not forget the quiet assurance with which, thinking of his family, he spoke the third petition of the Lord's Prayer with his last breath.

Just as a man cannot live a human life without joy, so he cannot live without jobs to do. Because the present had no value in our eyes, our life lacked any of those working objectives which are normally made necessary by one's profession or one's fellow men; this made us indifferent both to our work and our fellow men and did not allow us to take things seriously. Some close friendships certainly grew up but on the average, being always herded together in a crowd, we just lived alongside each other without really being aware of one another. Not until the eschatology of prison life was understood from the Christian point of view did the man on the next bed achieve any importance, and living together became a duty. I often observed with silent joy how when one of the few enthusiastic Christians ("a Christian is a rare bird", said Luther, and how right he was!) was moved into another brigade, without doing anything special, except being a good companion and (in later years) not taking part in obscene conversation, he grew in authority and people responded to him. Men became visibly enthusiastic when asked for news of him, and seemed to have been waiting for someone with a new and unwearied purpose in life to fill the emptiness of their lives.

Our relations to our work were similar. We could now understand fully what those passages in the Epistles must have meant to the slaves to whom they were addressed: they opened the door which enabled these men to preserve a human attitude towards tasks which according to reason could offer no human relationship. These passages told them that they must conceive of their work as done "to the Lord". Every thrust of a spade could be transformed from a task undertaken with reluctance into a service done to the Lord. Someone may say that this is

more easily said than done. It was not an exhortation from
outside imposed from above, but was a possibility promised as
a gift—and thereby a door was opened indeed: forced labour
need not remain forced, it could be transformed from a
meaningless drudgery into a service full of meaning (although
all the external meaninglessness persisted!), into a service
offered to the Lord. That is more easily said than done. Everyone who, like so many men, is the slave of some hateful
drudgery, learns daily, but the prisoner does so doubly. To me
it was a completely new experience. The dullest routine was
made easier because I consciously took an interest in it.
Now, feeling weak at the knees, with our strength dwindling
daily, urged on by a Russian master who was a veritable slave-
driver who meted out kicks and curses and entered up less than
we had achieved in order to get a higher premium for himself,
we would load tree trunks for eight hours on end during a
night shift at the saw mills, carting them to the saws, with
growing hatred of these voracious machines which consumed
the trunks and never stopped shrieking for more, so that in
rain, snow and storm, in an increasing rush, we had to perform
tasks which always demanded the last ounce of strength. How
could we, the slaves of men and machines, refrain from drawing
in a scornful breath when, to the annoyance of the master, the
current failed again—a frequent occurrence with the Russian
electricity system—or when a trunk got stuck in the frame, and
thereby offered us a pause, which we hoped would be as long
as possible? With an air of indifference we would throw on to
the fire the most beautiful wood which we would have wept
over at home, would hurl a sack of cement into the lorry so
that it burst, would kick a box of nails so that they were all
scattered and lost in the grass; we watched the lorry sticking
in the mud and did not push it out before the owner had
entered up a sufficient percentage for it. If anyone sorrowed
over the good things that were thrown away, cared for the tools
and hammered old nails straight, the others would wring their
hands and say, "You idiot, who are you working for anyway,
yourself or the Russians? Look, in prison you have earned your
breakfast by getting up, the midday meal by marching out, and

supper by marching home again—what's the point of working?" Only the passing of time was important, and I am sure that not since the days of boring school lessons has one of us asked what the time was and how long it was till the end of the period as often as we did during our imprisonment. Often I quoted that horribly appropriate verse from the *Odyssey* (xvii. 323):

> *For of man's virtue when he is enslaved*
> *Zeus the Far-sounder takes the half away.*

A slave is only half a man. And in communal life this becomes even more apparent. Perhaps the first shock which accompanied this realisation was greater than the shock of being taken prisoner. In Hitler's army we had experienced friendships and terrible disasters both at the same time. Here, all that was done away with.

During the first week's work in the forest camp this fact was made apparent by a small incident. One member of a brigade stayed at home for a day because of illness. For three days we received the "percentage-Kascha" (an extra portion of soup made from millet, pearl barley and such things) that we earned by our work on that one day. The men of the brigade were still thinking in terms of former army friendships when they quite naturally wished to share it with the one who had stayed at home for that one day, who was now back at work and just as hungry as they were. Two old prisoners, however, who were working with the brigade, objected indignantly saying that he had no right to it and should therefore not have any. We spoke a different language from them when we said that he was after all an old comrade whom we did not want to see starve beside us, and that one more helping among twenty did not make much difference. They could no more understand our appeal to their sympathy and comradeship than we could understand their pitiless reckoning of what was due to them—a method of reckoning on which the whole system of living in the U.S.S.R. is founded.

Besides that, there were the first thefts of bread. Only someone who knows how the prospect of the evening slices of bread is the solace of the last hours of work can picture the fury of those from whom it was stolen. The brigade leaders are ordered by the Russian camp commandant to report to him for punishment anyone who refuses to work. We do not take that seriously, because we cannot believe that one of us would denounce his fellow-prisoner to the Russians—then one day the unthinkable happens, to which we soon became accustomed, that a leader reports a weak member of his brigade as unwilling to work. And soon an even more unthinkable thing happens: that group leaders obey the orders of the commandant and beat lazy workers. Those who do this belong to the "upper-class" of the camp, they do not have to suffer half as much as their inferiors from the rigours of prison life. They only have to supervise, they do not need to use up their energy in work that is too hard for them, and are mostly on such good terms with the cook-house personnel that they get from them "extras" and better food, while their fellow-countrymen sit and stare at their potato-water. In the same way they get the best shoes and clothes from the stores while the wind whistles through the holes in the clothes of their fellow-countrymen. On top of all this there is such an atmosphere of spying that everyone learns to guard his tongue. "Friend, give me a corner of your paper, I want to roll a cigarette." "What's this about friend? All our friends died at Stalingrad!"

The Russians encouraged the breaking-up of all friendly associations. From the first they regarded the Germans as a solid block of Fascists, which they must at all costs break up. They made the officials appointed by them keep a sharp watch on the men, gave them better food and then incited the men to complain against the officials about this. Men were lured by the offer of privileges to join the "anti-Fascist club" and the anti-Fascists were incited to work against the "reactionaries". By means of the conditions of work, of which I shall speak later, they created sharp distinctions between those in the more favourable and those in the less favourable positions, between those who earned a large amount and those who earned only a little, between the skilled and the unskilled workers, between the strong and the weak. Thus any solidarity disappeared, envy and distrust poisoned the atmosphere, gossip played its part in this closely knit life; any community spirit, any appeal for a communal sharing of the burden or for the strong to stand-in for and be sacrificed to the interests of the weak were always illusory questions. When an attempt was made to bring about genuine equality, possibly by dividing the duties equally among them all, it was always stifled by the Russians. In their own system of work, which curiously enough they call socialist, they have organised everything on a basis of personal incentive so that they cannot imagine that the common enjoyment of a common reward could lead to anything but a lowering of the working capacity of each individual.

If our own moral powers, our own sense of community and of belonging together had been stronger we could have stood this test. Why was it that the years of collective education under the Hitler regime resulted only in the fact that, at the first test, any sense of community gave way at once and turned into cynical egoism? It should not have been so; not only general and natural human weakness was to blame. The old men who had been prisoners during the First World War told us this, and assured us that in those days things had been better; the young men confirmed this by their behaviour, since the Hitler Youth education had instilled into them a frightening cynicism. The Hungarians and Japanese exemplified another possibility. The Japanese, in a camp near ours, succeeded where the Germans had failed, in that the Russians did not hinder the sharing out of rewards to all the inmates of the camp. The Japanese community did not disintegrate under political temptation. The discipline which the Japanese soldiers observed with regard to their officers always impressed me, and it stood out from the plebeian lack of respect with which the Germans felt they had to treat their "dethroned" officers. In that forest camp we had fifty Hungarians, all civilians, who had been captured while on the road and had just come from a camp at Tula, they being all that remained of seven hundred men. Some of them were respectable middle-class people, some of them gypsies, but all in a pretty bad way. They stole like magpies, but never from each other, and if a man quarrelled with one of them, he had the whole lot coming after him—a thing that never occurred among the Germans. Thus, "German, beware of the Germans," was a household word not without foundation in the camp. This was an evil saying, uttered violently by many a man as though, after the self-glorification practised by the Germans up till then, he wished to express a negative racial doctrine. Did the evil really lie in the German way of doing things? Was this really worse than that of any other nation? At the same time, I have often been comforted by plenty of proofs to the contrary. How often has my heart warmed to the simple German people! What a fund of loyalty and constancy is still preserved in our country! How the urge to work and to create things of value broke out again and again in the midst of our slavery! How much lonely courage, too, in carrying out a responsible decision which was recognised as the right one! It was even possible to arouse the roughest man's sympathy for the weak and to bring out the best in him if one approached him in the right way. What delicacy, what respect for religious convictions was shown by those who had fallen away from the Church! How many examples there were of a servile attitude of mind, but how many also of upright defiant natures! No, they were certainly no worse than other people, and perhaps even something good might grow out of them if . . . yes, if! . . . How many things would have to be mentioned that would make this possible!

It is appropriate at this point to make some general observations about the Russian treatment of P.O.W.s, since at this time we were moved from the labour camp to camp 27/I where political questions were allowed to come once more to the fore. The tremendous number of men "missing" in the East, the miserable transport for those who were unfit, whom the Russians sent back to Germany after the war, and finally the crime of retaining tens of thousands of innocent German soldiers as war criminals have been the cause of many false ideas which need to be corrected. If someone wishes to object that the U.S.S.R. has by its own behaviour forfeited its right to just and reasonable estimation, then I can only answer that those false ideas must be corrected. This should be done if not for the sake of justice (to which even a criminal has a right, as long as we do not wish to become totalitarians ourselves), then at least for the sake of necessity, in order to gain a correct picture of the U.S.S.R. and not a picture of horror and panic.

In November 1947 I was able, with a small delegation from camp 27/I in Krasnogorsk, a suburb of Moscow, to take part in a conference with a delegation of the East German trade unions, which was at that time travelling through the U.S.S.R. The hall of a Russian officers' club was packed with about a hundred P.O.W.s from all the camps in the district; on the platform sat the delegation composed of ten men, among whom were Hans Jandretzky, Bernhard Göring (to inspire special confidence), Roman Chwalek and Hermann Schlimme. Behind them sat prominent representatives of the Russian P.O.W. administration. The afternoon session was divided into three parts; first, the members of the delegation gave accounts of the situation and the problems at home, then we were able to ask them questions about various details, and finally they questioned us. The first part impressed me most of all. The last we had seen of official representatives of the state were the Nazi "high-ups" with their poverty of intellect and their arrogance—and here we had the impression of simple, solid, sensible and modest men who were easy to talk to, who obviously did not wish to rule but to help, and with their lower-class attitude seemed much more like former Social Democrats than Communists. Only a few of them had even been members of the Communist Party. Their accounts were factual and straight-forward—this was at a time of transition when the split between the two worlds was not as pronounced as it is now. In all the speeches could be heard the echo of those good resolutions which in the prisons and concentration camps of the Third Reich had bound together the left and right wings of the political opposition: the resolutions to recognise each other, to overrule nobody and to work together. Anyone who took part in these meetings knows that these resolutions were taken seriously even by the German Communists because of their experience of dictatorship; there is no doubt that the developments in the Eastern Zone of Germany would not have followed the course that they have taken today—with such results for the Germans and for Communism itself—if those German Communists, who had experienced life in Germany under the Third Reich, had been able to take action freely in the light of their experiences, and if the Russians and their underlings who had emigrated to Moscow had not taken absolute control of affairs. The internal and external conflict to which many sincere old German Communists were subjected is a tragedy which ought not to be ignored.

The third part of that afternoon's programme was, however, most important in connection with our own problems. The questions which the delegates put to us were naturally all about living conditions. The answers satisfied them completely. The German club-member who was acting as spokesman emphasised the fact that we had complete freedom to answer; everyone could say what he thought. One should not expect, however, a prisoner to answer freely. Many of those present could expect not direct but certainly indirect reprisals if they gave unfavourable reports, which might mean the loss of their positions—and all of them held some position in the camps. For, of course, the Russians had not just picked out any working group and brought it here, but had sent members of the camp aristocracy who had everything to lose. For that reason nothing negative was said, all the "Plennis" were wonderfully looked after and were all most grateful for the benefits bestowed on them by the Soviet Government. The delegates were surprised and extremely pleased; so all the terrible stories that were told by many who had returned home were only anti-Soviet propaganda instilled into them by some incorrigible Fascists. By this time I was bursting and offered to speak.

"I am astonished that only the positive side of our life has been discussed. What the P.O.W.s tell when they get home is of course not only horror-propaganda, but is also based on the bitter experiences that most of us have had. I come from a camp in the district where there was the great drought in 1946. Our rations were certainly somewhat larger than those of the civil population. But they could always find extras and we could not, and for that reason our rations were quite inadequate for all the heavy work we had to do, and men grew so weak that they were sent home. One cannot counter anti-Soviet propaganda by believing that everything the returning prisoner tells is a lie, but by asking such a man three questions: 1. Whether during his captivity he has not seen some good in the Russians, or only evil—if not, then he is just being ungracious. 2. Whether he can contradict the fact that the orders of the directors of the Soviet P.O.W. administration were good but badly carried out by the lower-ranking officials. Every P.O.W. knows this is true; for he realises from the famous thick 'inspection soup' which they get on the days when one of the many inspectors comes to the camp, that the authorities wish things to be better. The fact that these orders are badly carried out is due to the difficulties of organisation and to a local inadequacy of personnel; for even today the old saying is still valid: 'Russia is big and the Tsar is a long way away.' But the Soviet Government cannot be blamed entirely for this state of affairs. 3. Whether he does not realise that we should have expected something quite different considering the treatment of Russian P.O.W.s in Nazi Germany. There inhumanity was ordered by those in command, here they try to prevent it—a difference which always carries weight with us sufferers. I am an Evangelical pastor and would like to add something else: I knew already that the relationship of the Soviet Government to the Church cannot be spoken of as a bloody persecution of Christians. But I have been astonished to meet in the camp officers such a willing understanding of our requests with regard to our religious welfare, since most of them have a very different philosophy of life."

Following on this verdict which I have reported almost verbatim, and to which the delegates had listened with worried expressions, there came unexpected applause from the Russians. (Herr Lothar Bolz, later chairman of the "National Democratic Party" in the Eastern Zone, which was nothing but a great confidence trick, and at that time editor of the newspaper News for German P.O.W.s in the U.S.S.R., printed such an abridged and altered version of my speech in this paper that my companions could not recognise my words.) The Russians, indeed, knew that being a P.O.W. was not like being in a sanatorium, they too had been surprised that everyone had stressed only the positive aspect of conditions, and were now heartily in favour of eliminating these bad conditions from every camp. In short, we saw, what had so often been experienced in the Eastern Zone, that within certain limits one can sometimes (though "sometimes" is a mark of uncertainty) find that the truth has a better reception with the Russians than with their German "stooges".

I still stand by what I said in that speech (apart from the last point which later experiences corrected, as I shall explain), although my general outlook has since changed a great deal. The three questions which I put forward are an exact outline of what even the most embittered home-comer cannot ignore. If the Soviet Government had wished to retaliate in the Nazi style for the treatment of their soldiers in German camps, then we should never have seen our homes again. Above all, two of their instructions meant for us a relief which cannot be sufficiently praised and which saved the lives of many: the prohibition of ill-treatment and flogging, and the regulations about being graded unfit.

A group of German prisoners were to be escorted back from the front. The captain gave the sergeant in charge strict orders that there was to be no flogging. The sergeant contradicted him in that unceremonious manner which we had often seen used by Red Army soldiers towards their officers. "These Fascists deserve nothing better than to drop down dead." To which the captain replied sharply, "You know the Party line. You will be held responsible if you do not arrive with them all unharmed." One could hardly say that that was the line of the N.S.D.A.P. (the Nazi Party)! During my captivity I twice received a blow from the butt-end of a gun; each time, as a result of my complaint, the guard concerned was promptly relieved of his post. Of course, beatings did occur during the first few years (though hardly at all during the later years—except in the trials; but these form a sad chapter in every country!), but what occurred is not to be compared with what might have happened had there not existed these strict instructions. The indignation with which our fellow-countrymen used to react to every blow shows what good grounds they had for doing so.

As far as the grading unfit was concerned, every month "inspections" were carried out by the camp doctor (often this was a woman), i.e. inspection of all the prisoners to see whether they were fit for work. We all marched past the doctor (naked or half undressed) and were looked at, prodded like slaves in a market; we could also make complaints about our health, all with the result that we were graded category 1 or 2 (fully fit), 3 (fairly fit) or O.K. (unfit for work). Just as there were doctors who sent men to work when they were really not fit, so there were doctors we knew, who, even in the face of protests by the commandant, gave verdicts in our favour. At any rate, it was a definite help to know, when our strength began to dwindle, that when we reached a certain limit we would be no longer forced to work and could count on recovering, and, if our health was not completely broken, on being made physically fit again. We knew from the very beginning that we did not need to go on working until we collapsed. This limit saved the lives of many of us, and it was not a matter of course, as prisoners from the First World War and Soviet prisoners of the Third Reich know well. At Stalingrad, ninety-five thousand men were captured, and today the survivors number only six thousand. I spoke to many of them and they all claimed that the high death-rate could be ascribed to the state of exhaustion and the terrible conditions (and thereby to a government which did not capitulate soon enough), and also to the long marches from the battle-front back to the reception camps, but not to the Russian guards and hospital staff. They were full of praise for the devotion with which the Russian doctors and nurses gave their last ounce of strength to save as many as possible of the Germans, and many of them fell victim to spotted fever themselves. It was this unexpected experience that made many of those fighting at Stalingrad regard the Soviets with new eyes, and join the "National Committee of 'Free Germany' ". In most of the camps the hospital was a gem, and the care of the sick exceptional. While the war-fever was at its height, there seem to have been some doctors, who, after the daily report of the number of deaths said, "Potschemu tak malo?" (Why so few?) But later on every life was valued, and everything possible was used to save life, from penicillin (I knew a woman doctor who bought this precious medicine with her own money) to specially selected diets. This was often true of doctors, especially Jewish doctors, who had sometimes lost all their family through the Germans. Every prisoner could tell of such things, and often these stories are very moving.

The sanitary arrangements, the supervising of the cooking, the improvement of the sleeping accommodation witnessed also to the strength of will of those who resisted this war-fever, and to their efforts to treat us as human beings. The "cultural encouragement" system had this end in view also, and was not only intended to influence us politically. In the autumn of 1945 a high-ranking officer visited us in the forest camp and in his talks persuaded us to organise musical activities, choirs and instrumental ensembles, in order not to grow listless and homesick. We, who had hoped to hear from him news of an early return home, were disappointed; but later I realised that he knew better and was concerned only for our welfare. *Kulturni schisn*, the cultured life, the Russians called it and spoke of it constantly, when they demanded cleanliness in the barracks or wanted flower beds laid out; yet they never made such a systematic fuss about cleanliness as was made in the German concentration camps.

"To let us live as human beings"—it cannot be denied that that was the aim of the Soviet Government. This was the difference from the German concentration camps. In November 1945 someone who had spent the year 1934 in Dachau told me that his first five months in Russia were worse than the year he had in the concentration camp—but in Dachau he had been in a privileged category and his experience is not general. One can say, however, that in general the system of loss of rights and utter degradation which makes life in concentration camps hell for the men, from the giving of a number instead of a name and the endless cunning to the terrible punishments and liquidations, is not to be found in Russian camps. Even in the "Sakljutshonnyi" camps (camps for civil prisoners), this system is apparently not in force. The accounts of Kravchenko and above all the reliable account of Margarete Buber-Neumann reveals this, too, and I myself noticed in the Sakljutshonnyis in the Urals, near our labour camp, that the prisoners had less freedom than we did, but the food and the treatment did not seem to be any worse. (These were criminals and not political prisoners who would be treated much worse; for in every Soviet inspection prison the criminals pride themselves, as some of my companions told me who had come from these, on the fact that they are not "politicals" and are careful to guard against expressing any political opinions.) This is connected with a fundamental difference between the Soviet and the Nazi systems (cf. my lecture on "Christianity and Marxism" in *Unterwegs*, Vol. 6, 1950). The humane tendencies, with which Marxism began, are still preserved today, in so far as the sadism, which made the S.S. State so bestial, is completely lacking. The cruelty of Sovietism is a bloodless cruelty. Its scorn of men is not cynical but Utopian; scorn of the present-day man as a pre-historic being compared with the man of the future who will be the true man. Or to put it another way: its cynicism is that of cold utilitarianism, not the cynicism that satisfies impulses. I am not analysing the reasons for the humanity of the Soviet Government's treatment of us, but I am confirming the fact that whatever utilitarian designs it may have had, this treatment was humane within limits.

Within limits! Therein lies the answer to the question of how it was possible, granted such humane treatment, for hundreds of thousands of German P.O.W.s in Russia to die. I cannot prevent the Communist press from reprinting the above remarks out of their context, without mentioning what came before and what followed in this book, but I also cannot let this risk stop me from saying it. Communist propaganda is itself to blame that the reports of returned P.O.W.s were so damaging, and that in Germany today not even a dog will accept a crust from Communism. The idiotic thing about all totalitarian propaganda is that it outbids itself and tries to destroy the force of an old, old story which is true enough in itself. The Communists felt the urge to make propaganda not only out of their aims but also out of the success which the Soviet reconstruction policy had already achieved: yet here they came up against all those who had had the opportunity to see for themselves. They were not content to speak of the privations which the inhabitants of the U.S.S.R. have to endure today for the sake of the future: they were not content to praise their success in the industrial, military and political fields. But they thought that they must praise everything, in fact they praised the Soviet man and the Soviet people as being already the new mankind. It is obvious, however, that in thirty years it is possible to organise and industrialise a country, but not to change fundamentally a nation about whose "backwardness" Lenin had constantly complained. *Naturam expellas furca, tamen usque recurrat* (You can drive out nature with a garden fork but it will always reassert itself)—these lines from Horace kept coming into my mind in Russia. They explain the suffering and deaths of P.O.W.s in Russia.

"When the Red Army moves into Central Europe, the world will see for the first time what a proletarian army is: a real army of liberators, more disciplined and humane than any before it," said a German emigrant in Moscow in January 1945 to one of my friends. He was thereby—and in his later disappointment he realised this—a victim of his own propaganda. What the world really saw was the same *soldateska* of a backward people that had laid waste East Prussia during the Seven Years' War. Only one who from the very beginning considered that when dealing with the Russians as well as with their satellites we were dealing with a backward race in the European sense of the word, with a race that in the mass is still raw material, untreated and in its original state, expected so little from them when he was a prisoner that he was surprised and grateful for the treatment he received. I am taking into consideration various points; such as the Russian conception of "living as a human being" which is quite different from the European conception, and I am not denying the Russians' wonderful characteristics, nor their unique Christianity nor the real fruits of their culture.

"Why are you always thinking about your return home? What haven't you got here? You've got food, a cinema, you can have women, too—what else have you got at home?" We often let ourselves be asked these questions, and by them measured the difference between our conception of life and theirs. The most significant difference, however, lay not so much in the highly developed needs of the Central European as against those of the Eastern European—but rather in the desire to order their own lives—a desire felt very strongly by us in the West. This was felt even by the simplest men (and was in no wise lessened by years of Hitler's domination), but was felt not nearly so strongly by the Eastern races, whether from disposition or because of the long years of regimentation and levelling-down.

This applies particularly to a time when war dominates a nation's life. For three and a half years the Hitler regime did not dare to subject the Germans to the real privations of total war. Stalin did this from the very first day, indeed the war here was only another aspect of the subjection under which the Russians had suffered for two decades; since the Revolution, conditions had been those of "total war", under which they had to sacrifice their own well-being for the sake of "higher ideals"; the Revolution, the Socialisation and the Industrialisation.

> *There are sacrifices here,*
> *Neither lamb nor steer,*
> *But human victims, as never before.*

The civil war swallowed up millions of human lives; collectivism meant that hundreds of thousands of Kulaks were sent to Siberia as "dregs of civilisation" (I have been in Ukrainian villages in which hardly a home had been spared this tragedy of the early 'thirties), while hundreds of thousands died of overwork and under-nourishment while being evacuated or in the labour force in the Urals and in Siberia during the Second World War. To the question put by a reporter about the effect of war experiences on the Soviet people, Konstantin Simonov —one of the most renowned Soviet writers who visited Berlin in 1948—replied that in the Western sense the Russians had had no real war experiences, for they were no longer individuals, but so much a part of the social structure that the war merely altered the part they had to play. He cannot have realised what a terrible state of affairs he had revealed by saying this. Since, however, prisoners all over the world are never better off than the native population, it was not to be wondered at that they had to undergo the same privations as the local inhabitants. Because of this, numbers of German P.O.W.s in the U.S.S.R. perished.

Indeed, we had not been taken to Russia for a rest cure. Nothing was wanted of us but work. This wish had of necessity to clash with the humane principles of letting us live like human beings, and when the clash came, it was no wonder that work had to come first.

I am sure that our major in the forest camp when he took over the command did not feign his sympathy and that his promises to improve our living conditions were not vain. But he was under contract to set to work for the combine 80 per cent. of the camp, and he had to ensure that the camp was run at a profit—and he had to ensure his own salary too. Every morning when he came on duty he stood with all his staff officers in front of the miserable groups of unfit men and made an examination to see if they could not perhaps send one or other of the men to work; thus the relief at being graded category 3 was to all intents and purposes quite illusory, and in the evening, too, he would fetch the poor men from the barracks to load the lorries. He would not have been a Russian, i.e. a man who laid stress on theoretical rather than on practical consequences, if he had not expressed sorrow at the thinness of the soup while inspecting the kitchens every morning, and then let himself be cheated by the manager of the collective farm of a few pounds of fat and a sack of flour. He would accept for our consumption the carelessly piled up stacks of half-rotten potatoes, for which normally the farm manager would have been sued, or he would exchange the 90 per cent. ground bran for the fine flour which we received from the central stores. This made a kind of bread which gave cramp to those with weak stomachs, and a soup which only made us wonder how the water got even a faint colouring from the small amount of potato-peel. They themselves hadn't much—no wonder that they made it up out of what was destined for us. While in the forest camp we had eight Russian storekeepers in sixteen months, i.e. each stayed for an average of two months until his fraudulent dealings (mostly of course in the high-class products like fat and meat) stank to high heaven, so that he had to be relieved of his post. Eventually a lawsuit was brought against the responsible maintenance officer at which some of our men could also bring complaints against him—but that did not bring our dead friends to life again. The higher authorities did their best to control everything by frequent inspections, but it is well known how deceptive these inspections are, especially if the inspectors let themselves be deceived. It is not to be wondered at that so many died, but rather that so many have survived!

II
KRASNOGORSK
DIARY

KRASNOGORSK
DIARY

12 June 1947

There is always something surprising about the unexpected, in Russia more so than elsewhere. For ten days on
the O.K. list waiting for the next transport home, completely
worn out, with a body which, suddenly suffering from all a
prisoner's ailments at once—boils, diarrhoea and urinary
disorders—protests against exorbitant demands made upon it.
Then all at once I was summoned to the commandant's office:
I am to travel alone to Moscow! "It is sure to be only so that
you can be released from there," says the commandant, and
impresses upon the sergeant accompanying me to show me
round Moscow thoroughly, so that I can tell them all about it
at home in Germany. Release does not seem improbable. So the
petitions of many of my friends to the Russians in Berlin have
been successful. At any rate they have caused the attentions of
the Russians to be drawn to me and aroused hopes and doubts
in my mind. Yet in captivity the old saying of the Stoics, λάθε
βιώσας—or, as my fellow-countrymen say, "never be noticed"
—is more than ever valid. I was moved alternately by fear and
hope.

13 June a.m.

An old rule: the farther east one travels, the more interesting does travelling become. Especially in Russia. The trains are
overcrowded, people are clinging to the running-boards like
bunches of grapes, there is a bitter and inconsiderate battle to
get in. Nobody finds it worthy of notice that the young fellow
next to me hurled the old woman down on to the rails. With a
constant cry of lament, "Bosche moi, oi, oi, bosche moi!" she
crawls out again. My guard prevails; two places are left free
for us without argument. Officers travelling too, obviously

111

intelligent men, are highly excited to recognise in me a Plenni and try to make use of their smattering of German. My escort told them that I was a *bolschoj doktor*. "What sort of doctor?" they ask. Theology. What was that? I try to explain to them. They come down to earth: that is not a science—and eagerly they inform me that science and religion are diametrically opposed to each other. That we can study theology at a university is for them proof of the incomprehensible backwardness of the West. Had I not studied anything else as well? Philosophy? What was that? Again I try to explain in simple language. In doing so I mention Hegel. Their faces light up. Ah, Hegel! Dialectics! Now I ask them what dialectics are, and they rattle off the four principles of dialectics, as Stalin had laid them down. Kant, Plato, Aristotle? Unknown! I might just as well have asked them about Brown or Miller. It is strange that the striking fact in the philosophies of Marx and Engels is repeated in those of Lenin and his successors, that the giant Hegel distorts everything that went before; Kant is as good as unknown (in Engels he is mentioned only in connection with the Kant-Laplace theory and with Kant's theory of tides). Democritus is known in Marxism because he is the subject of Marx's *Dissertations*, and every Soviet man of letters, inveighing against idealism, quotes dear old Berkeley, because Lenin, in the introduction to his essay against the criticism of empiricism, alleged him to be an example of the prototype of idealism. Everywhere I have found that Hegel is the only one whose writings are read and dutifully discussed— but naturally it is always said that Marx was the first to make possible the triumph of dialectics by purging it of all mystic rubbish. Over one-sixth of the world it is like listening to a gramophone record, whether one hears G. Alexandrov or Rosenthal from Leningrad or Victor Sturm in Berlin: whoever knows these men can always say the second sentence when he has heard the first. An intellectual life, completely secure from all surprises!

13 *June noon*

We have seen Moscow! While we were still on the train my good-natured sergeant kept on nudging me: "Skoro vidish

Moskva! Metro! Krassivij!" and his face shone like that of a pilgrim reaching Mecca. In such a way must a man have spoken of Rome in olden times, of the city in which is united all the glory of man's greatness.

We travelled hither and thither, on trains and trolley-buses, along past the Kremlin, over Red Square to the great Opera House and to the Stanislavsky Theatre, along Gorki Street and from one underground station to another. A dream city—that is the first surprise. Everywhere there are armies of women sweeping the streets. A giant city. The garland of suburbs, through which one has to travel a long way before reaching the centre of the city, is very extensive. The great stretches of underground railway lie well distributed over the city. It must be the most modern underground in Europe, built on a vast scale, constructed at an expenditure which only the building authorities of a dictator state can afford. The roomy stations are of ridiculous magnificence, like the foyer of an opera-house. This railway is the first instalment of the future; the worker is expected to weep with joy at seeing this example of what magnificence the future has in store for him—or for his children —or grandchildren, well, sometime anyway! Everywhere one can buy a little book giving the history of the Metro and emphasising particularly Stalin's personal intervention in the difficult building problems. Feverishly we travel to and fro, my companion cannot marvel enough at those subterranean stations, each one decorated in a different colour, and built with different materials. So we move about, more under ground than above ground and at last we travel out to a little station in the suburbs. This neighbourhood is worlds removed from the beauty of the façades in Gorki Street and the splendour of the Metro. Here, unchanged, lay the world which housed Raskolni-kov: the stinking back-yards, the poverty of the small shops, the tumble-down hovels, the pale children. That is all still un-changed. Of course, that cannot be done away with all at once, it will take time; but they are setting to work on it, and in a few years it will all have gone. You must just regard it all dialectically—not only stare at the present, but see the future in the present! All right, I will do that and not forget. But could they not progress more evenly, so that all our contemporaries might have an equal share in it—I had imagined that that was what was meant by socialism. But now there are some who are profiting by it today and others who will profit the day after tomorrow; there are the Metro and the palaces in Gorki Street, and here are the back-yards. You must just wait! Perhaps you see here a dictatorship with everything just as it was under Hitler, but the form and the content are quite different!

13 June evening

To think that there could be such a camp! Not a German from Brest to Vladivostock could have dreamt of it! The barracks shining in the sun are set on the hills on the bank of a little lake, the whole camp is a jewel-casket of flowers, on the lawns lie dark-brown figures, reading, sleeping or playing chess. Yes, it is Friday. Are they having a *wychadnoi* (a workless day)? I questioned the man who, after I had carried out all the formalities on entering, took me from the guard house to the barracks. "Tell me, what sort of work do you do here?" "We don't work here. It's a strange camp this, as you will see if you just look at the generals walking around." Those in the group wandering towards us at that moment certainly did not resemble any of the generals I had seen hitherto, but the most shattering thing of all was to be addressed as *Sie*. Nobody had used that form of address for years.

The N.K.V.D. bring to this "professional" camp all the people who interest them particularly—for favourable or unfavourable reasons. The unfavourable reasons no doubt applied to the many generals, staff officers and diplomats, and the favourable reasons to the technical specialists, scientists, parsons and so on. If the reasons are unfavourable, then this is mostly nothing but the "ante-room of Lubjanka", if favourable, then it is the next stage of the homeward journey, as I hoped it would be for me. Thus promise and danger live side by side; whoever crosses the threshold of this camp does so with anxiety in his heart—or with hope, as I did.

14 June 1947

Here, then, we do not work, that is, not productively. The various duties for this camp of about five hundred inmates were carried out by the available troops and subalterns, but in what a leisurely manner and without the use of that objectionable word *davai* (forward) which up till then I had heard a dozen times every hour! What work was to the labour camps, politics was to this one. In the labour camp political propaganda was nothing more than a side-line and an unwillingly performed "must"; one had the definite impression that it was all the same to the Russians what we thought, so long as we held no Fascist demonstrations and did our work properly. Here, however, everyone has propaganda fired at him from all sides, and is asked for his inmost thoughts. The thin young man who reads the news at morning and evening roll-call (a special office translates it all from *Izvestia*), almost preaches a sermon and seems to be in it heart and soul. Several wall-newspapers, a full programme of seminars, study circles and lectures testify to the activity of the anti-Fascist club. A library, which fills one whole room, arouses my enthusiasm; the catalogue contains an abundance of all kinds of classical literature, modern belles-lettres and everything essential from among the classics of Marxism. The delivery, too, of German newspapers from the Eastern Zone seems to be better here than anywhere else; other camps have only recently enjoyed this longed-for luxury. Life may not be too bad here: I am revelling in these possibilities like a fish which has just been thrown back into the water. I am planning, in the short time which I hope to spend here, to refresh and increase my knowledge of Marxist theory.

15 June 1947

As I have been told, this camp is directly under the highest directors of the P.O.W. organisation. It is often visited and inspected not only by the inspection commission but also by other high-ups, German emigrants from Moscow are often guests here, and the German section of the editorial staff of the P.O.W. newspaper (*News for German P.O.W.s in the U.S.S.R.*)

has its headquarters here, as has the central administration of the P.O.W. postal service; last winter the central anti-Fascist school for German P.O.W.s was held here and will be held here again this winter. All this means that irregularities in the treatment of prisoners and any fraudulent dealings as regards their care are out of the question. If there is any occasion for complaint, a member of the camp has the right and the opportunity to turn at once to the highest authority, and no camp commandant will dare to suppress his petition. The Russian officers are reserved, and the commandant is equally circumspect and correct in his behaviour. They are less talked about than the commissars, of whom several work here. One is responsible for censoring the letters, another is in charge of the group of engineers and their work, a third and particularly feared man conducts the trials. Over these, however, are the high officials of the N.K.V.D. who are often seen in the camp, among them Karagadse, alleged to be an erstwhile prince in Georgia, and a general who speaks fluent German and whose name is Stern, although we do not believe this.

The camp includes as mixed a company of people as one could wish for. Among the troops there are no fewer interesting people than among the officers. A dozen or so generals live in their own barracks, together with diplomats, economists, the famous Berlin traffic-controller Engel and several professors. In another part of the camp, separated from ours by a fence, live civilian internees with their wives and children, among them the Polish pretender to the throne, Prince Radziwill, who had been arrested by the Russians soon after the collapse of Poland, then set free and finally arrested again, also some high-ranking Japanese officers and generals. The German camp leader is Lieutenant-General K., an upright and completely trustworthy man who had risen from the ranks, and who seems to do the job very well. There are a few Roman Catholic and Evangelical clergymen who welcomed me with open arms. Many of them were members of the "National Committee for Free Germany", and thus their names were already known to me from their proclamations; now, however, they seem to have altered their ideas. Last year a special transport train took some ten Evangelical pastors home; for that reason they conclude from the fact that more Evangelical theologians, myself among them, have been brought here lately, that another special transport is due for home soon. Every Sunday there are both Evangelical and Roman Catholic services, although these are attended only by a small group of people. Since none of the officers above the rank of major do any work, and many others—the engineers for example—are doing office work, this camp, bedecked with flowers and set in such a picturesque spot, gives the impression at all times of the day—and especially in this warm summer-time—of being populated by holiday-makers pottering around, playing chess, discussing, chatting and reading. To me it seems like a fairy-tale. To the Russian officer who asked me today how I was enjoying it, I replied that the difference between this and my former camps was perhaps not that between heaven and hell, but at any rate between heaven and earth. That means, however, that anyone who has seen only this camp knows as little about camp life in Russia as he would know about the U.S.S.R. having only seen Moscow.

16 *June* 1947

My present wretched state of health was sufficient for me to be graded unfit immediately. So I have plenty of time. Anyone who sees me sitting or walking around with one of the thick blue volumes of the Marx-Engels books or one of the red-covered volumes of Lenin's collected works in my hand, probably thinks I am an enthusiastic club-member. But that does not worry me at the moment; I must get things clear.

The young Austrian lieutenant, who stands next to me at roll-call, has done better. He has already got things clear. He points scornfully to the volume of Lenin in my hand and asks why I am reading that, the theory of Marxism was long out of date, and I could see with my own eyes how it was working out in practice—where was now the need for long explanations? A great number of people here share his beliefs, the so-called "reactionary wing"—and the broad mass of P.O.W.s in the labour camps think much the same. But what does this spirit of rejection reveal? The narrowness of their bourgeois ideas, the German middle-class fear of socialism? The unteachable nature of many of the younger ones as a result of all the Fascist intellectual regimentation? This spirit of rejection can survive so long as one is not sucked into the Communist sphere of domination and can keep it at a distance, as the prisoners were still able to do. Yet as soon as Communism dominates and determines the course of the world around, then it must become pliable and turn into resignation and conformity. In the Eastern Zone this very thing is happening. All those who declined to take Marxism seriously because it was out-dated and because in practice its theories are contradicted, have to take it seriously now and can avoid coming to grips with it as little as they can avoid responding to a sermon which thrusts itself upon their attention and in the face of which they must finally realise why they responded to it in such and such a way. Thus it is of vital importance to get to grips with this understanding in time, while they are in a position to observe, test and hear arguments on both sides in freedom, and gain a stronghold for this rejection, if it must take place, which cannot be shaken. Men who are prevented from understanding Marxism in time are more liable to fall defenceless before it when it finally triumphs.

I am trying to get clear where I stood up till now; before 1933 there was nothing outside the Church which held my attention more than Marxism. The analyses of Marx and Lenin helped me to understand contemporary events, the crises, the war and the rise of Fascism; it seemed a matter of honour to be "left-wing". The K.P.D.[1] would have turned my sympathies towards it had its leadership not been so inadequate and had it not so much resembled the Nazi Party in its worship of force. Already I regarded the Soviet Union with lively interest, alternately sympathising and criticising, because I was opposed to my own environment; here, too, it was only the dictatorial element which irritated me. I did not think that I ought to weep over the atheism of its system, since in it I saw only a reaction against the hypocrisy of Christians. The hardness of the revolutionary measures could be explained by reason of the greatness of its aims, and justified in view of the great human

[1] German Communist Party.

sacrifices demanded daily by capitalism. The romantic anti-capitalism to which the young people of the middle classes paid homage and out of which Hitler made capital, made of socialism something to which one had naturally to say "yes". The question was no longer whether it was to be socialism, but, what kind of socialism? I did not want to answer that question romantically but with sober rational clarity—and so the answer was, Marxist Socialism. That meant as far to the Left as possible —up to the limits of the K.P.D., which was unfortunately so inefficient, so sectarian and which had such an uncompromising philosophy of life.

The year 1933 cured me definitely of any love for a dictatorial system. To a certain extent Hitler freed us from any love of Communism—not by his own anti-Bolshevik propaganda but by his own example of totalitarianism. The Moscow trials in 1935–1937 did the rest: there was nothing to choose between Stalin and Hitler, they were both tarred with the same brush and we had to guard against painting the one white in order to make the other black. I followed the disputes between the Trotskyists and the Stalinists very closely—and I knew which were right! The tourist-like accounts about Moscow written by such sympathetic intellectuals as Heinrich Mann and Leon Feuchtwanger were too much like what the Hearst Press and the *Daily Mail* wrote enthusiastically about Berlin in Hitler's time, and in André Gide's accounts the parallels which he drew horrified us more than him. The same year, 1933, however, made us unexpectedly into fellow-sufferers with the German Communists. The Gestapo attacked us, the Confessional Church, drawing our attention to the Hindenburg Legislation of 28th February, 1933, and thus accused us of preparing for and encouraging Communism. We could dispute this, horrified —we could however let this accusation serve to make us consider whether perhaps from Hitler's point of view we had not something in common with the Communists, and whether Jodl was not right when he said to one of my acquaintances during the war, "For Hitler, Christianity and Bolshevism are fundamentally the same, and I agree with him!" Now the common persecution formed a link between us; in small resistance groups, at the trials, in prisons and concentration camps we met our opposite numbers, and the bugbears of "bolshie" and "parson" were done away with by these encounters. The impressive resoluteness, the comradeship, the readiness for sacrifice and the manly dignity of some of the Communists let us see for the first time the ethical background of Communism; a way of life which was supported by its partisans with such devotion and, at the same time with such well-thought-out theories—a fact which distinguishes them from the fanatical sectarians—should have been taken seriously a long time ago. Now, they were taking us more seriously. Just as we saw a new side to the manifestation of Communism, so they saw a new side to Christianity and realised that up till now they had dismissed it too casually.

New possibilities seemed to be opened up on both sides. The problem of dictatorship took on a new aspect. The Communists had now themselves realised from their own experiences, what happens when the leadership breaks away from democratic control; they, who had always denounced democracy as being the "dictatorship of the bourgeoisie", began at last to see in Fascism the hoofs of the devil which they had talked of for so long. They also knew that the German working-man had not grown more ready for a Soviet system because of his experiences under the Third Reich, but rather had become still more disinclined towards any such totalitarian experiments. One could see that all this had given them something to think about. These problems would become more pressing if the hopes which they had set on the Soviet Union were fulfilled. Had not Roosevelt good grounds for his expectations? There was the alliance with the Western Powers and the contacts made by the Red Army soldier with the western way of life. Certain definite American demands had been fulfilled in the domestic life of Russia (there was even talk of suspending the collective farm system), the Comintern was abolished and the desire for a world revolution had changed to strong nationalist feelings. The distinct conservative tendencies of Stalin's system were evident in such things as education and the laying down of family rights. The Soviet regime had changed in its attitude to the Church, and had ceased its official godless propaganda. Russia had introduced her manifold contacts and influence into every aspect of international life, from U.N.O. to the Olympic Games. Would all this really lead to a softening of the rigours of Communism, to its purification and to a more democratic way of life? Can we believe that it is possible to fight against Fascism as the Russians have done without freeing oneself from anything resembling Fascism and without becoming more democratic? We can—but may we not hope also?

Behind us lies a world which can no longer solve its problems, and which stumbles from one disaster to another. Marxism, which can so cleverly analyse the reasons for this state of affairs, should also be taken seriously in its programme for salvation. With this programme is linked Messianic hopes; very well, but these had nothing in common with our Christian knowledge of the true salvation of man. But could we not impartially examine it, and, perhaps, approve of it, disregarding these hopes, and disregarding the philosophical aspect of the practical and political content of this programme? The Marxists offered to work with us, without demanding of us an acceptance of their philosophy of life. Could we reject this offer, since any way the East could offer more to broken-down Germany than the West could? We were a proletarianised nation. The West could mean only temptation for us—the temptation to rebuild rather than to undertake the harder but more rewarding task of starting again from the beginning; a temptation not to bear together the common burden brought about by a common guilt, but to become divided into those who still have something and those who have nothing; a temptation to return to the sins of the past. The socialist people of the East offer a form of society which seems to suit our needs so much better. The alliance with the East will help us to find a new definite way into the future. I feel much the same as Christopher H., the sensible engineer from Frankfurt, felt when he said, "When I was taken prisoner, I was almost glad. I felt great sympathy with this Russia and its daring new way of life, and was full of desire to get to know it better. If I had found here the sort of socialism praised by the Communist propaganda, I would have been an anti-Fascist long ago." He did not find it, and was bitterly disappointed. But perhaps he let himself be frightened off too soon by its imperfections. I cannot come to such a decisive and unfavourable verdict so quickly.

18 June 1947

"I judge every man by whether he adopts an uncompromising pro-German attitude."

"What do you mean by pro-German?"

"Not to yield an inch to the Russians and not to treat with Marxism."

"Have you ever read a single line of Marx?"

"I do not need to read him, I can see for myself what it is like!"

Another conversation:

"I hear that yesterday evening you went to General B.'s discussion group. Allow me to say that I was very sorry to hear it."

"Why? It was a very interesting discussion; one is not bound to anything by attending a discussion group, and one must get a clear understanding of affairs."

"I don't try to understand swine."

"Whom are you calling swine?"

"Every anti-Fascist! Anyone who still takes the side of the Russians in spite of what they have done to us and the way they treat us here, is for me nothing but a paid agent and a traitor to the Fatherland."

"Do you not think that there are among these anti-Fascists some men with honest convictions?"

"There are madmen everywhere. But most of them are just bought. I find it strange that pastors go to these circles when Communism has increased the amount of godlessness."

"Firstly, these groups are not based on Marxism but only on anti-Fascism; secondly, the Marxists don't force me to deny my faith; thirdly, National Socialism was a decidedly godless institution, wasn't it? If godlessness annoys you so much then you ought to have rejected it without compromise."

"National Socialism was still undeveloped and there was some good in it. Communism is satanic."

"I myself would almost reverse these judgments. But perhaps for you they don't depend so much on godlessness. Perhaps you have so biased a view of the two movements because Communism is taking more away from you than National Socialism did, and just because you are 'bourgeois'."

"Bourgeois—that's only one of these ideas belonging to the ideology of class-warfare. We are first and foremost all Germans. I am sorry to have to tell you that as long as you and your fellow-countrymen maintain such a pro-Soviet attitude, I cannot attend your services."

These two conversations were with members of the so-called "reactionary" wing. The camp is sharply divided into two groups, the "reactionary" and the "anti-Fascist". As in all the camps the opportunists belong to the latter group; those who are more definitely Marxist have generally less integrity than the others; some of them doubtless have honest intentions, and many, I am sure, belong only because of a real dislike of National Socialism. In the former group one meets men who are now really being loyal to the Führer; they confuse obstinacy and strength of character. Others think much the same as I do, but keep away from the discussion groups because they are afraid of appearing opportunists; many have been cured of love for the "Brown-shirts", without having aroused any enthusiasm for the "Reds". To try to exist between these two groups means to fall between two stools. That will no doubt be my fate in this camp.

20 June 1947

Today I visited the "club president", the man who is responsible for the flourishing intellectual life of the camp, while the German camp leader is responsible for the German administration. The latter was formerly in command of a regiment, and rose from being a quarry-man to the rank of general, yet in spite of the fact that this career was only made possible by Hitler, he has now got the idea into his soldier's head that Hitler's Socialism was only demagogy and that Stalin's Socialism is the real thing. The president is, however, a slim, handsome young Saxon bank-clerk, intelligent and half-educated. In him, as in the majority of the "professional" anti-Fascists in the camps, one can study the typical new generation of officials in the totalitarian states. These are mostly men of lower-middle-class origin—not quite artisan—who are obviously not worried by problems. They joined the S.S. as light-heartedly as they joined the club. They look well, and want to live well, and are intelligent enough to learn the necessary language to do so.

What he says is sensible and well thought-out: "I am glad that you are taking part in the discussion groups. In our anti-Fascist work we want to create common ground on which all those can work together who want a democratic Germany!"

"Unfortunately the word 'democratic' today has more than one meaning. The question is whether it means freedom of speech for all those who accept certain fundamentals."

"You will have read Grotewohl's lectures on this programme. There it is clearly stated that for Germany today the subject for debate is not socialism but a parliamentary democracy. Not until that is created can the next step be taken, a long time afterwards."

"We still have to consider, however, whether having got so far, we are likely to be surprised with a dictatorship again."

"A dictatorship is a battle-order, which is necessary in Socialism only if the ruling class refuses to give up its privileges. Herein lies one of the Church's tasks—not to range itself beside the ruling classes but make its followers see the necessity of a social revolution. I am glad to see that so many Evangelical theologians agree with us there."

"The co-operation of the Church depends upon whether the Marxists for their part will give up the fight against religion."

"You can convince yourself in this camp that you are free to hold your religious services. Every Sunday we put the room at your disposal for your services, and we do not wish to take away anyone's beliefs. The same is true in the whole of the U.S.S.R. I have travelled around a good deal, and everywhere I have seen open churches and the freedom to go to church. Mistakes have been made on both sides, but we must not

prolong them. The world is in the grip of a tremendous upheaval. The Soviet Union has gone ahead on the road to the
future. It will spare us a great deal of unnecessary suffering if
the rift between Marxism and the Church is healed."

Just as I was taking my leave, a German emigrant from
Moscow entered and on being introduced was very pleased to
learn what my profession was.

"I need your help."

"We have just been talking about how we must all help each
other to find a new way forward together."

"Oh, you mean help in the wider sense. Yes, we do indeed
need it, and why should it not be possible? Do you know
Niemöller? We don't want to fight against such Christians but
to work with them. Christian humanism and Marxist humanism
—their starting points are different but they converge later on,
and that is what matters. At the moment, however, I meant
just 'help' personally. We are translating into German Alexei
Tolstoy's novel about Peter the Great. You must tell us where
the biblical quotations come from."

"I should be glad to. But why does he quote from the
Bible?"

"Oh, that is all connected with the historical background.
But you will be astonished to see how much that is Christian
comes into this novel. Did you know that, though we Marxists
do not really believe in God, most of us have got over our anti-
religious prejudices?"

As I went out, the words of the president still sounded in my
ears. "Mistakes have been made on both sides, but we must not
prolong them." It should hardly be our job to condemn and
reject these advances from the outset as hypocritical tactics.
Doubtless something has softened that was formerly as hard as
stone. It is now up to us to show that Christianity is not a class-
conscious supporter of the "reaction", that is, of those powers
interested in keeping things as they are; that the Church is
able to free itself from the chains of class distinction; that our
"no" to Marxism is directed to its Messianic claims and not to
its social revolution. Up till now they have heard nothing but
"no" from us. They see that the Church with its vast majority

was firmly saying "no" only to them, not to the present state
of affairs with all its injustice. In National Socialism, in
capitalism, in Fascism, both good and evil were admitted, but
Marxism alone was condemned out of hand. With this "no" we
did not help them, but we still owe it to them to preach the
Gospel. They have always seen us only in the front rank of the
opposition. We must not be to blame if nothing new comes of
the present more tolerant attitude in their ranks.

24 June 1947

I have hurled myself on the pile of newspapers and
periodicals which are available here, and am catching up on
events in the world during the past two years. The Nuremberg
trials—U.N.O.—the increasing difference of opinion among the
victors—and developments in Germany. Anton Ackermann's
essay in the S.E.D.[1] periodical *Unity* on "The German Road to
Socialism" and Eugen Vargas' essays on the character of the
new "peoples' democracies", reveal what stirring times we live
in. There is evidence of a possibility that what have hitherto
seemed to us to be the dangers of Communism are disappearing.
Lenin's words, "All nations arrive at socialism, but not all by
the same road", are often quoted and given a good deal of consideration. The Russians are now placing a strong emphasis on
their own traditions. (Not long ago I saw that outstanding film
about Peter the Great, which, with its glorification of this
alleged "people's Tsar", contradicts strongly the Marxist
teaching that hitherto the State has been the instrument of the
exploiting ruling classes!) If the Russians have a little historical
sense, then they will not demand from us Germans the con-
demnation of our own history up till now; they will seek to
link up with those conditions which have become history for
us and allow us to find a way towards socialism which will
correspond to our mentality, our intellectual background and
our experience. Vargas' description of the "people's democracy"
reveals this. For him, although he does not admit it openly, it
is in fact an evolutionary way to socialism; a way free from the
dictatorship of the proletariat, from a one-party system and the

[1] Socialist Unity Party.

terror of revolution, a way of peaceful co-operation between the various classes, of a peaceful doing away with the hitherto ruling classes, and the carrying-out of social reforms, of the temporary co-existence of state economy and private economy, leading to the gradual assimilation of the latter. Is that not that evolutionary "growing into socialism" which many people expected, any idea of which the orthodox Marxists derided? Has the renunciation of the Marxist dogma of the inevitability of violent revolution not been shamefully side-tracked by Vargas' assertion that revolution was unnecessary, since the original state-apparatus had been broken down by war and by Hitler's occupation, and since the peasantry and the proletariat had already taken a hand in the government? If this "road to people's democracy" is not a snare and a delusion, and not merely a fleeting episode, then it could lead to the avoidance of the terrible manifestations of Communism: the bloodshed of civil war, dictatorship based on a philosophy, and Russianisation. If the Communists, including the leaders in Moscow, take this road, then it will be a sign that they have changed their spots and are now amenable to discussion. I know that in the last few months several things have happened which have descended like a frost on the spring flowers of these hopes, in the east and in the west, as well as in the "people's democracies" themselves, but it must be clear to every serious-minded person that there can be no progress without some setbacks and some obstacles. Too many people are determined that this road shall lead to nothing. But we must not help them by being sceptical ourselves, for we ought all to be interested in seeing that something comes of it.

26 *June* 1947

Yesterday evening I again went to General B.'s discussion group, whose subject was to be "Marxism and Religion". B.'s introductory speech betrayed both his efforts to throw dust in our eyes about the difficulties of the problem, and his lack of knowledge about Christianity—an astonishing fact, considering that he is a clergyman's son. Christianity and Marxism, he announced, both wished to bring about the "Kingdom of God

on earth", the Church by means of religion and Marxism by
means of politics; so they were both wonderfully comple-
mentary. Marxism did certainly reject religion because the latter
did not agree with science, but it did not fight against it, and
allowed everyone freedom in his own way. Contrary to my
intentions, I took an active part in the debate; the fateful
thing about Marxism was that it had been founded by two
Germans. If Marx and Engels had been Englishmen they would
have planned a practical political programme for the liberation
of the working classes and for the reorganisation of society. As
Germans, however, and above all as disciples of Hegel, they
could not be pragmatists. Instead of contenting themselves
with the discovery that in a capitalist society all political strife
meant class-warfare, they immediately had to magnify this in
the *Communist Manifesto* into a problematical teaching concern-
ing world history; and instead of being satisfied at least with
historical materialism, they must needs put it at once into a
framework of dialectical materialism, and of an all-embracing
dogma about life in general. As a result we were faced with the
grotesque situation that any philosophical query—for example,
whether like Kant I denied that one could recognise the essential
nature of a thing, or, like Lenin, I held the opposite view—took
on a political aspect, and a political discussion became a metaphysical one. As long as Marxism did not only base itself on
Marx's political economy but also on his philosophy, it was
not in a position to allow genuine freedom of religious and
philosophical belief, but had to endeavour to make real not
only its political supremacy but also the supremacy of its
philosophy of life. However serious for the Church may be the
problem of freeing itself from its former bondage of class
distinction, even if the problem is solved, co-operation between
the Church and Marxism will never be really possible as long
as Marxism clings to its philosophical aspirations. On that
depends not the fate of the Church, but the fate of Marxism.
For as long as it does not fulfil this demand and does not throw
dialectical materialism on the scrap-heap where it belongs, it will
not be able to add anything to the sum of true human happiness
and will come to grief politically, because it will always repulse

the majority of the people of Europe, who are bound to the Church, and will drive them into the opposition camp. Therefore it will never win them to itself, but can only subdue them by force, thus putting itself in the wrong.

I spoke excitedly, but I saw that the Marxists were not in a position to accept this sensible proposition. Marxism is a unity, I was told solemnly, it aspired to being more than just a movement towards social reform; its power lay in this very universality. "I stand and fall by my philosophy of life," cried Willi L., the only old Nazi Party member among these neo-Marxists.

"Then you are at least admitting that it is also a religion," I answered.

"No, it is not a religion, it is a science! Scientific socialism is true because it is scientific, as opposed to religion, and—as Lenin says—Marxism is all-powerful because it is true."

"Then destiny must take its course," I said finally.

Today, one of those who took part in yesterday evening's debate brought me an essay in *Unity* (the organ of the S.E.D.) in which it is explained how whenever in the past there has been any deviation, however insignificant, from orthodox Marxism, the whole system was at once at stake; only by guarding the principles could one guarantee the road to victory. That only proved to me how great a part fear plays in all this, the fear of losing oneself while one is correcting oneself. In the worshipping of knowledge, the very freedom to acquire knowledge is lost. But is Stalinism really orthodox Marxism? Or is it Leninism? I shall have to look around me carefully.

28 June 1947

Yesterday, while we were all taking our evening walk around the camp, I met General B., and at once asked him the above question. But I might just as well have asked an automatic machine; a penny in the slot and out comes the prepared answer all nicely wrapped up—there are never any surprises here. Certainly, Marxism was not a static thing, it was developing alongside the changing conditions of history. Lenin and Stalin had developed it further according to the prevailing conditions, and to that extent it was no longer the Marxism of 1848, but the basic principles were the same.

I had already heard that umpteen times, but I could not give in. "All right, but development does imply change, all the same. In the dispute as to which changes are permissible and which are not, in the disputes about all the theories from Bernstein and Kautsky to Lenin, who determines which are the principles that cannot be discarded? Who decides which of those who carry the development a stage further may give up certain principles and which may not?"

"The Party does that, and everyone else has to obey its decisions."

"Let me be more precise: the Party today does not agree with Marx that Socialism necessarily does away with money! For Marx—think of *Das Kapital*—that was essential. Max Adler was of the opinion that the link between Marxism and Hegel could be exchanged for a link with Kant. Lenin fought that idea. The Party therefore has to decide whether in future we pay cash or not—I see that, for it is a question of practical consideration about which Marx was not clear. But the Party also decides whether it may or may not agree with Kant that the essential nature of a thing cannot be recognised. It also decides whether I may or may not believe in the Resurrection of Jesus Christ and in the existence of God—you see, it is not science that we were calling on yesterday that decides, but the Party; the Party orders science to decide, and does not allow it to declare the Party incompetent—in this matter for example. Don't you see that something is happening here that must not happen under any circumstances—that only I can decide these very questions for myself, but must never let the Party leaders come to a decision on them?"

"If you come to a different decision, then you must leave the Party."

"No, I must not leave the Party—don't tell me that in Russia anyone is even allowed to leave the Party—but I must submit or else I am punished as a renegade! But a party ought not to claim such competence. It is, however, forced to do so as long as Marxism sets itself up as a philosophy of life."

130

He changes the subject. "Look, we must not worry about the competence of the Party to decide for the Communists. The decisive question is rather whether the Christian Church will sever every connection with the old world and the ruling classes. Nothing more is demanded of it. If it does not resist the Socialist Reconstruction, it will not be fought against. For Christians, only the practical political programme of Marxism is the subject for debate, just as you wanted it yesterday. Within the socialist community there will then be, so to speak, a free competitive fight between dialectic materialism and Christianity. For the Marxist it is an established fact that the more outward conditions improve, the more dialectical materialism will triumph because men will no longer have need of religion. You Christians are not prevented from believing that Christianity will triumph. But not one of us would think of deciding that battle by force. That would be contrary to Marxist principles. For that reason the Church has been given more freedom in the Soviet Union since it has renounced any counter-revolutionary activity."

"But you must admit that the conditions for competition that exist are by no means ideal for the Church."

"That is all part of the growth and cannot be altered overnight. But I am convinced that in the 'people's democracies' and in Germany everything would proceed with much less friction if the Church recognised the right moment and did not ally itself with its old friends."

This answer turned out better than I had expected from its beginning. There is no doubt that that is how they see it, and therefore they can, for example, see behind the anti-Communism of the Vatican only ill-will and disguised class hatred. Can we do anything about this? That will depend on whether Communism can respect the limits set out, whether it will use its political power as a weapon in the philosophical battle, and whether it understands more than we do by "freeing the Church from the chains of class distinctions", namely a positive decision by the Church in favour of socialism, the "league with the progressive camp", and therefore a new captivity for the Church.

15 August 1947

An enjoyable evening with Joseph R. Since he has been in the camp—which is just a few weeks—we have been told great things of each other, and now that at last we have met, I feel as though I have found a friend. He has had an unusual career, from being an actor in a Roman Catholic Mystery Play company in the time of the Youth Movement, and on the German radio programmes from Paris, to becoming a convinced Marxist, but he gives the impression of being a man whom one can trust. We had a very frank and confidential chat together. Here at last was a Marxist who does not say that everything the Soviets have done is good and worthwhile, and who does not hide his doubts.

"One must always remember that they are Russians. They have had to build up things for themselves under such different conditions. That is why they cannot understand why we are shocked by much of what they do. They were dealing with Russians and therefore had to use other methods than those approved of in the West, and they themselves are Russians— Lenin and Stalin and those around them—and therefore they have their limitations as we have ours. What really matters is whether they are on a road that will lead to a real future, i.e. a future in which everything is not the same as it always has been but in which we can once and for all get away from all the madness which we have just experienced."

"And why do you promise yourself that exclusively from Communism?"

"Because it states categorically that those who are the rulers according to the present social structure have interests different from those of the masses. Because everywhere it mercilessly questions people's interests and because it derives from the sober conviction that fundamentally everyone seeks his own interests."

"Is there not the possibility that someone might place duty above self-interest?"

"In individuals, yes, otherwise it would not be possible for single members of the middle classes to stand on the side of the proletariat, otherwise there would be none of your Christian

132

saints, whose existence I do not deny. But the great developments in history are encouraged by the interests of the collective powers and groups. When the ruling classes formerly supported the Church, then liberalism, and then turned to Fascism, and are now once again supporting the Church, one must always ask: What are their motives? Who is interested in it?"

"Very well, now I ask you: Who has interests in Communism?"

"All of us ordinary people. For the first time here is a movement which serves the need of the ordinary people, not one that appeals to the moral sense of the ruling class; for it knows that the ruling class as a whole can do nothing other than protect their rule and their own possessions. Therefore it does not make a moral appeal but removes by force the presupposition that one class should have possessions and thereby power. Marx did not command those with possessions to reform society—the Utopians did that, and anyone who still does so today is nothing but a Utopian—but rather he asked who would be interested in the reform of society, and that was the proletariat and now, in the days of capitalist monopolies, the broad mass of the ordinary people, i.e. all of us who work for our living."

"But you must not portray those with possessions as being completely blind. The realisation that society is in need of reform is very widespread today even among the upper classes of the capitalist world."

"Yes, they want small reforms in order to avoid a big reform. They accept the little discomforts of the small reforms —social insurance and the trade unions, just as they accept the discomforts of crises and wars which are unpleasant for them too. But these are less unpleasant than the big reform which they had to refuse. We, however, are all interested in the big reform. For it alone will do away with crises and war, in which we suffer so much more than the upper classes. It alone can make the world what it might be today. You have no idea of all that man could become! Just think how, with the present technical advances, the needs of all men could be provided for! Just think how senseless are frontiers, national hatred, the race for armaments! Who are the people out for the continuing of all this nonsense, who stir up mutual hatred, and will not allow the world to come to terms peacefully with its potentialities? It is always those who, as we have experienced, would rather submit to a Fascist dictatorship than allow a great fundamental reform to take place, a reform in which everyone has equal rights of access to the national larder, in which what we all achieve belongs to everyone."

"But surely to hope for that is very Utopian?"

"In former centuries it would have been so. But Marx's genius lies in the fact that he recognised that industrialisation had made possible something that formerly would not have been possible, namely a life in which, by means of communal work and the services of technical knowledge, everybody will be so well provided for that nobody will need to secure for himself a decent standard of life at other people's expense. The devastating thing about your objection is that this living by the few at the expense of the many is portrayed as something unchangeable, because it is alleged to be the result of original sin which nobody can change. Thereby you are depriving man of the courage to carry out what could be carried out today, and teaching him to make do with rubbish which is no longer necessary. And to whose advantage is it? Those who are interested in living at other people's expense. Look, I was brought up as a Roman Catholic, I was a pious Christian, but I had to come to Russia before learning to wonder about who really gives me everything in life; who paves the streets, who mines the coal, who made this box of matches, and this piece of material? And what do all the men who produce these things get for their work? Certainly less than anyone else, less than factory directors, civil servants, tradesmen or high-ranking officials. The others have to work the hardest and get least. I realised all this for the first time when I came here and could not stop worrying about it. What I don't understand is this: 1. Why the ordinary people in the world do not recognise their real interests more clearly, and always let themselves be misused to other people's advantage. 2. Why you in the Church do not recognise where you really belong. If you take your faith as seriously as I imagine you do, then there can be no doubt as to where your place is in the world."

"We shall want to discuss this further sometime. For the moment, I have just one small question. If we Christians put ourselves where you believe we ought to be, in the so-called 'progressive' camp, then that does not necessarily mean that we approve of all that goes on there, does it? Not everything here is as ideal as you make out."

"I am not saying that it is. I myself told you before about a great many things that are not in the least ideal. The workers are still very badly off here, and there are more than enough 'bigwigs'. But it is definite that the preliminary steps have been taken to ensure that things can be different, and that the points are correctly set along the line towards the future. And they are. Therefore the difficulties will gradually be overcome. You can see that they are learning more and more about it. In the 'people's democracies', many of the mistakes which they made here are already being avoided, and here, too, many things which we did not like are being altered. Conditions in the punishment camps have much improved—many men have seen this with their own eyes—and they have also learnt by slow stages that one cannot simply drag off a man and make him disappear. One must be patient about these details. After all, we are speaking of Russians."

16 *September* 1947

Heinz A. is the other young Marxist here who knows how to do things in an impressive and credible way. He seems to be held in very high esteem by the Russians. He is recognised to be the best horse in the stable, and, in the "Anti-Fascist" School, which is a special department in the camp for giving the cream of the anti-Fascists from all the camps instructional courses lasting for several months, he is given ever more important duties. His talks reveal an upright and idealistic ardour, he has an excellent command of theory, and this has obviously become for him the key to the world of truth, a key which he had not found hitherto. As a student of national economy he was taken prisoner, suffering from the same perplexed state of mind as the majority of young Germans: sceptical of the Nazi regime, a stranger to the traditions of the Church, without ever having had any striking religious experience. He had occupied his mind only by dallying with literature and philosophy, with no guiding principles and with nothing at stake and seeing nothing in the world around him that called for sacrifices. He entered into captivity with the usual terror of the Russians—and found something quite different and unexpected; not sub-human Bolsheviks, not a "materialism" whose god is its belly, but men filled with one idea, men who knew what they were here for, and before whom he must creep away to hide the emptiness of his life. His sense of gratitude was too great for him to be made bitter by his illtreatment when taken prisoner, or by the miserable conditions in the camp. He was, rather, astonished at the correctness, even humanity, which he saw over and over again in the attitude of individual Soviet officers towards the prisoners. He was interrogated—and the Commissar is nothing like the terrible figure depicted by the Czechs in anti-Communist literature; he is an educated, friendly man who is willing to listen to one's life-story and to whom Heinz had to confess that he had lived up till now without worrying about the world, the Nazis and the Communists. The high-flown phrases crumble away in his hands, Heinz sees that he has still a lot to learn, a new world is opened up before him, and at the same time he is shown a way —the way in which these men are fighting for a better world. There is such a way then, it was framed by great thinkers as a result of great intellectual effort, and it is now being trodden by a great army of people. There is, after all, some sense in thinking and in finding out, the truth does exist and to this truth belongs the future, and it is worth fighting for. The disappointed, perplexed, characterless, blasé, self-centred middle-class youth sees himself invited for the first time to pledge his life for a purpose that has a meaning; the joy of sacrifice and a teaching which satisfy both heart and mind beckon to him. Marxism has become for him a decisive spiritual experience. He thinks of his life as it has been till now with a shudder, he thinks of his home environment with all its "song and dance" about careers and business, with its Christian and national hypocrisy which was always fostered by naked egoism, with its petty cares and thoughtless pleasures. Ashamed now, he sees how till then he had taken the division of mankind into rich and poor, high and low, privileged and non-privileged to be natural and unalterable, which is not so. His eyes are opened to the fact that this differentiation determines everything, and de-humanises and poisons all human relationships. He realises now that things can be different, and he is joyfully prepared to cling to everything that here in Russia seems to point to the new reality, and to despise everything that still remains of the former life.

We are sitting on the seat behind the barracks in the twilight. This is not a chance meeting, but a pre-arranged interview which is to be the beginning of a systematic discussion of the problems.

"The Devil must be behind it when two people, who are honest, and only want what is best, fail to agree. For me, Marxism is not an end in itself. Therefore it is of the utmost importance to me to try to understand your point of view and, if possible, to clear away what lies between us. I know that the Party is in earnest when it declares its intention of coming to a peaceful understanding with church people. Many of our anti-Fascist pupils think to demonstrate that they are Marxists by acting like bitter enemies of religion. Then only with great unwillingness will they obey the order prohibiting anti-religious demonstrations, and believe that it is nothing but a cunning and temporal tactical move by the Party. But I repeat: you misunderstand the Party; to the Party this is not merely a tactical move, but a firm and definite wish. What do we want? Men's happiness! We do not want to take from them what is important, but to give them something. We do not want to free them from religion, but from exploitation. We want to make them so free that they can really live their own lives, without any compulsion, some religiously, some irreligiously."

"I hear the message but lack faith. I have heard and seen

much that leads me to doubt this. They don't all think as you do."

"I know that many are still dominated by the old anti-religious resentment; not everyone has heard that the Party has adopted a new line and that it means it seriously. But I assure you that discriminating people think as I do."

"Why are you so sure?"

"First of all because of the instructions that we receive. They all point in that direction. Next, because of the outlook of contemporary Soviet life. The period of revolution, during which one could see enemies everywhere and had to hit out on all sides, is over. People now live naturally as Socialists. The instructions we get now are not only to be taken as tactics but are an indication of what the future is meant to be. They all show that the Party, after this extremely severe struggle, does not wish to press its claim on the people, but desires to let them live as they will. The deepest impression I got in the first few months of my imprisonment was that these were not a people oppressed by a minority, but I saw them building together the 'new life', and everyone knew how much he himself would gain from putting this first."

"You are idealising. Surely you must see that among the people there is great discontent and that they are dominated by a sinister compulsion."

"Needless to say, I am not blind. I know that many of us think it necessary to pretend to be blind. But that is wrong. I can see all that, but what really matters is to see it in its right perspective, that is—and you must forgive this well-worn phrase, of which you are probably sick and tired—to see it dialectically. This means that one must regard all details from the point of view of their connection and as part of a scheme of development, and must ask of every detail whether it is the after-effect of some past event or a prognostication of the future. I know that many Germans believe that we are blind or bribed because we accept the Soviet Union in spite of the many injustices in the Soviet system. They see that many people here live in greater poverty than many in the West, that only a small class of people can reach a higher standard of living, that the

N.K.V.D. keeps a good look-out everywhere to ensure that there is no freedom of the Press in the Western sense of the term, and that everyone is forced to work. After most of them were at first quite willing to break with Nazism and to give some thought to Communism, they are now fed up to the teeth with it, change sides again and then glorify Hitler who was in the right in his fight against Bolshevism, and finally become worse Nazis then before. Why? They come to a collective farm, see that the farmer's wife has only two old pots to use in the kitchen, think of their fine kitchens at home and say that Communism is a fraud. For my part, whatever I see, I ask myself: can it be explained from the point of view of the past? Then I realise that it is due to necessity, poverty or laziness, and I know that all that will be overcome. Or can it be explained from the point of view of the future? Then I see what great enthusiasm the youth of the land has for the communal tasks, and that it is impossible for a young man to give himself over cynically to an egoistic philosophy of life as many do here at home; I see many factories with their outstanding social organisations; I see collective farms in which the farmers live very well without farm-hands or casual labourers as is the case in Germany; I see the students in Moscow belonging to all the different races in the Soviet Union, whose scorn of racial barriers is proverbial, and whose ambitions are never directed towards individual achievements, but rather towards communal results; I have got to know families in Moscow and have seen their houses and their living conditions improve in the course of a year. And if some people live better than the average it is not because, as with us in Germany, they have chosen their parents better, but because they have done great things for the community. For this reason they are awarded larger incomes of which nobody is jealous because everyone knows that those achievements will benefit them all and that everyone who can accomplish equal tasks can have equal compensations and that one day everyone will have better living conditions."

These two conversations reveal almost all the arguments which moved many of our honest fellow-prisoners to go over to Stalinism. If we ask ourselves how it comes about that in face of the same facts some grew enthusiastic about it, and some were frightened away from it, then the answer is contained in these two sentences: "You must look at it dialectically!" and "You have no idea what good things the future has in store!" Anyone wishing to understand why Communism has had treacherous and unwilling followers as well as faithful and enthusiastic partisans must understand these two sentences. These phrases are of course the outcome of blind faith—although the Communists like to think they are the outcome of reason and knowledge. "Seeing dialectically" helps them to resist the temptation to see things as they really are; it is the buffer which absorbs the shock of disappointment. Thus they manage to dispose of everything that conflicts with their wishful thinking in such a way that there is no longer any danger. Nothing can disturb them any more; even if they themselves lost their lives in a Party purge, that would merely be a "detail" at which they must not stare fixedly and "metaphysically" as at an isolated incident, but which they must regard as playing its part in the broad scheme of development, not doubting that this is directed towards a definite goal. From there it is only a step to a deliberate blinding of oneself, and to propaganda which is not limited by reality.

"When you say, 'That is an old, badly pointed barrack wall,' " declared Professor Janzen to us once, "then you have given a metaphysical judgment, and singled out one moment in the present." But if you say, "That is a fine new wall, spotlessly white," then at the moment you are wrong, for it is not yet new and spotlessly white. Look at it dialectically, and you are right, because it will be so tomorrow. When you tell people at home that Russians live in old bug-ridden huts, then you are lying, although it is the case in many districts. If, however, you say they live in beautiful new houses, then you are telling the truth, although only a few live in them today. To see the future in the present, that is what 'seeing dialectically' means." The difficulties begin when someone no longer sees in the future what the leaders wish them to see. The selecting of those details in which one wishes to see signs of the future is an action pre-determined by one's beliefs. Supposing that the future is announced not in a spontaneous youthful way but in the mechanical manner in which propaganda is churned out, not in the present achievements of Soviet music but in the decline of the Soviet film, not in the brotherhood of nations but in growing nationalism, not in the old armoured cruiser *Potjemkin*, but in the Suvorov film which we saw recently with its glorification of war? Supposing the better living conditions of the upper level of society do not represent a promise of better things for everyone but rather the beginning of new class distinctions? Supposing force and despotic rule are not merely a temporary necessity but an indispensable and permanent feature of the system? An easy idealism says, everything that is bad comes from the past, everything that is good points to the future! Supposing it was the other way round? Anyone asking himself this begins to doubt, and doubt opens one's eyes. Therefore they have to fear doubt like the devil.

Marxism must be true because God does not exist. Because there is no God, Marxism is the only solace. If Marxism were not true, where should we be, since there is no God? Therefore they have an amazing ability to live in the future and to ignore the present. Recently we set out in a lorry to fetch potatoes for the camp. The lorry broke down. We stood around in the rain cursing. The driver popped out from under the lorry; he was thin, dripping with rain and covered in oil and wearing an old torn pullover, but he smiled and said, "Nitshevo, duazet ljat possle-budit kommunism!" (Never mind, in twenty years' time the Communist state will be here!)

An officer of the Polit-bureau gave a lecture describing the Siberia of the future; laughing cornfields, blossoming orchards, rich new towns, and so much space that the masses from the overcrowded countries of Western Europe would go there in throngs, "not deported, no, indeed they will be tumbling over themselves to get to this beautiful country, and anyone who wants to can spend his holidays on the Riviera; for then there will be no problems of air transport". We could see that he was already living in his dream world and that he could not understand why West Europeans feared the peace-loving Soviet

Union instead of throwing themselves into its arms in their eagerness to live in the Siberia of the future.

One cannot understand the Communists until one has grasped the fact that since the time of Marx they have all been fascinated by the picture of what man might be in the future. One speaker ended his lecture on Darwin's Theory of Evolution, which for him was "not a hypothesis, but an absolute certain, incontrovertible theory", with the enthusiastic words, "Anyone who follows the development from the uni-cellular organism up to *Homo sapiens* must realise that we are now only at the beginning of the history of man and that the real man is only now standing before us. His era will begin when Communism triumphs over the class-ridden society." Marx has already said this; not until this triumph comes will the "pre-historic age of man" come to an end. History up till now has been nothing but the laborious struggle of man to find his way out of the primeval forest; religions, racial hatred, wars—all these are the dead wood of the primeval forest. The man of the future will be able to penetrate and dominate completely the laws of nature, a transparently rational being with a will ruled entirely by reason and freed from everything that was stupid, irrational and sub-human. Gorki once said that Lenin was the only man alive then who lived entirely in the future; the land of the future lay before his eyes as though it were in the present, as faultlessly fashioned as crystal. This led to the unreserved emphasis on the technical aspect of life, with no romantic reservations and no tears shed over the sacrifices of the past. This was the reason why they are able to take in their stride problems which we struggle with so seriously. We struggle so earnestly because we take so seriously what has happened in the past. Roman Catholic–Protestant, Bavaria–Prussia, Monarchy–Republic, France–Germany: what do all these signify when seen from the point of view of the man of the future? They are only molehills which will no longer exist when the great plough of the new society has passed over the fields of human life. That is why they can convert the castles in the Russian Zone into piles of bricks for the new farm houses. That is why they can pacify us with regard to the Oder–Neisse Line, as General M.

did the other day, he having been converted from a loyal Hitlerite corps commander into a Marxist. He consoled us by saying that in the future world frontiers would no longer have any significance. How indignant Joseph R. was recently over the "reactionary stupidity" of someone who declared that the present was "the battle of slavery versus Germanic Rule", whereas it was really "the battle of the future versus the past".

These are indeed the children of the age of science! There seem to be two schools of thought which are hard to reconcile. One that thinks scientifically, thinks along evolutionary lines, continually discarding out-of-date explanations in favour of newer and better ones. It is concerned with the past history of its own knowledge only as a museum piece. The other that thinks historically sees every epoch in history as "directly from God"; for it each age has a personal value of its own, quite apart from its value as coming one step nearer the man of the future; the past is its school, it listens to the voices of its ancestors and goes back to its beginnings. These two processes of thought have little in common but are dependent on each other. The fate of Marxism lies in the fact that it has given itself over entirely to scientific thought. Thus it is continually offering violence to the past because it despises it.

One might object at this point and ask whether I am not overlooking the fact that the Soviet Union has recently shown a renewed interest in history by affirming its national traditions. But that only gives emphasis to the question of whether the U.S.S.R. does not increasingly contradict Marxist expectations. History is unreasonable; Marxism wanted to leave it behind but it is asserting itself in spite of this opposition—and this is made obvious by the fact that things are taking a different turn from what was promised by the Marxist Utopia. Man cannot and ought not to get rid of the irrational—"the primeval forest". The world of the future will not look like that transparent crystal which Lenin, as a child of his time, saw in front of him.

17 September 1947

I have just found an interesting example illustrating this relationship between Communism and history in a back number of *Internationale Literatur* (A Moscow journal published in German). Julius Hay, a Marxist playwright from Hungary, is discussing a performance of *Tartuffe*, in the Stanislavsky Theatre in Moscow in 1940, at which the Russian public were given the original ending with its apotheosis of absolute monarchy. He says that the fact that there is no longer any need to leave out this ending at performances in the Soviet Union as hitherto, shows the political maturity now attained by the Soviet citizens. There was no longer any need to fear that people would come away with dangerous leanings towards monarchy, but could be trusted to understand this ending "historically", that is, to realise that for the people of Molière's time absolute monarchy was a "progressive element" as opposed to the rule of the aristocracy, whereas, nowadays, of course, monarchy was decadent. "To understand historically", means to regard an event in the past as a step in the path of development and nothing more. I have seen beautiful editions published by the Moscow Academy: the memoirs of the Archpriest Avvakum, the *Dialogues* of Plato, the *Divine Comedy*; but they were always given a preface to guide the reader to this "historical understanding" and to prevent him from learning a different, more direct lesson from these texts, and therefore from taking them too seriously. In that way history is put into a glass case, it no longer comes to meet one, but is dead and gone. I can no longer listen to Plato nor converse with him, but "catalogue" him and view him from afar. Here it becomes clear how closely the real relationship with history, that is to say, having converse with history, is connected with the Incarnation of the Word in Jesus Christ. Because the Word became Flesh, there are historical texts which witness to the fact: the Old and New Testaments. They speak to me as though I were talking to them personally, they defend themselves against being deprived of their eternal value, and come to meet me directly. Then the conversation is extended to those who also took part in it: St. Augustine, St. Thomas Aquinas, Luther, and every epoch of Church history is also a partner in the conversation. In that way it is possible to gain a different view of the whole of history; Buddha and Plato do not only want to be regarded "historically" but to be listened to and taken seriously as living partners. The true relationship to history is based on the Christian exegesis of Holy Scripture; here too are seen the irreconcilable differences in the Christian and the Marxist conception of man.

29 September 1947

I am reading Dostoievsky's *The Possessed*, which I have not done for many years. While the camp band is adding pleasure to the Sunday evening promenade around the camp with its dance music, I am sitting beside Andreas R., a Bavarian who is well-up in literature, telling him about it. I quote Bukharin's words in his last speech before his execution when he said that nowhere in the whole of the U.S.S.R. can one still find a "Dostoievskian existence", and I express the feeling that this must be quite true; for a well-disciplined State could never be created with the aid of the kind of Russians whom one meets in *The Possessed*, with their extreme individualism, their endless discussions and their far-fetched logic. To which Andreas replies, "Look, with everything that repels me in the Soviet system I ask myself the question: if you were Stalin and had to deal with Russians, would you do anything different?"

This question leaves me non-plussed. It puts things in a different perspective. We certainly do react in too western a fashion and judge from a western standpoint (although Communist propaganda is to blame as well, since it always thrusts the Soviet system at us as the ideal model for all the world). Indeed, I would adopt different methods with regard to the Church and thereby the whole would be altered fundamentally. But would it work without any of the strict discipline, without the frightfully severe penalties for thefts and sabotage, without putting an end to discussions and setting up an undisputed authority? How would they have got along here with a parliamentary democracy? But what kind of question is this? Does it not presuppose that man exists for the State and that the setting-up of a "disciplined State" justifies everything? Certainly, without Stalin the Soviet Union would not now be the power, bristling with weapons, which dominates one-fifth of the world and arouses terror in the heart of everyone. But is that a misfortune for its inhabitants? They owe Stalin not only this well-ordered State but also their power as a nation—but at what a price!

20 *October* 1947

In the "Big Club" the anti-Fascists have put on a frightful exhibition, namely photographic copies of the reports of a German police detachment about the executions and liquidations which they carried out. There is no doubt that they are genuine documents, in the cold-blooded official language of which is revealed the terrible fall of our nation into the deepest shame. The unfavourable reactions of many of those looking at them ("And that's what Germans hang up for all to see! Hanging out their own dirty washing! They ought to put beside them pictures of what the Russians have done!") makes me very willing to agree to the request of the club that I should speak about "The Question of Guilt" at a meeting of the camp called for this occasion. I know that it will be difficult. Recently at a service a young East Prussian pastor of the Confessional Church was induced by the text to speak about this subject in his sermon, choosing his words carefully and well—and afterwards even the most faithful members of the camp, who fundamentally thought as we did, were indignant because "these things were always being brought up".

I began by telling of an experience which Alfred B. had recounted to me in the forest camp. During the war he drove his regimental commander to a town in the Ukraine. Towards them came a long procession of Jews being led to their liquidation. At the end walked a mother, with one child in her arms and the other holding on to her skirt. When she fell behind, too weak to keep up, one of the S.S. guards escorting them gave her a blow with the butt of his rifle. Blood flowed from her mouth and the screaming children threw themselves on her, whereupon the S.S. man shot them both. "That, General, was not what we were fighting for", said Alfred, and his commanding officer, not a hard-hearted Nazi, but a humane officer loved by his men, replied, shrugging his shoulders, "It certainly is hard. But perhaps the Jewish problem cannot be solved any other way."

In addition I discussed three phrases:

1. We knew nothing about it!—but why did we know nothing about it? Was it that we could not know, or would not know?

2. We did not want it! Did we, in our heart of hearts, really not want it, or is it merely that we no longer want it today?

3. We could do nothing about it! Did we do everything we could to prevent it? Did we do all we could for those who were persecuted?

Finally I told them about a scene in a leave-train in 1942 when one of us gave an account of the shooting of the Jews and said while we were all silent and depressed, "If there is a God, that must be avenged." "There is a God, and it has been avenged." Dead silence in the hall.

This seems to have been understood rightly, even by those who still mourn for the Third Reich, and it led to many profitable discussions with those very people.

27 *November* 1947

My speech at the reception of the German Trade Union delegation (see page 99) has had an unexpected result. In the evening of the day before yesterday I was asked to go and see General B., and found with him Joseph S., another anti-Fascist and Professor Janzen. In spite of his German name and his fluent command of the German language, Janzen is a Russian, the man responsible for the political education of German P.O.W.s in the U.S.S.R. What do they want? I am once again complimented on my frank attitude, which showed that I was "a man of truth". Now they wished, from the hundreds of reports collected from all the camps, to compile a book about the life of P.O.W.s in the U.S.S.R., which would present a true picture to those at home. The tales of horror told by those returning were unfortunately not entirely false, but they were only half the truth; this book was to present the whole truth. "The Soviet Union does not need to fear the truth." Would I take part in working on and editing the book?

One should always ask for time to think over such propositions, though in this case it would have looked as though I did not want to represent "the whole truth" at home. Unfortunately I said "yes" spontaneously, and thought it over afterwards. Then I listened while Janzen gave further details of the plan, and I realised quickly what I might have thought of before, namely that the matter of the whole truth was not going to be taken very seriously and that the book was destined only to be a glorification of the humanity of the Soviet P.O.W. administration. Finally I left the room without committing myself any further, followed by the gaze of the man whose eyes I had to look at again and again while he coldly regarded the others—who were after all his companions and fellow-workers—as though they were merely tools. "The ideas do not worry me, but rather the faces of those who fight for them" (Longanesi).

I walked round the camp for hours and reproached myself for my over-hasty assent. I shall definitely tell the whole truth at home and also do the Soviets justice, but it is certain that in this book much will be left out that ought not to be omitted: Eugen K., who froze to death because they were not allowed to light a fire while at work; Alfred S., who was shot in the stomach by a guard who also slashed his face—these will not appear in the book. Nor will the corpses which, during the winter in Archangel, were pushed frozen under the bunks and not buried till the spring, so that others could get their rations. I must be alone in saying what I have to say, and not in the company of those more tractable of my companions who do what they are told.

Next day I withdrew my consent; it was clear to me that it was nothing but political propaganda, with which I ought not to concern myself. Janzen said disdainfully, "Oh, as a Christian you want to have nothing to do with politics! Look, I had very pious parents, was myself very religious and prayed a great deal. But one must grow out of that!" Then began a long tug-of-war, consisting of offers and refusals, during which I learned that Marshal Sokolovski had issued urgent orders for such a book, because the German people were very anxious about the fate of their P.O.W.s. Again and again the same argument came up, "Either the Church joins the progressive camp or it goes to its destruction. He who is not for us is against us!"

At last I got clear of the matter, with some blame attaching to me, naturally, for having veered so quickly from "yes" to "no"; but then one has to take the rough with the smooth. When I was a child, one could buy at the fair strange little bags. One would tempt some unsuspecting person to put in his finger, then when he tried to pull it out again, the bag shut and he was caught. I am now convinced that it is fatal to proffer even one's little finger. To have anything to do with this business would mean being bound hand and foot. Of course, when I pulled my finger out, I left some hairs behind; I have lost my good reputation with them. I really had wanted to gain their confidence; I was quite serious in my attempt to bridge the gap between our differences. They, however, are not interested in honourable intentions; they are only interested in the prospect of enslaving men. If they don't succeed in this, their distrust knows no bounds. My behaviour is for them only a proof that hitherto I had concealed my enmity. "He who is not for us, is against us."

The further history of the book is very characteristic: first of all the resolution to reveal "the whole truth", since they were of the opinion that nothing else would go down with German readers; and at the same time the great haste, since Sokolovski had written, saying that the P.O.W. question was problem No. 1 to the people of Germany. In March the manuscript was ready—not a coherent account which would give those at home a clear picture of the experiences of German soldiers in the U.S.S.R., with all their ups and downs (this was what the German editors wanted), but a collection, in the Russian style, of documentary reports which gave only a fleeting mention of the unfavourable aspects. Then the book went to the Russian censor "right at the top"; when it was returned, every slight indication of anything unfavourable had been "blue-pencilled"; it was now nothing more than a song of praise. Then it went to the critics in the Eastern Zone; they, living "closer to the enemy", were horrified and said that it was completely without value. Finally it was decided "right at the top" that it must appear even so in its expurgated form. It was published in the summer of 1949—*Prisoners of War in the U.S.S.R.*, S.W.A. Verlag, Berlin—and had no effect at all. The contributions bore no resemblance to their originals, though this fact was not betrayed, and some of the writers have since been condemned to forced labour and have probably changed their opinions. Thus the whole affair is an enlightening example of the precarious position of the Soviet propagandists, whose efficiency is often overrated. They themselves are so hemmed in by the ever-present distrustfulness of the system that they have no freedom to mention unfavourable facts and to explain them in such a way as to blunt the head of any attack, but they must either keep silent or deny everything so that they do not attract the unwelcome attentions of the "high-ups" and become suspected of sabotage. Consequently they can only gamble on the blindness and stupidity of their readers and listeners.

2 January 1948

In a letter to the Austrian Communist Party last summer, Stalin had promised to send home all the Austrian P.O.W.s. A good many have gone, but here as in other camps there are an even greater number left, estimated at several thousands. They have hung home-made calendars on their bunks and still mark off the days defiantly: Dec. 32nd, Dec. 33rd, etc. I wonder how far they will get! And I wonder how long we Germans shall have to go on counting after the next New Year; for, according to the decisions of the Moscow conference of foreign ministers, the "repatriation year" has begun. This is announced in coloured lights over the entrance to the barracks, the Russian and German camp leaders give it out in their New Year speeches, and recently the East German Trade Union delegation were told of it too. But on the same afternoon Janzen had said, "We know that a great many things are still in a bad way; but we are working hard and in a few months there will be nothing but model camps everywhere." But why, if we are going home anyway? And why all this business about the book? One would like to believe them, but it is impossible.

"What is the difference between an absolute monarchy and a dictatorship?" Otto H. asked me this morning.

"There are some very characteristic differences, but they don't really signify much."

"You are wrong. There's a very important difference; in the monarchy one can still rely on the word of the king, but in the totalitarian state only the lies of the dictator count." He sat down excitedly on the potato-bin in the pantry, where I am an assistant, in order to regain his strength. "Don't you agree that the chief distinguishing feature of these dictator states is their shabbiness? I have often had interviews with Hitler. In some respects he was phenomenal, otherwise he would not have got the reins into his hands. But to any man with a sense of nobility, he was the personification of shabbiness, in his thoughts as in his outward appearance. Every time I left him I felt sick. And the situation here is just the same. They play about with promises; they flatter you as long as they want something out of you and curse you if they don't get it. Look at their crafty attempts to bribe you to support them, and the lack of any respect for honest, independent opinions! Look at the way the Party has its own little squabbles, which make people call them a band of ruffians! Look at the way they cheat and deceive any who work with them, and the utter lack of any fairness! That is all so shabby that it stinks day and night! It's the same at the top and at the bottom. Every time accounts were settled up at the labour camp, it developed into repeated attempts to find fault with us and to injure us in order to grab what profit they might out of our efforts. Have you ever known an official, a firm, or any representative of the Soviet agree to anything unless you have some means of forcing them? If I had to use one phrase to describe the whole of the Soviet Union I would call it an 'unsafe business'. There is just that mixture of cunning, unreliability and shabbiness which we see in a business house which at home we would call 'unsafe'. One has the impression that when they killed off all the aristocracy in the Revolution they killed everything that was noble, all generosity, all honour-ableness, all chivalry." This was a violent outburst, to which I could have added plenty of examples. But I only said, "That is what the Party is like. But you can't apply this formula to the people."

"The people, oh, yes, the famous Russian people! Listen, for years I did the accounts in a labour camp and came into contact with Russians of all kinds. There were many fine people among them. But it's no longer possible for an absolutely honourable man to be found among them. Think of Homer, 'Man loses half his virtue when he is enslaved.' The only thing that can be said in their favour is that in their position we Germans would have been corrupted much more rapidly and more thoroughly. We have given proof of that. I am always surprised at what a measure of humanity of every sort, of naturalness of individuality, of 'human-ness' has been preserved in this nation under such oppression. This applies more to women than to men, to the old rather than to the young, to the farmers rather than to the artisans, but in no level of society is it completely lacking. A wonderful nation—you can't help loving them!"

7 January 1948

During our "last months" we are to be given the best impression of the Soviet Union to take home with us. So the whole camp is to go in groups on excursions to Moscow. To-day, the second of these took place (it was also the last!) and I went with them. Our "Polit" officer (he is not one of the com-missars of the N.K.V.D. but an officer responsible for the political education of the camp), a kindly, cheerful man, was highly enthusiastic and bent upon showing us as much as possible, and rushed us round untiringly. Compared with that of the previous June, the picture presented by the streets was astonishing, the people looked much healthier and were better dressed. In the centre of the city ragged figures were no longer to be seen. The currency reform of December 1947, added to the higher purchasing power of the rouble and together with better stocks of goods, had brought about a great change. The streets were thronged with people, elegant cars and fur-coats were no longer a rarity. In front of two large stores which do not open until 11 a.m. we saw, at about 10 a.m., a queue several hundred yards long stretching round two corners. When we passed again in the evening the shelves were no less full than in the morning; nothing was sold out. There are, then, enough wares but still too few shops. The prices are, of course, still very high. But a lot of people must be able to afford them, for until the shops closed, the crowds were as thick as ever. The "Central Stores" were larger and more magnificent than anything I have ever seen in the West.

There is not much for the tourist to see in Moscow. When he has been to the few museums, in which are concentrated history and art, and has walked along the fine streets and wandered round the Kremlin, there is not much left to do— except go to the excellent theatres, ballets and concerts, which delight the hearts of all Russians and for which they, more than any other nation, always seem to have enough money and plenty of talent at their disposal. That is probably due to two things. First of all, Moscow did not grow gradually over a long period of time, as did most of the cities of Europe, but was hammered out of the ground by its various rulers at various times. Thus anyone going for a walk is constantly being repelled by tastelessness and poverty, after enjoying short moments of architectural pleasure. If one turns the wrong corner, one sees how the ugliness of the suburbs penetrates to the centre of the city. "But in twenty years' time there won't be anything left of all this," our leader consoles us.

The second reason is connected with the new order of society. Here, everything is lacking which makes a Western European city so exciting; the shop windows (there are only a few good ones showing model dresses, furs and ugly tasteless furniture), the luxury shops, the Kurfürstendamm, the lighted advertisements, in short, all the visible attractions of the capitalist world. And there is no night life, no bars, no cafés, no night-clubs, no hotels. Where do the inhabitants find their evening amusement? I believe there are a few expensive cafés. These public eating places are not such centres of social life in the east as they are in the west, and since the Revolution, social life has been restricted to the "factory clubs". Thus to the traveller Moscow seems to be a monotonous, colourless city, hardworking and earnest.

In the morning we went round the Lenin Museum. A large building, the spaciousness of which would fill every German director with envy, contains documents, pictures and relics of Lenin's life, well set out at great expense. We saw Lenin in all the stages of his life, autographs, first editions of his writings, his library, his study in the Kremlin, the coat with the bullet-holes in it—the result of an attempt on his life—impressive pictures of the young Krupokaya with her sad and pitiless eyes. Many of the rooms seem to be more the centre of a cult than a museum. Yet is it, as one would expect, a museum of the history of the Revolution? Here the visitor is led to believe that the Revolution was the work of one man, Lenin, and that "men make history". I am reminded of the well-known essay by Lenin's teacher Plechanow, "On the role of personality in history", in which he relegates the importance of a "great man" to the "surface" of the course of history. The people need the cult of the great man, and here it is offered to them. The working class takes a back seat, and with it, of course, Lenin's collaborators, most of whom ended their days against the walls of Soviet prisons, facing the firing squad. The great "Creator of the Soviet State" stands alone—with only one man beside him—Stalin. Whoever is against Stalin is disloyal to Lenin: that is what this museum seeks to impress upon the people.

The afternoon was devoted to the Tretjakova, the famous Moscow picture gallery, limited to Russian art, the entire history of which is represented here. Our captain fortunately did not try to act as guide, but left us free, and I was able to get away from the others. In the first of the new halls is the wonder of Russia, the icons, excellently restored and very carefully hung, among them the famous ones of Rublev, and many others like them. I spent two hours looking at them—those two hours are among the best in my life. A few of the many visitors to this gallery paused with the same reverence. I will not repeat what has been said about the icons so much better by other people. The fact of my being there just at that time was a great help to me in the decisions I had to face.

Going on from the icons, which came to an end in the sixteenth century, to the more modern Russian art, which begins at the end of the eighteenth century, is a painful step. The courtly rococo painting, the trivial everyday pictures, the picture book of the narrative painter—anyone who sees the icons first sees the absurdity of the belief in progress. What has happened here? What source of inspiration has dried up here? The Russians are not allowed to be told; they can compare nothing, the Leningrad Hermitage is far away, nothing stops them from feeding their patriotism here and from believing that in the field of painting Russia has always marched at the head of modern art. But there can be no truth in that. As with Scandinavians, their talents do not seem to lie in the direction of painting; only Ilja Repin, some of whose works are hung here, has attained the heights and stands on a level with the Impressionists. Nearly everything else is well executed but decadent. The "Union Exhibition" of 1947, the great representative art exhibition of the U.S.S.R., which fills the inner halls, is just as dull as the "House of German Art" in Munich in every aspect, every choice of subject, style and quality! Totalitarian levelling triumphs over all the differences of nationality or ideology!

Finally we went on a pilgrimage to the Lenin Mausoleum. It lies up against the wall of the Kremlin, a vast edifice, with the tombs of leading Communists on either side; in front of it a long queue of visitors which we joined. We went along a bare corridor, past Red Army soldiers standing stiffly to attention, up the broad staircase past the tomb. While we walked we looked at Lenin lying embalmed in a glass coffin as though asleep, involuntarily comparing him with the portraits of which we had seen so many in the museum, and struck by the feeling that this unique personality was present here. Then we left, with mixed feelings at this parade of death.

13 *January* 1948

Having been here for exactly six months, and not knowing how much longer this will last, it is appropriate that I should get straight in my mind my impressions of the past months. I have plenty of time to think it over. At the moment I am in the so-called "tea-kitchen", cutting up vegetables for the camp kitchen, a job conducive to meditation. Living in this camp it is possible to make a survey of the life of German P.O.W.s in the U.S.S.R. This camp is not typical, but one can learn how they are getting on. For specially selected men come here from all the camps, into the camp itself for various favourable and unfavourable reasons which I mentioned before, and also to the "Anti-Fascist" School which has been going since last October, and which now and then has courses for German camp doctors from every part of this vast country. I am taking advantage of my returning strength and of all my free time to have long conversations with these men, and I am beginning to get a clearer picture of everything. Here is my picture of Russia so far:

1. Outside Moscow, all the people in Russia live the same sort of life as those in the district round Briansk, which I know. There are different national characteristics, there are differences in the crops and in the climate, but these cannot alter the awful monotony of their life and work, of the management and the regimentation which the Soviet way of life has forced upon this sixth of the world. In the Baltic provinces, which I have discussed with many who know them well, the population is still resisting the regime which has increased its efforts to make them conform to the Soviet way of life. The terrible sufferings of the people prove that what the newspapers in the Eastern Zone have been saying more and more openly during the last few months is true, namely that the regime is unable to tolerate any other economic system, any other form of rule or any other way of thought in its own sphere of domination, and is determined to mould all the lands under its control to its own shape. That means (a) that it is an illusion to believe that any land under Soviet control could attain the same measure of independence as is possible under British or American control. To come under Soviet rule—not at one fell swoop, but gradually, yet with the absolute certainty of complete domination at a foreseeable date—means to become an integral part of the Russian Soviet system. If Europe were made part of this "empire" it would inevitably become an insignificant appendage of the vast Russian State, robbed of its own traditions

and of all its national characteristics. I cannot imagine that the moral power of the European nations to withstand successfully the pressure of the Communist regime would be any stronger than that of the nations already subject to this rule. Many Communists hoped that they could develop a separate "European" Communism, but those hopes are no more likely to be fulfilled than were those of some of my Nazi acquaintances in Austria in 1938, who hoped that a specifically Austrian form of National Socialism might be developed which would avoid all the mistakes which the German Reich had made. One small proof of this is the penitent way in which the former S.E.D. official Anton Ackermann has just disavowed his former beliefs in "Germany's own road to socialism" as being a "nationalist deviation". I had at one time let myself be led astray by these illusions, but now I shall have to break with them completely.

It means (*b*) that it is an illusion to believe that the disadvantages of the regime which I have so far observed were only local, and were due to the poverty and war damage in the district around Briansk and to the facts which I have just mentioned. "It is the same all over Russia!" said one man who had spent many years of his life here. "I have known it in peace-time and in war-time, I know Siberia and the Caucasus, Leningrad and Kasau, and I can only repeat that, whatever differences may exist, what you have seen is true of the whole country—and you have only seen a small part of it!" All the other accounts confirm this statement. As far as the character and the structure of the system is concerned, one can and must generalise about these, and about their consequences. If one wishes, one can admire the Bolshevists for having set the stamp of uniformity on this vast land since in 1917 they were so small a minority, but one must also reject any illusions one may have as regards their ruthless determination and ability to repeat this performance elsewhere.

2. The whole of Russia is a camp, i.e. the methods they employ in dealing with P.O.W.s are not specially designed for us but adapted from those in general use. There are secret agents in the camp, because they are everywhere; our efforts in

the direction of culture are not supervised and limited merely because they fear Fascist activities but because people everywhere are led by the nose in the same way; anyone who was weak got trampled on in the camp because everywhere those who can work hard get extra pay, while the weak ones are penalised. Numbers of our companions starved because everywhere the system and productivity are more important than men, and because people everywhere are starving. The calculation of pay in the camp is always such a revolting battle between employers and work brigades, between the brigades themselves and between the members of each brigade—a battle which splits up any comradeship and reveals clearly any class-distinction—because it takes place also on every pay-day in the factories. The appeal to personal egoism by their system of incentives and extra pay and so on was not invented to get the most out of the P.O.W.s, but it pertains everywhere and prevents any thinking along social lines, any sympathy with those who are not so well off, and any social equality. For that reason any firm and lasting comradeship was always systematically squashed, because throughout the Soviet the State, in order to serve its own interests better, discourages in every village and working group any solid community spirit which might make the people more independent of its control and its favours. This is because the system everywhere demands the kind of nomadic ant-man who is free of any other loyalty and serves no other community besides the State. It was an illusion of mine to suppose, for instance, that the establishment of the collective farms really did for the peasants what the statute said—brought them out of the atomisation of private property into the larger village community. On the contrary, the organic community of the village has been turned into a casually assembled business controlled from above. This system recognises no subject standing over against it—whether an individual or group—and that means that here nothing is able to *grow*. If life is really free growth in accordance with its own laws, then this is the worst thing that can be said about the system, and the results both for the economy and the spiritual and intellectual life in the community are bound to be fateful.

All there is, is planned and contrived; all that grows of itself arouses suspicion.

3. What Joseph R. says is just a fairy-tale, namely that in this "movement"—it was once a movement but is now a system run by a quasi-religious group—"the ordinary people" had at last taken the matter into their own hands, and that their interests were being served. At best, something is being done for the working classes but certainly not by the working classes who here more than anywhere else in the world are considered not to have reached years of discretion. But is what is being done really being done for their benefit? Is it really a case of solving a social problem? Are the points on the road to the future really set correctly, as Joseph maintains? It is now growing increasingly questionable whether what appealed to me first as social progress is in fact such. Yet I still hesitate to pronounce judgment. It is very hard to free oneself from one's sympathies and expectations—how much harder it must be for a doubting Communist to free himself from his beliefs!

17 January 1948

Are the points on the road to the future really set correctly? What proofs have we? Lenin himself stated that the socialisation of the means of production was the most important thing; not that men should begin to think along socialistic lines, nor that ideas could create a new society, but this important change in the economic system, common ownership of the means of production, of factories and of the land. But these are still in the hands of the men who manage and direct them. Whether these men merely enjoy the great power which is new to them, or whether they live as the rulers or as the servants of others—these are the questions from the answers of which we shall be able to see what the others will gain from this system.

A war-time friend of mine, whom I met while he was taking part in one of the special courses for doctors, and who, in his capacity as camp doctor with a good knowledge of languages, is able to move about freely in an industrial town farther east, has given me some very interesting details about the life of the population in that neighbourhood. In everything they are restricted and supervised, especially in their intellectual and private affairs. Nothing can grow. The N.K.V.D. commissar to whom I spoke freely about these things during a friendly interview, denied it flatly, saying that everyone had complete freedom so long as he was not working for class dictatorship or as the agent of an imperialist power. Even the German anti-Fascists have not achieved this total disregard for reality; they admit it, but say that it is a necessary state of affairs during the transitional period of Socialism which will disappear with the final change-over to Communism. A unique article of faith in the dialectic handbook—that the greatest lack of freedom leads to freedom! Children tied to their mother's apron-strings are expected to behave like adults all at once. Men like our commissars and all the other high functionaries of the Soviet State, who have always seen men tremble before them, are expected all of a sudden to exchange willy-nilly this enjoyment of power for the enjoyment of living in a free country among free people, and to be capable of tolerating contradictions and differences of opinion; indeed they are even expected to aim at leading those in their power to this very state of liberty. Because of such hopes, Lenin could not pour enough scorn on the Socialists and their programme of co-operation with the upper classes. But surely the same beliefs are demanded here, except that they have less sure foundations and contradict even more every reality and everything that one sees every day.

Joseph R. and his companions afford me a good example of this state of mind. I have been watching them for months. What he told me previously in our conversations may then have been his honest convictions. Recently, in a "political cabaret" which he wrote, he himself played the part of the glass-blower "Nante Eckensteher", the personification of the old Berliner who learns that the Third Reich has come to an end and is pleased that freedom is returning once more, that one can again speak freely, and that small people can again criticise the great. But what does he do himself? He tells me in a *tête-à-tête* what he does not like about conditions in Russia, but outwardly he is the first to act as though he approved. He is never openly what he professes to be in secret, one who understands, one who meditates, one who respects the other's point of view. He never corrects us, but is just a hundred per cent. propagandist like the others. And he knows too, judging by what he has told me, why he does not do what he ought to do; he knows that he has given his support to a system which does not require the co-operation of men of honest convictions, but only wants submission. And because the privileges which he enjoys are so important to him, because he fears the labour camp like the plague, he has chosen submission. He is obsequious and calculating, and is a lesson to me not to let myself be impressed by words and theories.

His friend Willi K., who worked with him on that book about P.O.W.s, does not seem to suffer so much from internal conflict. Before 1933 he was an official of the "Revolutionary Trades Union Opposition", the Communist group in the trades unions. They seemed to me then to be the most energetic, brave, self-less and incorruptible representatives of the interests of the workers. I have been finally cured of those romantic ideas by seeing him wandering round the camp, well-fed and resplendent in civilian clothes. He is the privileged man, who is no more moved by the thought of the life our comrades lead in the labour camps than by the thought of the life of the Russian working man. He has chosen the road that leads upwards, and will press on relentlessly.

How unimportant the various theories are beside the uniform type of man produced and encouraged by the new systems of government is well illustrated by the neo-Marxist T. as well as by the obsequious Joseph and Willi, the former Communist. He was a "Junker" from a Nazi "Ordensburg", an S.S. officer and an enthusiastic Hitlerite. Now he is a respected anti-Fascist and is soon to take up a high official position in the Eastern Zone. Nothing has changed about him except the phrases he uses, and these only to a limited degree. Instead of parsons, Jews and plutocrats it is now parsons, right-wing Socialists and plutocrats who are the subject of his vicious tirades. His brutality, his terrorist manner, his scorn of men, and his need of power are unchanged. All three of these men are not serving either an idea or the working man, but themselves.

Are the points on the road to the future set correctly? The socialising of the means of production brings about nothing but a placing of power in the wrong hands. It increases the danger of unlimited and uncontrolled concentration of power. But men are the most important, in the past as well as in the future. The Soviet regime has not achieved any of the things which Lenin had promised for it; by its economic changes it has not left men free, it does not foster altruism, it does not protect them from the temptations which power offers, but rather gives them up to these temptations.

1 *February* 1948

The first time I appealed most strongly for "co-operation" between Communists and non-Communists was also the last. Not knowing any better, I thought that I ought to do my bit in this camp so that the hopes aroused at the end of the war might not be entirely vain. The repercussions show that it was an effort with an impossible object in view.

A few weeks ago the "club culture leader" asked me to give a public lecture on "The Problem of Spiritual Regeneration in Germany". It was due to the latest "Party Line" with regard to political work that I, who had refused to join the club, was asked to speak at all. They realised that the persistent trumpeting of Marxist propaganda was only falling on deaf ears, they remembered that originally they had wanted to win over all the non-Nazis, and they allowed non-Marxists to put in a word. I accepted, but after some time, during which I had thought out what I was going to say, I went to the club members and recommended them to withdraw their invitation. Since I could not be false to myself, they were likely to hear some unusual and unwelcome things, and thereby they might get into trouble with their own people. They pondered and discussed the matter—but lo, they took their courage in both hands and persisted.

Yesterday the great event took place. Everyone was there, I spoke for two hours, their attentiveness left nothing to be desired and tomorrow afternoon there is to be a private discussion about it. I began with a description of the state of mind when the Third Reich collapsed, gave a survey of the position in the Russian Zone only, since we know next to nothing about Western Germany. I gave the only two groups which still have any influence over the spiritual life of men the names Christian and Marxist, and said that whether or not they co-operated was the decisive question which underlay any re-building which was to have a real meaning, and outlined the conditions laid down. Co-operation must be honourable and trustworthy, and in the event of its being impossible either to bring about an amalgamation or else to kill off the other side, it would depend on the strict fulfilling of two demands: that there should be mutual toleration (which meant giving up totalitarianism and the terrorising of minorities), and that they should take each other seriously (which meant getting to know each other and being prepared to learn from each other and be of service to each other in finding out information needed).

This speech was a test; if they accepted it good-naturedly and did not take offence at the lances I levelled at them, that would prove that they were capable of some community spirit, which one ought not to ignore. There would be a sporting chance that at least in the small sphere of our camp a better example might be set. The effect was quite the opposite, however. They reacted like men whose power was being tampered with; what I had meant for a warning they took as an attack, and my assertions of independence as enmity. I had now revealed myself in my true colours, said one of the teachers of the anti-Fascist school—and thereby he showed his own colours.

4 *February* 1948

Yesterday's discussion only served to confirm my opinions. Anyone who does not see co-operation as submission must be exposed as a hypocrite. All my sins were added up. I had set the "conservative opposition" against Hitler on a level with the Communist opposition. I had conceived "liberal ideas of freedom", I had thrown suspicion on the Communists' totalitarian tendencies, I had not, above all, strengthened faith in the

Soviet Union. It all went to show what a commotion is caused when, in the midst of all this monotonous, monomaniac propaganda, someone uses different figures of speech, and when someone talks calmly and quietly in the midst of all the shouting. The totalitarian world is a world full of shouting. Whenever someone broke in on the Nazis' anti-Semitic bellows with a quiet word about the Jews, the atmosphere was immediately cleared, men calmed down, began to think and to ponder. But that must not be allowed to happen here; for that reason everyone who does not either join in the shouting or block his ears is considered dangerous. Whether they talk of peace or of capitalist monopolies, of Fascism or of the Anglo-Americans, of human happiness or of friendship with the Soviet Union, they all shout, afraid that someone might begin to think. One of the instructors praised the fact that Marxism treasured freedom of speech. I asked him whether he agreed with me in drawing the line at tolerating men who themselves would not acknowledge toleration.

"No, but I would not tolerate reactionary ideas."

"Why?"

"Because they are a danger to mankind."

"Then you would not tolerate religion, idealism, and pacifism, since in your eyes they are all reactionary ideas?"

"Only in so far as they grow dangerous."

"Have you never considered that thought is always dangerous?"

It is important to realise that this is not just one man's reaction. The directors of the school and of the Russian political education react in exactly the same way, if not even more violently. One might ask why I was so naïve as to expect a different reaction. I was not naïve, but it seems to be right to take every opportunity of accepting the hand of friendship rather than rejecting it—as long as one does not thereby sell oneself or submit.

20 March 1948

Up till now the results of the "new line" are illustrated very clearly by the above remarks. With all the storms in our teacup here we are getting a taste of world problems. Anyone who knows about Lenin may well laugh at a man who believes that one can get anywhere with the Communists. I have studied him, and yet I cannot help believing that some day—because after all they are men—some kind of understanding must be possible. Now things have gone wrong again—fortunately without my taking a hand. First of all the slogan "a broad policy of political co-operation" was passed round: "Not a Marxist, but an anti-Fascist club!" Close co-operation between all the democratic forces in the camp! Such "democratic forces" were absorbed into the club, the non-Marxist wing saw a good opportunity and announced its demands: the political equality of all who belong to the C.D.U.[1] and L.D.P.,[2] lectures and discussions with speakers of all political colours. A few concessions were made—then the authorities got cold feet. The Russian directors of political education who had founded the club, ordered an old Communist to act as the "proletarian conscience" of the club; for with all this broad policy one must not lose sight of the goal—this was drummed into the new club-president day and night—and in a few weeks the situation was just what it had been before; behind a democratic façade nothing but Marxism was taught, and the proletarian conscience was at rest.

One could laugh at all this if it were not so typical and if it did not have such serious consequences. One certainly cannot wish the Germans to become Communists. But what one can and must want, is that the Germans should be purged of National Socialism and of all that made them its easy victims. This anti-Fascist propaganda, however, is driving them back to it. It is like trying to put the bridle on the horse's tail. They are trying to turn our fellow-countrymen into Marxists before they have purged them of National Socialism. Therefore they have passed over National Socialism and have immediately begun to allege with high-sounding phrases and a wild distortion of history that the system of capitalist monopolies is the one and only background of National Socialism, which explains everything. In their fear that "Fascist" opinions might

[1] Christian Democratic Union.
[2] Liberal Democratic Party.

be expressed they have not dared to allow those free discussions about Nazism, which are so desperately needed to give an outlet to so much repressed resentment. Anyone who is to become an "anti-Fascist" must first swallow the Marxist doctrine—and most men refuse to do that.

They give their refusals without explanation, because they sense that all is not right with this doctrine since the lifeless repetition of Marxist formulae leaves their questions unanswered. These German and Russian propagandists are themselves so afraid of slipping off the prescribed "line" that they take refuge in a mechanical and stereotyped language. Thus they have lost the freedom to make any impression on the German mentality.

But must they lose this freedom? Yes, for they all have to fear for themselves. I have never met any "Polit" officer yet in whom I have felt the slightest genuine missionary zeal, or that in any circumstances it would be of paramount importance to him to win men over to his cause. Their first care was always to show their superiors that they had fulfilled their commands with regard to all arrangements even to the hanging up of coloured lights and to the use of stilted official phraseology. Among the German anti-Fascists there are a few who serve their cause and try to go their own way, because they see that all propaganda has the reverse effect. Recently I was discussing this question with Otto A., one of the most active anti-Fascists. "You are the worst saboteurs of anti-Fascism," I said to him. He agreed sadly, "We know that, but our hands are tied."

"Why don't you shake off all this nonsense for the sake of your cause?"

"In order to prevent anything worse happening."

"That's an old yarn!"

(Later he did try to shake it off—and is now paying for it by being condemned to forced labour on account of his "anti-Soviet propaganda".)

22 March 1948

It is a peaceful Sunday. I am sitting with Emil H. drinking tea and eating "Knatterpriem" (a cake which we made ourselves by mixing together bread crumbs, sugar, butter and various other ingredients which we saved up; whether and to what extent this saving up could be carried on in a camp was a test of the state of its catering!). Emil is a former German Communist workman, having spent a long time in a concentration camp under police supervision; he succeeded in deserting to the Russians from the probation battalion. Today he is still here, naturally much respected as a veteran Party member. After a long period of observation he is convinced he can confide in me. The disappointment of a child who, instead of the promised Christmas present, finds among his gifts a cane and book, can hardly compare with the disappointment which he revealed to me. He talked to me for a long time. He has seen a good deal here in Russia and has kept his eyes open. For a long time he would not believe what he saw, but now he could not stand it any longer.

"But you knew already," I said, "that things were not so very ideal here. You knew that one had to look at things 'dialectically'. Why don't you do that any more?"

"Because it's not only a question of the conditions—I could put up with those—but because I look at the people. For the Communists have died out."

"Now look, I have met people here who have shown me their Party cards, saying that these were the most precious of their possessions. I worked at the sawmill under an employer who had no more to eat than we did, but who was on his legs from morning to night, ceaselessly, and what we could not do because we were too weak, he did for us—and he was an enthusiastic Communist."

"You can see dutiful people and sacrifice everywhere. That does not make Communists. I have just been looking at the leaders and I have realised the difference: the war-time Communist, the Communist in Western Europe is quite a different type from the Soviet Communist. What the one must be is just what the other must not be. Look, I did not need to become a Communist. I earned a good salary and the Socialists would have welcomed me with open arms. But I am a thoughtful man, I have read and studied. I did not only think of myself but of the working classes, I did not want to be a working

167

aristocrat. That was why I was proud to be one of the Communists in our trade; I spoke openly, even at Party meetings, risked my own skin and kept my self-respect. And now the rulers here are men who will not speak openly and will risk nothing, and I myself shall have to become one of them, for I have undertaken to go to the Eastern Zone just to get out of here. But I can't look at it 'dialectically' any longer because I see that it has got hold of the wrong people."

His faith was broken on one particular point: the difference between the Communist as a fighter and as an official. I remember what made such an impression on me in the Communist acquaintances of my youth. In the case of the intelligentsia, but also of the working classes, the fact that they joined the Communists was due to a strong feeling of responsibility, a disregarding of personal interests, marked spiritual independence and a fighting spirit. These very characteristics which led them into Communism will be useless, indeed dangerous, as soon as Communism in the form of Stalinism comes to power. They must break with themselves or be broken.

23 *March* 1948

The tragedy of the people about whom I have just told you could only be a surprise to them. Only someone, who, like the Marxist, combines a relentless criticism of the past with uncritical wishful thinking about the future (even Marx did this), and who has done as little thinking as the Marxist about such realities as State and power, could not have foreseen this development. (It has always been a mystery and yet a revelation to me how Engels could write a book about *The Origins of the State* without touching upon the problems of power and the driving force behind the power!) New light has been shed upon this problem for me by the figure of Stalin in Alexei Tolstoy's novels about the Revolution, which I have just read (*Bread* and the trilogy *The Way of Suffering*). They are not only documents of the artistic decline of this writer who had begun so well with his haunted stories and then returned to the Soviet Union because he was homesick, but they also reveal involuntarily what kind of problems the Soviet system of today has raised for Communists of the old school. Tolstoy describes the moment in time when first the figure of Stalin the Silent stepped into the light of history. During one of the most desperate situations in the Civil War Lenin ordered Stalin to direct the defence of the threatened city of Zarizyn (later called Stalingrad), since on its preservation depended the supply line to Moscow and St. Petersburg and thus the victory of the Revolution. Stalin found nothing but chaos in the town, towards which the Whites were pressing from all directions; the Red regiments were practising democracy by calling a meeting to discuss and decide every wave in the battle, to discuss and appoint their commanders, to leave the bourgeoisie free to hold up proceedings. Stalin at once did away with these Augean stables of democracy, established martial law, backed up his authority with great brutality—and saved the city and the Revolution. The same system he later applied to the whole of the Soviet State: he may have saved the State by doing this, but he precipitated Communism's greatest crisis. He showed then which beliefs he had room for and which he rejected. He agreed with the Leninist doctrine—doubtless he went on "believing" in it; he was not a cynic without ideas, but the conception of democracy within the party and within the proletariat—in which Lenin believed and by means of which he won the confidence of the Russian working men—was strange and repellent to him. The question is whether he was not the most consistent Marxist of them all, more consistent than Marx and Lenin even, because he was the first to recognise that Communism and human dignity are incompatible, and that one must choose between the two.

12 April 1948

Communism is an idea. One can talk about it, there is both truth and falsehood in it, and one might perhaps mould it so that it could be compatible with human dignity—but it is not for me to decide. It is a human error, thought out by a perplexed and godless man, but it is no more satanic than any other religion or ideology. Yet the totalitarian state, the conception of which is one of the bases of Communism, appears to me to be something satanic. For the hand which it is now stretching out to grasp the soul of Werner W. is the hand of the Devil.

For the last three days he has been going around visibly upset, and yesterday evening he asked if he could see me. We are sitting on a pile of tree-stumps in the wood-yard. After seeing that the coast was clear he burst out, "What am I to do? I have got to sign on."

"What do you mean by 'sign on'? For specialist work, for the Eastern Zone, or as a secret agent?"

"As a secret agent!"

Anyone who has been in Russia for some time knows what that means. All the camps are bound up in a web of secret agents. The people I talk to, what sort of war experiences I relate, what I think about politics and religion, what remarks about the Soviet Union I let out involuntarily, whether I am toying with the idea of escape or whether I am pretending to be unfit—all this information is given about me without my knowing by whom, and anyone who seeks to gain my confidence may well be a secret agent. He has been won over by compulsion or by bribes, by an appeal to his anti-Fascist feelings, which he must now prove, or else he will be unmasked as a hypocrite, or else by a reference to his Nazi past which he will have to atone for. Many have only given in for the sake of form and try with all their might to give favourable instead of unfavourable reports of those whom they are set to watch. Many denounce others freely, many even invent things in order to prove their efficiency; but all are threatened with a terrible punishment if they betray to anyone the fact that they have signed on.

This system might be excused in some measure, or at least understood if it had been invented specially for P.O.W.s. Since the Russians considered us all to be Fascists they thought they would have to reckon with sabotage and acts of violence; they supposed that concealed among us were many S.D.[1] men and war criminals. It was understandable that they wanted to get to the bottom of our secrets and find out what we really

[1] *Sicherheitsdienst*—a branch of the Gestapo.

were and thought. But this system is only a part of the great web of observation which is laid over the whole population of this vast country. They have only repeated with regard to us what was already in force everywhere, and it never occurred to them not to carry it out, just as they will carry it out all over the world if they get the chance. The claim of the totalitarian state to be the god of mankind is nowhere more clearly illustrated than in this ubiquitous network of unknown eyes and ears. This network is an example of the omnipresence and omniscience of this god. "You have to tell us everything even if you consider it unimportant. You must not conceal anything, even if it means incriminating a friend. You need not fear that you will harm your friends for we do not wish anyone ill. Just leave it to us to judge the details. But we must know everything—you understand, everything!" So this god demands from his servants unceasing obedience and complete confidence. The servant knows, however, that he will never again be alone, that he can never let himself be taken into anyone's confidence without being a traitor by this very act, that he can never have a *tête-à-tête* with anyone without having to eavesdrop on behalf of his god, and that he must always count on his god listening in too. A spy wears a mask as long as he is trailing down his prey, but while he is not hunting he is still a man. A secret agent, however, the servant of his god, never ceases to be his eyes and ears, and he must conceal this even from his most intimate friend. So he carries his secret around with him, every contact with other men becomes a lie, and the more so the more intimate his friendships are; his whole life is a lie, he lies to his fellow-men, he lies to his god, he lies to himself, and realises how this god increasingly sucks all the humanity out of him and thus stands revealed as a demon vampire.

Werner sees all this ahead of him. He is a cheerful young fellow with the most candid eyes in the world, one of the most unsuitable men for these underhand dealings. He was, however, a leader in the Hitler Youth and they are holding that up against him. What makes him so afraid? Simply this, that if he agrees he can see his life developing into a lie, and knows that he will never again be able to breathe freely. How many of us

171

have ever really suspected what it meant to sell one's soul to the Devil! Do we not think of it as a medieval superstition? Now I know that this expresses better than any other idea or image what man is really like.

"All things around him go forward, governed by the power of another will; he is his own keeper and holds his life in his own hands. And it is not a matter of indifference to him whether he turns to the right or to the left" (Matthias Claudius). Man is the creature to whom it is not a matter of indifference whether he turns right or left, who must decide for himself; any teaching about man which seeks to understand him from the animal point of view and not in the light of this decision, is false. Yet not in the light of the decision in itself, not in the light of the fact that he is able to choose between right and left and is proud of this freedom! Up till now that has not been a serious question for man. But man must be understood in the light of that decision from which Werner is now shrinking, that is, from the fact that it is not all the same to him whether he goes right or left. To the left everything is offered of which the prisoner dreams: better living conditions, plenty of food, health and imminent repatriation; this can be his, and all for a signature—a signature which takes away his life, shuts him out of the community of the living, cannot be revoked and makes him the servant of a lie. On the one hand everything of which he dreams is taken from him, but he is left with his life, he is alive even in death, just as on the other hand he is dead in the midst of life.

What more is necessary than to show him this? The Devil has made you get the two sides mixed up. Look carefully, and you will see where life and death really are. So you still need to decide? Do you still think that you are facing a difficult choice? Everything has been decided already. You want to live, don't you? Then take the road to life and not to death— and see that you don't lose the way.

We talked about the day when he would see his parents again—and we talked of eternal life. All at once everything fell into place. On the one hand was a picture as ugly as the plague, unwelcoming, and on the other was life that could not be lost. For the first time for years he prayed. When he had jumped down off the pile he turned and laughed up at me. While I was climbing down I remembered that touching story which old Joinville told about his king, St. Louis of France The latter asked him once what he would do if he had to choose between becoming a leper and committing a mortal sin. It was a difficult question and Joinville did not dare to answer. Then he was deeply moved when the king, who was indeed a holy man, confessed that he was afraid he would prefer mortal sin to leprosy. I thought about that, and realised that St. Louis had worried about the wrong question at the wrong time, as we so often do. He worried over a hypothetical question, for it had not yet presented itself, he had only imagined it. When this question does crop up, however, our life depends, not on our power to resist the temptations of mortal sin and to accept leprosy courageously, but rather on whether we have the vision to see mortal sin as leprosy and to see life beyond leprosy.

Today Werner saw me again for a few seconds. He had come to a decision. Was he afraid? No, he would never have thought it would be so easy. When he was fetched he had some doubts, but then when he got there, was asked for his decision, and refused, it all seemed quite natural. He had felt as though he were unassailable. What would happen now? *Po smodrim* (We shall see). (Soon he was sent to a worse camp, and then home.)

15 April 1948

The elections for the "Anti-Fascist Committee", that is, for the leading members in the camp's self-government, which took place recently, have at last brought home to me what Soviet elections are like. Whenever totalitarians come into power it is particularly instructive to observe the technique with which they demolish democratic control and yet leave a façade of democracy standing. Hitler's technique was relatively primitive. He dissolved the constitution, he openly established the principles of dictatorship, and both the Reichstag and the elections now gave nothing but opportunities of acclaiming him. In the Soviet Union, however, a much more water-tight system of dictatorship had been established behind a much broader façade of democracy. The system of councils, the trade unions, the wall-newspapers, the elections, and all the achievements of the Revolution were retained and considerably expanded in the Stalinist Constitution of 1936—every year we celebrate this as the "freest and most progressive constitution in the world". Freedom for the press, freedom to hold meetings and demonstrations, and everything that was dreamt of during the French Revolution is solemnly promised. "The Soviet citizen holds his head up more proudly than anyone else," said the Leningrad poet N. Tikhonov recently at a great demonstration. "In other countries men are ruled by the state, but here they rule the state and are the people with the greatest freedom in the world." Above the entrance to our barracks in large letters is the motto: "Everything for the people, everything by the people, everything with the people!" "Everything for the people"—that may indeed be true and they may really be of that opinion. If one wishes to pass a benevolent judgment on the regime, one might call it "enlightened absolutism". Everything is done for the people, but nothing is ever done by the people themselves. Not even the Nazi regime showed so deep a mistrust of the people as the Soviet regime does. Absolutely every show of spontaneity is suspect and needs watching and directing so that it shall not become dangerous. The existence of the Stakhanov movement,[1] and the Tcherkassova movement for the rebuilding of Stalingrad, would seem to contradict this. But it is obvious how artificial this spontaneity is. It is a system of leading-strings. Yet how do they succeed in preserving the appearance that everything is done by the people, and at the same time protect the constitution from being used by the people to produce unpleasant surprises?

One must have studied closely the Stalin Constitution, and have experienced elections in the U.S.S.R., in order to see through the Russians' technique of protecting themselves from the will of the people by democratic means and yet of being

---

[1] The Stakhanov-brigades consisted of high-speed workers, created to set the pace for the ordinary worker. The movement was named after Stakhanov, who mined fourteen times the normal output of coal in one shift. Cf. *I Chose Freedom*, chap. XIII.

able to call on the people. Safeguards are provided unobtrusively by two things: the overwhelming power of the Council of the Supreme Soviet, the few members of which can overrule the whole government, and the public nomination of candidates for all elections (safeguards which can be relied upon only in conjunction with the stronger safeguards of the N.K.V.D., which makes it possible for this body to work in the background.)

All the elections are secret and quite fair—there is no lack of democracy in this respect, even in our camp. First of all, however, single groups or organisations—here in the camp it is the club—announce the names of the requisite number of candidates, who then have to "canvass" for themselves at a public meeting of the electors, that is, they give an account of their lives and careers and have to answer questions. Queries about something not made clear in his account of his career, reproaches about former activities, questions about his attitude towards this or that subject of public interest—he has to answer all these.

"What are your opinions about land reform?" This question is put to a western German landowner, who has been nominated by the meeting to stand against the club's candidate. What is the poor man to answer? If he agrees with land reform then nobody will believe him. If he disagrees with it then he is condemned as a Fascist and is violently abused. So he declares that he is in favour of a limited reform with some kind of compensation, and it is easy for the opposing speakers from the club to make him out to be a hypocritical reactionary, which of course he is not, After all this questioning, the meeting has to decide whether the candidate concerned is to be put on the final list or not. And that is just the trick in this matter: the later elections are secret but these preliminary nominations are public! Thus everyone knows exactly how he will appear in the eyes of the influential members if he should, for instance, support the landowner.

Here in the camp, however, this procedure is not quite so rigid. For all the supervision and discipline imposed on us, we prisoners still have considerably more freedom than the Soviet citizen to express our opinions. When I think, however, of these methods of election transferred to the Soviet Union itself, then I can understand why a nominated candidate never says anything he ought not to, and why the people never nominate an undesirable candidate. The secret ballot which comes later is just a farce, since it is preceded by all the public meetings at which candidates and electors alike have to act under the stern gaze of the N.K.V.D. The authorities can thereby guarantee that among any who oppose the official candidates there is never any unanimity, that such people see themselves as solitary creatures amid the mass of enthusiastic supporters of Stalin, and that undesirable candidates can never climb up the democratic ladder.

6 May 1948

We ought never to forget how much easier the life of a P.O.W. is than the life of a Soviet citizen. It would naturally not be advisable to call out "Heil Hitler". Hans Y. recently underwent a severe interrogation because while he was painting a notice for the barracks he gave a capital F such an extravagant cross-stroke that anyone with a suspicious imagination could have taken it for the hint of a swastika. We are, nevertheless, allowed a good measure of fool's freedom. We are allowed to be "bourgeois", to argue against Marxism, even if only in polite terms, and the spy-web does not frighten everyone; many have already told the commissar quite plainly what they think and now they flourish according to the saying, "When one's reputation is ruined, one can live untroubled." Above all, we have the freedom not to join in, to boycott everything political and to live our own lives. Many Germans had this freedom under Hitler. It was dangerous to say anything against the Nazis but if one kept silent one could survive fairly well. For the Russian even silence is dangerous. Any avoidance of politics at once labels him as an enemy of the state. Woe to him who does not shout with the crowds! And every intellectual worker knows that he is watched with mistrust to see that in his artistic and scientific work he fulfils his political duties. During the last few weeks we have been very excited by the manifesto of the central Party executive, who have accused the

glory and crown of Soviet art—namely the great Soviet composers Shostakovitch, Prokofieff, Khatchaturian and others—
of the worst blasphemies of formalism, cosmopolitanism and of
Western decadence, although they had been responsible for the
amazing popularity of this art in the Socialist society. These
men were ordered to compose folk-music, melodious and
harmonious. We were struck by the pitiful, humble declarations of repentance and promises of improvement with which
these composers *laudabiliter se subjecerunt* to this command of
their sergeant-major. Up in the wood-yard, where for some
time, having now recovered my strength, I have been spending
eight hours a day chopping the tree-stumps into firewood with
a heavy hammer and iron wedges, we are sitting in our little
circle, having a serious discussion on the position of modern
music, and the merits and demerits of this manifesto, and we
are enjoying a lively debate. Outside, beyond the barbed-wire
fence, civilians are going by, workmen, clerks, mothers with
their children, and two intellectuals holding an eager discussion.
Andreas pointed to the latter and said, "Who is really behind
the barbed wire, we or they? Here we can talk so freely. Yet a
short time ago I tried to talk about the manifesto to Professor
O. from the Conservatory of Music, who is lending us some
music for the band, and he only grew embarrassed and pretended that he had always been against Prokofieff, although he
had played some of his music a few months before with the
greatest enthusiasm. Sometimes it seems to me that the whole
world is sitting behind barbed wire, and that we here are a tiny
separate island of freedom."

12 *May* 1948

Under the seal of the greatest secrecy someone has just
pressed a surprising treasure into my hand: a West German
newspaper from Essen, only a few months old, which found its
way here by an unknown route—the first printed evidence from
the Western world to reach our captivity! Why was the arrival,
a year ago, of the first eagerly awaited German papers not the
great experience that we had talked of? I have only just realised
the reason for our disappointment: they were papers from the

Eastern Zone and the only difference between those and the Hitler papers was the terminology and the names of the enemy, the general tone was the same. Just as in the Third Reich the Party Press with its pamphlet-style had absorbed everything. One opened a paper and was shouted at. One knew at once that one was not meant to be so much informed as schooled. That Essen paper had its axe to grind and wanted to influence people—who could prevent that—but its wish to influence one did not stand in front of my wish to be informed. It fulfilled my needs and put forward its points of view in a dignified manner, letting those with opposing views have their say too, so that I could get a clear picture. I should never have thought that the humanity of a more humane world, which I had missed for so long, would be conveyed to me through anything so questionable and much abused as a daily paper, nor that a paper could become a human experience.

Is the West really a "more humane world"? I would never have believed that I could ever make this statement. Yet it is not now a theory which I have thought out and of which I have found proof, but it is a definite experience, such as we all have here. This is experienced also by the anti-Fascists, these poor captive people who are full of fear and who cannot get out of the spider's web.

Perhaps the difference lies in the fact that the West tempts one to be inhuman, while the East forces one to be inhuman. The temptation may be the greater danger. More humanity can survive under compulsion than under temptation; the latter can corrupt more than compulsion. But anyone in prison will not let the love of freedom be taken away from him even when the moral dangers of freedom are pointed out to him. Anyone on a bed of sickness may feel the purifying influence of suffering in itself, but will still long to be well again, "For he that hath suffered in the flesh hath ceased from sin" (1 Peter 1. 4). This phrase from the Epistles has become a favourite during my captivity. Suffering and compulsion can serve a good purpose —that is an inspiring promise when one has lost freedom and health. The Eastern system contests human dignity from without, the Western system constitutes a danger from within; in the East as in the West this dignity can be asserted only in the freedom of the children of God, about which we used to pray as children: "If Satan tries to overpower me, let the angels sing and say: may this child be free from harm".

20 *May* 1948

I am continuing my reading of the Marxist classics in spite of everything else. I shall probably go on doing so till the end of my captivity, undisturbed by the disapproving glances of my companions, who cannot understand what I see in "that stuff". The simple man says, "No, thank you, I've had enough. What I see is sufficient for me, I don't need to read any more!" The more thoughtful ones echo the words of General R., one of the best officers here, when he said to me yesterday, "I am sorry to see from your reading that you have not yet got over your Marxist sympathy. You have that fateful German superstitious belief in theory. As soon as a German comes up against a political power which drapes itself in a clever theory, he is fascinated and thinks, 'There must be something in it!' "

"Do you mean that Communism is today no longer an idea which one must at least know in order to understand the problems of the contemporary world?"

"We must decide, of course, whether we are now going to talk philosophically or to discuss the present state of the world. There is sense in both, but they ought to be kept separate. I am more concerned with the Soviet Union than with Communism."

"But the Soviet Union is based on the idea of Communism, you can't deny that."

"It all depends on what you mean by 'based'. I don't deny that the Soviet owes its existence to that idea, and that it makes use of it today, in order to woo fifth columnists in every country and to keep its own population on the right road; I don't even deny that those who hold the whip hand believe in this idea themselves. I make this statement guardedly since I cannot see into Stalin's mind, and since I know anyway that it does not matter so much what a man believes but whether he is ruled by

179

his beliefs. But what I affirm is this, namely that the Soviet State, that is, those in power, are ruled not by their beliefs, but by the overwhelming weight of that power, and by the instinct for self-preservation of the system which entrusted that power to them. Look at the way they carry on. Their beliefs never came into critical contact with this power as Lenin's did, nor are they able to prevent those in power from doing just what they like, but rather they form a delicate instrument to justify the deeds of those in power. It has always been the same, starting with the pact with Hitler right up to the business about the Oder–Neisse Line."

"The reason for that may be that today the aim of Communism, the new society, stands or falls by the existence of the Soviet Union. Thus the interests of Soviet power and of the idea are identical, and therefore every Communist in the world will have to put the interests of the Soviet Union before the interests of his own country for the sake of his beliefs. It is in that very way that he thinks he can best serve his country."

"No, one cannot say that that is the entire reason, so long as one does not live with one's head in the clouds wallowing in theory, but rather with one's feet planted firmly on the ground. You should have progressed so far in your studies of Marxism to have learnt from Marx that interests are always stronger than ideas. That means practical interests—the Communists, and people like you who are always seeking the idea behind them, forget that the most sensible thing about Marxism is the sobriety with which interests are always revealed behind all the pompous ideas in politics. The Russians are interested in holding the reins of world Communism; the little circle round Stalin is interested in remaining in power—sweet intoxicating power; the officials are interested in keeping their jobs and in climbing up the ladder. The interests of the man with possessions are not the same as those of the man without possessions— that was one of the first principles which Marx set out so excellently. When talking of the capitalists, he called it a fairy-tale when anyone expressed the hope that the ruling class were capable of caring selflessly for those without possessions. Well, the hopes which the non-Russian Communists pin to unselfish

"Uncle Joe", the hopes which the people here pin to the social eagerness of the *arrivistes*, in short, the opinion that power will be the servant of the idea and that the idea will not always be the urge of power for self-preservation—all this is a fairy-tale."

"Of which the consequences could be hopeless cynicism!"

"One man may become a cynic, another may realise quite soberly that power needs exactly what the Communists have hesitated to give it: control by the masses, that is, not by mass organisations but by the individuals who form the mass—well, we agree on that."

21 May 1948

All this cannot prevent me from summing up in a few points all that strikes me as fine in Marx's thought. His witty style, his youthful desire to please, the more objective style of his later years. The seriousness with which he took his work, the warmth of his emotions as revealed in his letters to his family—all these may seem unexpected to one who has thought of him with horror. What makes reading him so fruitful, however, are the following facts:

1. He (and this applies to Engels as well) was the most modern thinker of his time; by which we must understand that it was he who recognised most clearly what was new in the modern industrial age, and the burdens and destiny of modern man, and who was most steadfast in siding with this new age. In a way that his contemporaries found impossible he was able to establish formulae suitable for the age in which he lived, and analysed the motive factors behind the machine, the banking system and the pool of casual labour, while the most able men around him were still struggling with the fetters of the past. For that reason he is so up to date in all his ideas. How old-fashioned Lorenz Stein and Bakunin seem beside him, how romantic and scurrilous Stirner, and even Feuerbach. The age of capitalism, the power of money, the reducing of the world into what could be calculated and measured, the age when no limits were set to the emphasis laid on anything with a utilitarian or a technical value, have never found so perfect an expression as in the man who believed that he was called to overthrow them.

2. The second is his unreserved avowal that he was an heir of the Age of Enlightenment. With even greater power than Hegel he resists the Romantic reactionary movements. He seems to be completely free from the mysterious theology of idealism in which Feuerbach was so firmly rooted. More than anyone else—and with complete lack of consideration and respect—he lays stress on the finite nature of man as a product of nature and on the powers of cognition of the human reason. Therefore he is equally a logical nominalist and a relentless critic, and as such stands on a level with the other two great "unmaskers" of the nineteenth century, Kierkegaard and Nietzsche. With his dialectic he is able to counteract the banality of the traditional materialism, but also to take into consideration the cognitive theories and the ontological problems of idealism; he does not ignore the individuality of man as exemplified in his spiritual nature, and in his ego, but rather he makes allowance for just these attributes. Anyone who tries to combat dialectical materialism with nothing but such arguments, frequently employed in the West, as can only be effective against mechanical materialism from Holbach to Haeckel, will fail dismally, surrounded by the mocking laughter of the Marxists.

Not until we acknowledge this will we be able to comprehend the significance of Marx and his personal magnetism, as well as the impetus and power behind his ideas, which have had such widespread consequences. In studying him we may also recognise how this logical naturalism and rationalism contained the seeds of its own destruction, and how theology, which he believed he had so thoroughly destroyed that not a trace of it remained, attacked him in the rear. The state of man before the fall, original sin and eschatology—all these reappear in his philosophy. He could not ignore the fact that he belonged to the Christian era, he was forced to regard history as a road leading to a certain goal, and he never penetrated the mysterious metaphysics of the theory of evolution. As soon as one begins to read his works critically, one finds everywhere vagueness, over-hasty judgments and contradictions. Marx was to blame for the fact that later on Engels involuntarily administered the death-blow to the amazing conception of historical materialism by introducing the theory of "reciprocal effect"; for even Marx had confined himself to affirming basic principles, to making mock of objections, and to providing examples only from the analysis of the capitalist era (in his essays on French history). Plekhanov's attempt at systematisation was only fragmentary; and the assertion, first made by Engels and constantly re-affirmed by Lenin and by present-day Soviet science, that Marx had discovered and described the laws of historical evolution in as scientific a manner as Darwin had set out the laws of natural evolution, is quite false, in so far as Marx never went to work with the same self-critical prudence, the same care and the same wealth of material at his disposal as is found so laudably in Darwin's work. Marx was nothing more and nothing less than a genius at arousing enthusiasm; yet he was the most un-suitable of men to be an expounder of theory.

22 *May* 1948

Today I came across a periodical in which there is a brief account of the lecture which Georg Lukasz gave at the first meeting of the *Rencontres Internationales* in Geneva in 1946. Once again I am kicking against the pricks; I wonder what is going on in the world outside the barbed wire, at this time when all these new beginnings are starting to bear fruit, while I am chopping up my tree-stumps! Lukasz describes the spiritual crisis as a crisis of middle-class society, and analyses it into three separate crises: of reason, of the idea of progress and of human self-confidence. His opinion is, of course, that this particular crisis is one in the capitalist economy and society, one from which there is no way out; because of it, the middle classes, no longer able to resolve the contradictions, are beginning to have doubts about reason and progress, and are taking refuge in irrationalism and mysticism and scepticism, in Fascism or religion, because they fear the only obvious way of preserving the value of reason and progress, namely the way of a socialist revolution.

This is the surprising thing about coming into contact with the spiritual life in the U.S.S.R. The West European would like, with a superior gesture, to consign to the rubbish-heap of the nineteenth century the extravagant worship of science, that is, natural science, naturalistic anthropology, the rationalistic scorn of religion, the unbroken faith in progress, and the confident trust in technics and in organisation. He believes that he has left all this behind him, yet he has to experience the fact that he in no way impresses the Soviet Marxist, who is not deprived of his belief in rationalism, but rather contests the claim that all this is in fact overthrown. He is said not to have overthrown it but to have fled from it. His theory of the limitations of human reason and of the relativity of progress is not "cognition" but the expression of his lack of courage to trust in reason any more. In reality nothing has been destroyed but the bourgeois illusion of evolutionary progress with no crises, and nothing has given him cause to doubt the ability of human reason, to recognise the truth, to rule nature and to organise society intelligently. Existentialism and the fashionable religiosity of the West are conditioned by crises, are transitory, are the products of the disintegration of a moribund order of society, and do not constitute genuine progress in cognition.

It is a good thing to be told all this. Inherent in all of us is a tendency to turn away from rationalism, a pusillanimous fear of things intellectual, a readiness for "Confucius on hand-made paper" (Spengler), for escape into the dream world of the irrational, for a religious narcotic, for the giving up of all intellectual responsibility; against all these, Marxist rationalism will always prevail. "Reason, which gives way to emotion instead of thinking, can never be forgiven" (Kant). Knowledge must recognise its limits, by coming up against them itself, not by having them imposed upon it. Nothing but a greater measure of intellectual responsibility can bring about a fundamental alteration of Marxist rationalism.

At all events, this is now in progress. People here are making things too easy for themselves by denying that in the spiritual crisis of the West there is a real and effective content of experience and knowledge. Behind our "scepticism" about reason and progress stands knowledge which these people here still have to attain, and problems which they have not yet had to face. This is probably due to three things:

1. They are a younger nation as far as civilisation is concerned. The man who is starving because the steppes are still unproductive, and who has to use a spade and dig canals because there is no machinery, may well be under the illusion that heaven will have to come on earth when man is not at the mercy of nature to such an extent. We have lost this illusion.

2. The Marxist has to be a rationalist because Marxism is his spiritual home, his religion—a religion which stands or falls by the assertion that it is not a religion but a science. If his faith were broken against science, if he thought of it with the moderation of the genuine scientist of today, then this faith would collapse and he would fall into nothingness.

3. Every conversation about such things is based on the supposition that the person to whom one talks is free to possess this knowledge. Here, however, rationalism and the worship of science are officially ordered. Lenin's saying, that "electrification plus the Soviet system", i.e. technics plus the organisation of society, "equals paradise", is a state dogma. One must believe that the Soviet Union is the concrete proof of the truth of this dogma. For who is allowed to say openly that man, even when he has succeeded in protecting himself thoroughly from the sufferings caused by nature, still suffers definitely through man, his fellow-man and himself, and that the proof of this lies, to us West Europeans, in our society, and in ourselves, and above all in the Soviet society? The knowledge which we have acquired is forbidden to them, however much this knowledge may force itself daily upon their notice. Forbidden knowledge—therein lies the tragedy of spiritual life in Russia.

25 May 1948

Not long ago I discussed thoroughly with Dr. S. the scientific part of Lenin's writings against empirical criticism, and since I have also read a good deal of Engels, I think it will be profitable to sum up the metaphysical dogma of this quasi-scientific teaching.

1. I believe in the ability of our five senses to transmit to us in an appropriate way the realities of the world.

2. I believe in the methods of cognition in the modern

natural sciences as the only legitimate means of access to knowledge of the world.

·3. I believe that in this way, and in this way alone, one can take cognisance of everything that exists.

4. I believe in the unity and the unique nature of the world which can thus be recognised.

5. I believe in continual progress, that is, that mankind, as Engels says, is "still on the ascending path of its evolution".

6. I believe that human nature can be changed, and that man will ultimately achieve goodness.

7. I believe that in the history of man, only that has any value which has become effective as an historical fact, and is understandable by everyone.

(I have just read the words of a Marxist in the Eastern Zone, "History is not interested in the private troubles and the *Weltschmerz* of individualistic intellectuals."—Fred Oelsner, in *Present-day Marxism and its Critics*, Berlin 1948, page 120.)

8. I believe in the proletariat as a solid class with its own interests, which can at the same time be identified with the true interests of mankind.

9. I believe in the Moscow Polit-Bureau, in its orthodox Marxism, its infallible wisdom and selfless idealism, and that it alone has the happiness of all mankind at heart, and needs no control.

1 June 1948

The Soviet newspapers are all full of the debate in the Moscow Academy of Agriculture, in which the dispute between the Mitchurin sympathisers led by Lyssenko and the geneticists has been settled in favour of the former. At first we were astounded at the space which the Press devoted to such a specialist scientific question. It probably is connected with the wide interest in scientific problems of the whole of this population, so thirsting for knowledge, a fact that is emphasised, naturally, as a Socialist victory over the alleged intellectual indolence of the capitalist nations. But it is a good thing, here as everywhere, to look at the other side of the question. This publicity given to scientific discussion is not intended merely for information. The mass of the people must "give their

186

decision" about a matter which they are not in a position to
decide, that is, the opposition scientists are to suffer the pressure
of public opinion, as well as all the other things they have to
fear, and down to the last commune everyone must know that
by sticking to their belief in the now rejected genetic theories
they are guilty of a political crime. That is why the up-
holders of the genetic principles—Schmalhausen and Orbeli
were the bravest of these men—let themselves be scolded like
abject schoolboys, could hardly manage to justify themselves
and knew that their institutes would be closed and their official
positions taken away from them. It is an unpleasant picture to
see these outstanding men of learning, who had never had the
slightest idea of upholding the much-maligned idealism, in such
an undignified position.

The German professors here in the camp are always singing
the praises of the Soviet Union with its well-equipped science
institutes, but on the other side of the picture is the complete
shackling of science not only in its results (science in the West is
similarly threatened) but also in its methods and its ethics.

"The Soviet people do so much for science that they should
expect from it the greatest benefits." That was the refrain that
was constantly being chanted, as it had been in the spring at
our music debates. The would-be elimination of theology from
Marxism, which I mentioned before in speaking of Marx, is
being avenged by the growth of a pseudo-theology. The strange
thing about the Lyssenko debate was that it only appeared to
be a scientific discussion, but was really a "theological" one.
The doctrine of the reality of the gene in modern genetics was
contested, not so much with new facts proved by experiment,
but with the consequences which this doctrine would have for
materialism. It cannot be true because it must not be true. Thus
they did not have as their bone of contention hypotheses
relating to the interpretation of the results of an experiment,
but rather they fought over "isms": Mitchurinism, Morganism,
materialism and idealism. They pinned one of these "isms" on
to their opponents and then shot them down. So all the judgments were pseudo-theological, it was a battle between ortho-
doxy and heresy in a scientific garb. Everything was made

crystal clear when Shdanov, the Secretary-General of the Party and presumably Stalin's successor, stood up and declared that up till a few weeks ago he had believed the genetic theory to be worthy of discussion, but he had studied the matter and could now confirm (after a few weeks!) that Lyssenko was right—which was the death sentence of the geneticists. I could say a good deal about the reasons underlying the opinion of the Soviet leaders that it was now necessary to counter Darwin's theory with a doctrine of the inheritance of acquired characteristics, but I cannot do so now.

It was obvious that here was a State having the monopoly of a philosophy of life, and that dialectical and historical materialism is the official philosophy of the U.S.S.R. But before I came here I had no idea what that really implied. The Third Reich was also a State with a philosophy, it launched terrible attacks on the work of individual sciences, and if it had lasted longer, it would perhaps have done worse. Yet there were many opportunities for research and the expressing of opinions, there was a wide sphere of intellectual exchange of ideas spreading far beyond laboratories or periodicals, a sphere in which we still had freedom to move about. The mere fact that the Nazi philosophy was such a hotch-potch of indisputable follies, preserved spiritual life from slavery such as the Marxist system has enforced here. The medieval State, too, had its philosophical monopoly, but what an abundance of variety, what opportunities for fruitful argument of all kinds, was revealed in the spiritual life of the Middle Ages. We have no historical analogy (not even the Spanish Inquisition was one) with what happens here in the Soviet Union, and it must be seen to be believed. Take away everything that has had any influence upon our life, every spiritual experience that has inspired us, every question and every thesis which have led us from an individual problem to the essential study of human life in general, every movement in art and philosophy, whether we welcomed it or not; put a ban on all religious discussion behind the walls of priestly seminaries which have just been allowed to get going again after a long time, leave nothing but the narrowest field of specialist research, its general results at once dogmatically laid

down, and a strictly guarded interpretation of art, spiritual life
and history fossilised into a monotonous terminology with an
interpretation undertaken by official Marxism commented on
by specially commissioned scholars: what is left then constitutes
the spiritual life in one-sixth of the world. The shroud of
dialectical materialism lies over this land—and it really is a
shroud.

4 *August* 1948

A new scholastic year has begun in the "anti-Fascist
School". For several months specially selected P.O.W.s from
all camps, in groups of 250 at a time, will be schooled to become
"anti-Fascists". At first this was with the object of sending
them back to the camps to organise the political education
there, but now it is with the intention of taking up positions in
the Eastern Zone, in all the various departments of the Party
organisation, German industry and the trade unions, etc. For
this reason it was mostly only those who came from Eastern
Germany who were accepted for these courses. A year ago it
was proposed to start a course for the intelligentsia, with which
I was also threatened, but later they saw, as an assistant master
told me, that they could not achieve much with the older
intellectuals, and wanted therefore to educate a new "working
intelligence". We can now see how this is being done. The
main subjects studied are political economy, the history of the
Soviet Union and of the Communist Party, German history
(according to Franz Mehring) and "philosophy" (dialectical
materialism). The teachers are Russians and German emigrants,
and each group of ten attending the course has an assistant
attached to it, that is a trustworthy P.O.W. already politically
educated who goes over with the group what they have heard
in the lectures and directs the whole community life of the
group. Food, clothing and general treatment are all such that
those taking part in the course feel that they are no longer
prisoners but "comrades". Most of them come from the
"lower" age-groups, among them many nice fresh, unsuspecting young fellows who bring with them the atmosphere of the
labour camp, and, in so far as they had really been workers and

had not belonged to the privileged class, had not let their anti-Fascist position worry them too much and still expressed their thoughts freely. Now they will learn to "see things dialectically"; they will learn that sometimes one must not even see a thing at all, that there are some thoughts which must not be spoken aloud, and indeed which must not be thought at all if one does not want to be a reactionary, an imperialist hireling, or an agent of Schumacher. They would not have been Germans had they not tried with the greatest enthusiasm to respond to this call of duty, and to this task demanded of them here, just as they would to any task set them by anyone in the world. In a few weeks they have reached the point where one can no longer talk to them calmly. It is all so inspiring—one must be a crazy reactionary or a paid agent not to feel this—and above all the philosophy is so wonderful that all at once all the problems in the world are solved by a magic key. Especially during the last weeks of the course, in which philosophy is dealt with, one can see them walking around, their faces lit up, learning and discussing. The air is humming with "Idealism", "Dialectics", "the change from quantity to quality", "Fideism" and "objective Truth", and one can only shake one's head at the way these bourgeois philosophers make everything so difficult when it is really so easy—but then they are bourgeois and therefore have no courage to face the truth. The "anti-Fascist" pupils finally leave their course with the unshakable self-confidence of the half-educated.

Morals are strict; for in comparison with Fascism, Communism has a high moral code. Such vulgarities as were usual in the S.A. courses are not tolerated here; a variety concert in the school having a slightly dubious programme is sharply criticised. At the beginning of the course each member of a group gives the others an account of his life, not merely superficially so that they can get to know each other, but he strips off every layer, and if he tries to hide anything it is dragged out of him by persistent questioning, until his life lies naked before their eyes. That is repeated again and again during these months, and every *faux pas* can be the cause of an inquisition by the rest of the group. Finally everything is clear:

I have nothing private, everything about me belongs to the Party; the Party must know everything about me, and about everyone else. Therefore I must practise "revolutionary wakefulness" and must pass on everything that strikes me about another man even if he were my best friend; for above every human confidential relationship stands my confidential relationship to the Party to which I belong wholly. In the same way the assistants give detailed reports of the members of their groups to their superiors. Everybody spies on everybody else. You may have doubts, you may not understand something, you may have done something wrong, you may have a skeleton in your cupboard—that is not so bad; what is bad is that you should conceal it and continue to conceal it.

From this it is only a short step to inviting the pupils to sign on as spies, an activity not only limited to P.O.W. camps, but useful also in preparation for life at home. To refuse to sign amounts to unmasking oneself as a class enemy. Henceforth they can reveal themselves only in one direction—in the direction of the Party—towards the Party yet not towards Party members—for they must conceal everything from their companions however much these may try to draw them out, but they can reveal themselves only to the secret Soviet police; otherwise their lives are closed in all directions, even towards their fellow-men.

Not all of them are suited to this. Hans, who secretly opened his heart to me, realised at the moment of signing his name the fundamental nature of the system. He understood all at once that something was happening which ought not to happen, that not even the most holy purpose could sanctify these methods, that something was being demanded of him that no man ought to demand of him. Everything had seemed wonderful to him. He believed everything and was ready to fight enthusiastically on behalf of this system. Yet now that this was demanded of him, everything crashed to the ground. In an hour, without hearing any further arguments, he became a sworn enemy of the system, filled only with a desire to escape from this net and warn the rest of the world.

Outside my window Dr. R. is passing, his face lined with

anxiety. I know what is tormenting him. He had been a Nazi administrator, but when he was captured he surrendered to Marxism with the same devotion and is now at the school. During his first course, at the demand for a general confession, he accused himself, genuinely penitent, of having been present when the Wehrmacht were killing Russian prisoners by injections of morphium—not taking part yet not objecting. This was taken note of, the information handed on and now he has been interrogated several times on account of it. He is trying to make up for it and prove his worth by throwing himself fanatically into his work, by devoting himself to active propaganda and by unreserved "correctness" of thought. It was of no avail. Soon afterwards he was fetched away and condemned to twenty years' imprisonment.

I have hardly spoken to Heinz A. We have not continued the conversations we had planned. It is my fault, but I cannot decide to do it. Perhaps I ought to, perhaps I shall reproach myself bitterly for not doing so. What held me back? There is not much of my own reputation left to be ruined here, but what will happen to him if I convince him? Can he still be convinced? Perhaps he is already so tangled up in the net that nothing but death can set him free. Recently I heard him making a speech, full of a believing spirit—what am I to believe? He must be able to see something of what I can see. He cannot be for ever using his "dialectics" to help him get over it. Does Goethe not say somewhere that emotional enthusiasts should be killed off at thirty years of age, since they could only grow into fools or criminals? Is he still an enthusiast, or is he already a . . .? What will become of him? How will he take it when his eyes are open? What can I do?

5 *August* 1948

In the school one of the men taking the last course has thoughtlessly begun to play a military march on the piano during the mid-day break. There was great excitement. A psycho-analyst could not seek the reasons for a failure in one of his cases with greater perseverance than was shown in the probing and questioning about the inner state of this poor fellow to see whether (*a*) there were any traces of "Prussianism" left in his soul, and (*b*) whether his repentance over his lapse was really genuine.

I have just learnt a proof question by which one can test a State to see whether one would like to live in it or not: supposing there were an apparatus which could observe every citizen everywhere and read his inmost thoughts—is the State so organised that its leaders would grasp at this apparatus and make use of it—or would they despise it or would the citizens stop them from using it? The whole of this system of confession, of laying bare one's soul, and of being under observation is only an imperfect substitute for this apparatus which, to the great regret of the N.K.V.D., is not yet at its disposal.

10 *August* 1948

Evening conversations among our men in the hut: one man is reading an old paper on the front page of which there is flaunted the photograph of some great Soviet celebration, where all the big-wigs of State and Party organisations were assembled on the platform. He said disapprovingly, "Just look at all the fat faces of these leaders of the working-class! How many fat men can you see anywhere else in the Soviet Union? I could count them on one hand!"

"What about General X! Isn't he fat enough for you?"

"Oh yes, in the army they live like lords."

A third said, "I will tell you what I saw today. We were in the collective farm at N. collecting potatoes for the camp. As we were driving through the village with our lorry laden, the children ran after us and begged for potatoes. In summer, after two good harvests, three hours from Moscow! Then we drove along a pretty valley, past high walls, behind which lay wonderful villas with parks and flower-beds. From the road itself you could not see in, but from the top of the lorry you could. Then 'posh' cars came towards us with such elegant ladies inside as I would never have thought to see in Russia; they were driving up to the villas. Our driver said they were the wives of generals and ministers who were driving to their country houses for the week-end."

"During the war I was in the Crimea. There we saw Molotov's villa. The Tsars could not have had a finer one."

"Molotov is not just anyone, of course. But do you remember Alfred K., who was once in this camp? He was our best wireless expert. They took him to Moscow once to install a wireless set for one of the ministers. What did he find there? Six wonderful German cabinet models of the latest design, which he had to set up in various rooms. And the rooms weren't made of cardboard either."

"I only need to think of the evening dresses which Walter B., the camp's master tailor, made for General R.'s daughter, and I know everything."

"You were working in the aircraft factory, weren't you? Didn't you see all the lovely children out with their nursemaids? They must have belonged to some high-up official or director. Not long ago D. said at one of our discussions that here in the Soviet Union everyone had equal opportunity and it didn't matter what one's father was. I would rather have one of these officials as my father. Or do you think that the children will start from the bottom again when their nurses have finished bringing them up?"

"It's not as bad here, though, as it is at home. And, moreover, they may very easily fall again. In the prison in Sverdlovsk, where I was searched, I was sitting next to a director who had done nothing except put a barrel of beer on one side to drink it privately with a few engineer friends. He was in an interrogation prison for six months, and then got twelve years."

"That was probably only an excuse because they wanted to get rid of him anyway. They can always find some excuse because everyone has some dirty deed chalked up against him."

"But in general you can say that here, apart from those at the very top, the differences are not as marked as they are at home. If you go into the commandant's lodging you see that it is clean, but very simply furnished, just like the house of a bank-messenger at home. And there are not such great class distinctions as with us. Whether one works in an office or on a turning-lathe, nobody looks down on the manual worker from behind the rampart of his stiff collar."

"That's true. They all treat each other as equals. In Germany people wash themselves after shaking hands with a workman."

"You needn't make us out to be all that bad. You behave as though we were all living in the last century. In our business at home everything went on quite democratically, and in America there's not supposed to be any arrogance where class is concerned, although it's a capitalist country."

"It's worse in some places than in others. It does happen here and is increasing. How do you think the Natchalnik children will behave when they are grown up! But what you said about marked differences is important. I thought formerly that it was wrong that one man had as much money as Rocke-feller, and the other had to count every farthing. But that was really only jealousy. For the difference did not affect me since I had my salary. Then I was taken prisoner and learnt to see the differences which then did affect me; we ordinary Plennis were starving, while the well-to-do ones, the company leaders and the activists, stuffed themselves in the kitchen. Then I recognised that there is only one real difference: the difference between those who haven't enough to exist on, and those who can eat their fill. And this difference is as widespread in Russia as anywhere, and the fact that they haven't done away with it although it's thirty years since the Revolution when millions of people died, is too much for me. I think that we could achieve it more cheaply without a revolution."

The next evening in the discussion group the question was raised about the differences in income in the Soviet State. They were told that there are indeed big differences. In 1929 Stalin declared that the demand for equality of pay was un-Marxist. Now they were living in a state of Socialism. Their guiding principle ought to be: "Everyone should earn according to his abilities and achievement!" If some day so many consumer goods are produced that the transition from Socialism to Com-munism can come about, then this principle will take its place: "Everyone should earn according to his ability and his needs—and everyone must continue to work for the common good."

But surely, if everyone can get what he wants to satisfy his needs, then nobody will make the effort to achieve more than anyone else?

Oh, yes, for men will have been so educated that they will feel the need to work and will do of their own free will all that they can do for the sake of the community, while now they have to have the added incentives of graded wages and bonuses, etc.

But then, as you can see, so many big distinctions have been created that everybody's interests are different. The manager of a factory is no longer interested in the welfare of his workers, but in the big bonus he gets because of their high rate of production.

The answer: Firstly it doesn't matter all that much for it is only a temporary condition. The main thing is that we should increase production as rapidly as possible so that when there is a sufficient supply of consumer goods the transition to Communism can be effected: that may be possible even in our generation. Secondly, the difference of interests cannot cause much trouble, because the present directors, like all the leaders of the Soviet Union, have themselves risen from the working classes and are therefore not separated from the people but bound together with them.

A worker from the I.G. Farben factory asked to speak. At home, he said, they had had a director who came of working-class stock, and he was the most un-socialistic of them all. When a man became leader of a group of workers he became their slave-driver and we must not forget the proverb that "The slave who has become the master holds the sharpest shears."

He was severely reprimanded for calling the workers slaves, and the answer to his remarks was as follows: capitalist society of course corrupted everyone who had risen to the top but had forgotten his origins and accustomed himself to the life of a master. Here in the Soviet Union that was impossible because everything was done for the worker, and the worker could criticise his boss, by means of the wall-newspapers and at business meetings.

Kurt D. who had the next bed to me, and was a worker from the Krupp factory in Essen, told me about this debate when he returned and had crawled beneath his blankets. "Tell me," he said, "you were once working in a factory here, could a worker criticise his boss?"

"Lenin intended that he should be able to. That was what he meant by control through criticism from below. But now, as far as I can see, that is all an illusion. I often looked at the wall-newspapers in the factory. There were suggestions for improvements, or complaints that in one department the work was badly organised or even that a foreman preferred flirting with the women to working, or perhaps a political article in the usual style, or the men were urged to step up production and beat the record. You could see that people were trying to achieve importance and get a good report. But there was never any real criticism of the director, never a complaint that too much was being demanded of them, that the pay was too low, or the target too high. They wouldn't dare!"

"Why?"

"A Russian worker whom I asked told me that if anyone wants to attack the director in the wall-newspaper then he does well to keep his ears open to see if the N.K.V.D. and the Party have anything against him and whether they would sympathise with the attack, otherwise the worker himself is liable to come a cropper. Also there is never any criticism of the target set or of the low wages, for that would mean criticising the State. In one of the factories where I worked we came at midday to go on the second shift. The Russians working on the same shift have to be there at 11 a.m. for the daily business talks. At these meetings they discussed how to increase production, they receive political education, but never anything else. You can imagine how fed up they got with all that—but what could they do?"

"Since we had the debate, I am relieved about one thing, it will be a long time before they can make a transition towards Communism. For we shall never see the Russians feeling the need to work. There would be more chance of that among the Germans; they are never happy unless they are working."

"Yes, I often wonder what to pity the more, Communism for having tried its first experiment on such an unsuitable nation as the Russians, or the Russians themselves for being the guinea-pigs of the Communists. Oh, well, good night!"

12 *August* 1948

What they were told at that discussion about the bond between the present directors and the people, as contrasted with the enmity and hatred of the upper classes in the capitalist society, was all humbug.

Things were certainly different at first. This is shown very impressively in Gladkov's *Cement*, a novel telling of how after the civil war the workers rebuilt those industries which had been destroyed. But when Lenin, with his realism, opposed Tomski and substituted individual management of business for collective control, the foundations of the new classes, which are beginning to be seen today, were already laid. Today the Soviet factory directors have power over the workers to an extent unknown in any factory in Western Europe. The opposing interests are very obvious: the directors receive extra pay for high rates of production with little wastage, the workers have to ensure that they get this bonus by stepping-up production and by accepting less wages, the highly paid Stakhanov-brigades get paid for running the factories by urging the workers to increase production, and by lowering wages. Thus the "bond" between the two classes becomes more than ever one of those "fairy-tales".

It remains to be seen how far classes of society, such as we are accustomed to, can be stabilised and handed on to succeeding generations. With the new class of officials in the State totally devoted to industry there will perhaps arise a new sociological phenomenon that is less stable. The leaders at the top are interested in inheritable stability because this may lead to a certain measure of independence. Hereditary privileges (wealth, titles, etc.) give to individuals a firm standing and lessen their dependence on the State machine. All this is continually being impressed upon the Soviet official by the frequent and sudden falls of his comrades from the heights to the depths.

It is certainly a fairy-tale, however, that in the Soviet society

198

(as I have just been reading in an essay by Ernst Niekisch) the struggle between the various "high-ups" for leadership which hitherto has raged in the class-society has been done away with and that instead the mass of the people lead and rule themselves. The Revolution at which Communism is aiming is nothing more than the ousting of one group by the other. The people never do the leading but are led, with less will of their own and less freedom in the Soviet Union than in any other middle-class society in the world. What is to be seen here is not a lessening of the State's power, which Marx expected would take place after the proletariat had seized power, but the promotion of a new élite; there are no signs that, "seen dialectically", the future will bring the removal of the new élite but rather there is evidence that the power of this new class is being consolidated. How do I know all this? It is enough to look at the faces of the men around me. There ought to be some signs that, even when they are in power, these men will have as their sole aim to fight for those who helped them to power and have now lost their rights. There ought to be—and I cannot avoid this word—some small signs of love towards the people who still live in such poverty. These signs ought to be revealed in the fact that the new élite do not enjoy their privileges (while there are men living beside them in misery) as shamelessly as did the old aristocracy of the capitalist countries, and do not salve their consciences for this enjoyment by comforting the people by the thought of future life in a classless society—instead of by the much despised Christian belief in the life after death. The German P.O.W.s have found not only a great deal of misery in the Soviet Union, but also a class which finds this quite acceptable. What makes them return home completely cured of all sympathy for Communism is that they have missed the link of fellowship of this class with the mass of people living in misery, just as they missed it in Western Europe, perhaps more so because the lack of charity is so widespread among this class in Russia. The two bath attendants at the baths in Beschiza in the spring of 1947, who had only one meal a day and yet envied me although I too was hungry, had no one to whom they could turn for help. "There's nothing like that here," they said sadly when I told them what could have been done for them at home. When I think, with my present experiences, of the faces of the Communist leaders whom I heard speaking before 1933, it is quite clear to me that nothing matters to them but the ousting of the old élite in order to be the new élite themselves. The question is not: how can the under-dog be helped, but rather: who is to be the top-dog?

11 *September* 1948

This morning's delivery of post brought Wolfgang O. a surprise which made him think. He is one of our wood-yard brigade, formerly one of the S.S. officers who defended the Reich Chancellery to the end, and is one of those careless young men who are indifferent to the events of the world, because they are not really interested in anything beyond their own noses. When we distributed the post in the wood-yard hut, he got a postcard. His face was frozen into an expression of utter stupefaction, and he handed us the card, quite speechless. On the card was the photograph of a youngish woman with a little child, and the message from this woman was that she had at last discovered the address of his parents, and thus his own address, and could now inform him that several years ago she had borne him a lovely little daughter. The explanation that he gave us put this communication in its true perspective. During the war, on his way back to the front after having spent his leave at home, he arrived at a German town where they had a longish wait. On the station he got into conversation with a respectable-looking girl, who invited him to spend an hour or so with her family. He had coffee with a middle-class family, the father being a civil servant, then the parents retired tactfully. The two spent a short time together, after which he continued his journey and forgot the experience and the names. Now he learnt that he was a father. Although the consequences of this act left him dumbfounded and shaken, the occurrence was not all that extraordinary and for that very reason was a clear indication of the state of confusion into which the German black-coated middle-class had been drawn—a class of people not so very long ago leading such well-ordered lives. It was again a symptom of this state of confusion that Wolfgang recovered from his astonishment by saying that after all she should be proud to have a child by an S.S. officer.

Recently, he told me of another experience that is worth mentioning. Two years ago, when he was in another camp, he had thought out a trick to get himself sent home. He pretended to be mad in the hopes of being sent back to Germany. One night at 3 a.m. he walked naked into the guardroom, declaring that he had been called by Stalin and must go to Moscow immediately. In spite of flogging and detention he persisted with this delusion, otherwise behaving quite sensibly until the commandant and the doctors were baffled and could think of nothing but to send him—not home, unfortunately—but to a mental hospital. He stood it for six weeks and kept up the pretence until he saw that it was useless, and afraid that he would starve, pretended to be cured, whereupon he was without more ado sent back to his camp. The weeks he spent in the mental hospital had given him a foretaste of hell. With about fifty other lunatics, among them some German and Italian P.O.W.s, stark naked as were they all, he was locked up in a hall, against the walls of which were bunks with straw mattresses. Here they lived like animals. The only duties the warders had to perform were to wash the prisoners now and again, and to bring them a pail of soup twice a day, upon which they all hurled themselves. Since there was not enough for them all, the stronger ones made sure of their share while the weaker ones usually got nothing, but they were all as thin as skeletons. When one died, the warders fetched him in the evening. The doctors only came round occasionally to carry out their duties, or when there were any serious accidents during the battle for the soup. He thought that the Nazis had been more humane in killing off their lunatics with injections. I remarked drily that in that case he would not be here, and couldn't he think of a third possibility. Thus began a long conversation.

This story, however, is quite characteristic. Wolfgang is one of those whom I have tried particularly to wean from his glorifying of the Nazis, from his obstinate rejection of anti-Fascist propaganda and his scorn of everything in the Soviet.

He has, he says, practical proof that all the accusations levelled against National Socialism were only hypocrisy on the part of the victors, and that all over the world the same thing was happening. One of his statements cannot be contradicted, namely that Fascism and the Soviet system are so alike in regarding man merely as an animal and in their consequent despising of the individual, that for the Soviet Union there is no fundamental reason why they should not deal with lunatics just as Hitler did. If they had not used Hitler's methods hitherto, that was only because they were held back by a remnant of the Christian tradition; Hitler having freed himself from this tradition no longer found it a hindrance, yet in the Soviet system it only had the effect of preventing them from killing the lunatics directly. Really to care for such people is possible only when one has quite a different conception of man.

27 September 1948

A strange period in the life of the camp has now ended: a few days ago the N.K. course went home with great ceremonial in an express train, accompanied by several commissars. I will give you a detailed account of the whole story.

Before Easter there were strange signs of a change in the camp: one hut was cleared and made spick and span and, instead of the double bunks, iron bedsteads were put in with white bed-linen over the straw mattresses. Who was to be put in there? Rumours flew round the camp. Our countrymen betrayed their sub-conscious wishes by saying that female German internees were coming, but instead it was the N.K.— the "National Committee of Free Germany"! We were astounded to see that these people, whom we believed to have returned home a long time ago, were still in Russia.

Before the disaster of Stalingrad, political propaganda in the camps then existing was undertaken mainly by German emigrants. Pieck, Ulbricht and others travelled around, talked to their compatriots and found little response. After Stalingrad all this was changed. Faith in Hitler's victory began to waver. Those who had survived Stalingrad had had their eyes opened about their leaders, and also saw a different Russia from the one spoken of by Goebbels: a Russia that was strong and determined, treating the prisoners as far as possible according to their deserts. The Russians saw new opportunities and supported the formation of an anti-Nazi "party" among the German P.O.W.s, which in the summer of 1943 was finally constituted as the N.K. at a conference in Moscow of men sent from every camp. The chairman was the Communist writer Erich Wienert, the vice-president, probably only on account of his name, was the flying-officer Heinrich, Graf Einsiedel: the president of the officers' organisation, the "German Officers Union", affiliated to it, was General von Seydlitz. The members came from the most varied classes and held varying opinions, but only a few could have been Communists; the "conservative wing" was strong; well-known and long-established Prussian families were represented, together with quite a large number of clergymen of both confessions, who took part in special conferences. There were probably many opportunists among the members, but there were certainly many too who were driven by the feeling that Hitler had deceived them, and who now did not wish to look on inactive while the Fatherland was being conquered. Those who saw clearly may have had doubts whether the Russians and the emigrants would give the N.K. a square deal as partners; one could not deny this at this early stage, but had to take their promises on trust when they said that the N.K. would not become a unit of the Communist Party representing the Soviet Union but would be a free union, enjoying equal rights with the Russians, of all those who wished to prevent Germany from being ruined by Hitler and to rebuild it as a democracy. The settling of differences of opinion which existed among them could be put off till the end of the war.

The N.K. then began broadcasting from the Moscow radio station "Free Germany" with the signature tune "God who made iron to grow" (*Der Gott, der Eisen wachsen liess*), and published broad-sheets and the newspaper *Free Germany* with a black, white and red border, copies of which were sent to the battle-front. The whole set-up, including the well-advertised names of the generals, showed that the Soviet Union recognised, with a quickness not usually found in its propaganda machine, that the German soldier was mesmerised by National Socialism to such an extent that he would respond only to a call for nationalism and not for class-warfare. The N.K. was always all out for propaganda: there were never any armed detachments. The Russians never armed German P.O.W.s to fight against Hitler, and any talk of a Paulus or a Seydlitz army was all nonsense.

When Hitler was defeated, the fate of the N.K. was sealed; it no longer had any value in Russian eyes, all promises were forgotten, and in the autumn of 1945 it was disbanded; its paper *Free Germany* had its black, white and red border removed and was turned into *News for German P.O.W.s in the U.S.S.R.*, edited solely by Marxists; some of its most prominent members were allowed to go home, the rest were divided up over various camps where they either became active anti-Fascist club members, or else joined the ranks of working Plennis. Some of the non-Communist members were so embittered by the deceit practised on them and through them, that they now took up a definitely anti-Communist attitude.

Now they have been brought together again from out of their scattered places of concealment. What were they wanted for? They were to hear a series of lectures. But for what purpose? Many people tried to guess the answer to this riddle, but the Russians did not let anything out. It seems that in fact they had intended to proclaim this circle of men, who had only been told that they were to perform "great national tasks", as the government of Germany, that this purpose could no longer be carried out owing to the confusion resulting from the West German currency reform of June 1948 and that now, after an indefinite period of waiting, these men were to be sent to various places in Eastern Germany. "We have all got our marching orders," said one of them to me, the day before they left.

From the first, some of the original members had not been included in this scheme. Seydlitz was not there, nor were the Roman Catholic priests, except one, nor some of the "conservatives". Instead, one or two well-trained anti-Fascists were being sent with them. In the Anti-Fascist school these were now having a course of instruction along the usual lines. It appeared that the majority of them had meanwhile developed into complete Marxists and were therefore undertaking the task without opposition and apparently unreservedly. Only a few of them retained any independent opinions, made these plain by attending the camp church services, by stating their political views openly in the written résumé which all those attending the course had to hand in at the end, and by refusing to undertake duties in the Eastern Zone which were demanded of them. Of those few who thus did not comply with the "must", the majority were divided up during the last few weeks and sent to other camps; they fell into great disfavour and we ought to be much concerned as to their fate. (Some of them were repatriated with the last batch of returning prisoners in April–May 1950, others had meanwhile been sentenced to hard labour on some pretext or other.)

I got to know some of them, and the times we spent together were among the most enjoyable experiences I had during my captivity. It is easy to pass judgment today on their original decision to join the N.K. With the beginning of the course of instruction here in the camp, the old arguments about the N.K. flared up. At Easter, a first-rate staff officer, who agreed with my view on the Third Reich, answered when I asked him why he was looking so gloomy, "What is there to laugh about when we live in the company of fifty traitors?" It was only with difficulty that I could bring him to think it over. "These traitors may have worked towards the collapse of the front line—well, and what did you do? Up to the last minute you led your fellow-countrymen to die for a cause which you already knew to be lost and for a government which you your-self recognised to be destructive. You may be rubbing your hands in glee now because you have not broken your oath, but the question is whether the honest members of the N.K., out of love for the Fatherland, did not make things as difficult for themselves as you did. Did any one of us know of any course he might have taken and not have been guilty in some respect or other? That is what is so uncanny about these regimes, whether they be 'brown' or 'red', that all the rules of conduct

by which one could normally regulate one's life were broken—
rules, that is, contained in the conception of the words 'oath',
'betrayal of one's country', etc. In my circle of acquaintance,
men who, like me, were bound together through faith in Christ
and in the truth, did not act lightly, and tried every possible way:
one was shot as a conscientious objector, another deserted to
Holland, was caught there by the Gestapo and shot, one deserted to Switzerland, many did their duty as soldiers as I did:
one, complete with medals, fought like a lion to the bitter end
as an officer in a tank regiment, some who were prisoners here
joined the N.K. and several lost their lives on July 20th. I had
my reasons for acting as I did, but I cannot with absolute
conviction, as you seem to think possible, go up to one of the
others, and say, 'You are a rogue, because you did not go my
way.' Every way was the wrong one, whichever way we went
we are in need of forgiveness, and can offer no excuse except
that there was no better course open to us. Should we not see
this at last, and admit it openly?"

It will be necessary for us to make that clear to those at home,
not only as far as the N.K. is concerned, but also we must
condemn any generalisations in judging those who were anti-
Fascist during their captivity. Any such judgment would fall
on the innocent as well as on the guilty, and is therefore wrong.
It is impossible to generalise. In almost every camp conditions
were different. There were some camps with reasonable Polit-
officers who avoided forcing opinions on anyone and made
possible a broad programme of cultural work. Among the
anti-Fascists there were honest and dishonest men, fanatical as
well as tolerant men, Marxists and non-Marxists; there were
some who, as far as they could, made the lives of their companions easier, and some who made them more difficult, and
who deserve to be called to account for this. Many Germans
generalised unjustly because they resented all the meanness and
were envious of those with privileges. The complaint that the
N.K. and the anti-Fascist have the sufferings and deaths of their
comrades on their consciences is ridiculous. Our political
differences caused many psychological difficulties, but our outward life would not have been any easier if we had formed a

"closed front". Differences were unavoidable since we all had to come to terms, not only with Communism, but also with Hitler's legacy.

15 *October* 1948

For some time Werner A. and I have been going over our previous studies of Marx. Weeks ago I put these on one side and have, so to speak, been taking a holiday from the Soviet Union and have forgotten the troubles of the moment. First of all Stifter's *Nachsommer* (Late Summer) led me into a fairy-tale world, in which the life of man is a well-ordered one. Then Gotthelf's Uli-novels gave me inspiration, and *Kristin Lavrans-datter* and Ina Seidel's *Wunschkind* stimulated me just as much as intelligent conversations about physical and natural sciences would have done. I have just spent several long evenings reading Plato's *Republic* which I discovered in the library in a German-Greek edition, and I was divided in my feelings about the humanity of Greek thought and the inhumanity in the construction of this aristocratic state. Now I wanted to spend what I hoped would be the last months before our promised repatriation talking to Werner, who had also been doing a good deal of reading about Marxism, and formulating some general conclusions. Carefully we discussed our findings point by point. Because of his outstanding intelligence, the sincerity of his conversion to the Christian faith during the war, his un-prejudiced study of Communism and his readiness to accept it, we had been close friends for a long time. His opinions had developed along the same lines as mine.

"What then," I asked him this evening, "do you think Marx prophesied correctly, and what do you think was illusion?"

"He was right in thinking that the productive powers of the new age, that is, technics and vast sources of man-power, had made the old system of private ownership of the means of production out of date, and would therefore bring about a revolution in all spheres of life. He was right in believing that the society of the future would be socialist and that technical development would bring about a socialist economy."

"In what way socialist? Are either the West or the East

socialist today? And why only 'bring about'? Marx thought it should be 'force'."

"Do not take the word 'socialist' in its moral sense, but as a description of what in fact happens. Think of all the duties which the modern state, as opposed to the state which Marx knew, has taken over, such as social insurance, workers' protection, education and the health service. That the U.S.A., that last stronghold of individualism, has been forced in this direction too, is a sign that all this is still only in its beginnings. The humanitarian motives are only secondary; although I should not like to despise them as Marx did. The primary motive is the common interest which forces the state and society to act socialistically. The modern state can no longer afford such a wastage of the strength of the people as was prevalent in the time of the Tsars, in early capitalism and even in the early Soviet State. If it wishes to remain capable of competing with foreign countries then it must be a socialist state; it must raise the general level of health, it must abolish illiteracy, encourage talent, and give the lower classes the opportunity to develop their talents and rise in the social scale. Marx shared the prejudice of many of us who supported social reform, namely that it was a matter of morality, and therefore he declared that capitalism was incapable of these reforms because this morality contradicted the profit motive; he believed that only a socialist society was capable of doing what today was being done by every state, and what will in the future become even more widespread. When the Communists here began to carry out such social reforms their propaganda declared that this revealed that they had reached a higher standard of morality, and many well-meaning people, you and I among them, fell for this and believed that in fact more was being done for these people there than in the un-moral capitalist countries. In reality here was only a modern state which had freed itself in a more determined manner from the dead-weight of those who were just carried along by the current. The illusion in this was that this was all done for the sake of the people. It is really done for the sake of the state, however; man's value has not risen by one jot or tittle. He is the material which the state now treats better and uses to better advantage than the old state found necessary or possible. The more socialist state is the state with the better human material and therefore more powerful."

"But you say that Marx was right about all this?"

"Marx was right in saying that this 'socialism' has been made possible by the technical advances, while formerly it was merely Utopian. He was right, too, because he saw that those very people would press for it, who up till now had been victims of the stick-in-the-muds, the wasted human material, namely the proletariat. One of his mistakes was to believe that only those who were directly interested in it, only the proletariat, could achieve this by their own revolution. He did not see that those who now bear rule in the state also had interests in that revolution. I need only remind you what kind of effect was produced during the recruiting in the Westphalian industrial regions by the bad state of health of the recruits, and what effect this had on the social legislation of Bismarck's Reich."

"Then the real mistakes made by Marx and by most of us was that we saw unqualified progress in these socialist conditions?"

"It is hard to deny that it is a sign of progress when men no longer live in misery and can develop their talents. The *naïveté* consisted in accepting without question that this progress was naturally progress towards what Marx, in the Hegelian manner, proclaimed to be the 'coming-to-themselves' of men, the end of man's 'self-estrangement', and thus freedom, human dignity, becoming human, and a true community spirit. However, what is seen as progress in one respect need not necessarily be the case in all respects, but in other respects may mean the danger of regress and of dehumanising. This naïve error is the fault of secularised Christian eschatology, which was the basis of the conception of progress and to which not only Marx had fallen a prey, but which had also hypnotised Christians."

"It looks as though you don't particularly want social progress."

"I have suffered too much hunger in my captivity not to know what kind of progress it is when one can eat one's fill.

I cannot despise this kind of progress, then, because I see how inevitable it is if a state wishes to exist today. In so far as the people of the Western world still resist it they are malicious as well as stupid. But I think I can see it without illusions. In itself, it cannot prevent men from being regarded as so much human material, in fact it can increase this tendency if other things do not happen at the same time. Here I see the second fatal mistake of Marx and his successors: in his secularised eschatology, which he inherited from Hegel, he saw development simply as something necessary and inevitable, something positive and progressive. Both these ideas seem to me to be false. Because he held it to be inevitable, he could only imagine resistance to it as senseless; this he called reactionary, and since then nobody has liked being called that. Because he held that development was unquestionably a positive thing, it meant necessarily for him a rise in man's stature, the way towards a better humanity which one could only welcome with open arms; therefore there is this superstitious belief in what is modern, and this scorn of what is old that you find in all Marxists.

"The questions that are most important to us are asked neither by him nor by Engels nor by his decadent Leninists, namely: what could be done to protect us from the destructive potentialities of the new, and from the harm caused by this development. He rightly believed that development is inevitable and cannot be prevented, and he understood mechanisation and socialisation better than most others: the way we put these into practice, however, is not inevitable, and if we cannot completely do away with them, we can at least put a brake on the harm they might do, and only in this way can the human element be preserved."

"I presume that was what you meant by using the words, 'bring about'; development brings about a socialist system of economy and society but it lies in our power to limit or to carry out logically what is produced, and to give it free rein, to check it or to rectify it."

"Another observation impels me to question this second possibility ignored by Marx. What I said before about the necessary social character of the modern and future state would not impress a Marxist because class-distinctions in society are not removed thereby. 'The State', as he rightly sees, is not an independent hypostasis, but is an instrument in the hands of the men who rule over it. These rulers are the men who own the means of production, that is, the so-called ruling classes. Both Marx and Lenin believed that in a state in which the means of production are socialised and production is planned from the centre, even if it is a world-state stretching over all the earth, the mass of the people are themselves the owners of the means of production. This, however, is an illusion which today cannot be imputed to a man who is not under the thumb of the Communist Party and who therefore still has the use of his five senses and his reason. The transition from private owner-ship of the means of production to their socialisation is not the same as the transition from the exploitation of man by man to common ownership, nor the transition from slavery to free-dom, but is rather a change-round in the systems of govern-ment. The first sentence of the Communist Manifesto ought to be altered. 'History is not first and foremost the history of class-warfare, but the history of the battles between different systems of government', and if Marx thought he saw indications of the end of the era of class-warfare, then we can certainly see no indications that the battle between systems of government is coming to an end."

"That leads to a pessimistic view of history, which seems to me to be no better but rather worse than the optimism of the Marxists. It declares that man is always either a tyrant or a slave, and will always remain so."

"Let me remind you first, though, that the Bible too is not very optimistic regarding man as he is. There is no cause to think Darwinism is Utopian about what might become of man. But fortunately we have not yet to choose between a reactionary pessimism and an illusory optimism. 'Rule' must not mean tyranny and slavery; it is only denounced as such by one who promises a 'ruler-less' state of affairs when we entrust the government to him. Because his promise fools us, it is time to see clearly that he has not offered any other alternative, nor does he, nor can he bring about anything but a new system of government. Whether we ought to help him to set it up, remains to be seen. But what can our criterion be? It is just here that Marx's two criteria are not far-reaching enough, namely, whether the new system of government, which he thought of as a condition of affairs without government, of a dead state, was consistent with the purpose of technical development, and whether it would bring about a higher social standard of living. The latter is prophesied for the next twenty years by every Polit-officer, if all can be carried out peacefully; by 1965 the Soviet standard of living would be miles ahead of that of all West European nations. There is much to contradict this: but however that may be, the other criterion is much more decisive: which factors in the new system will force us to view man as something more than mere material in the hands of power? Pareto—and I should like to know whether, and to what extent, he had any influence on Lenin—saw a different picture of the decisive problems of the future from that seen by Marxism. Those in power are always prone to regard those under them as nothing more than so much material: you can see that from any high-ranking officer you meet. The question is not whether the lords of the Kremlin have only their power in view or even their former idea of improving human well-being, but whether they still retain in their system something which forces them to regard man as something more than the mere material of their power or their ideas. And you know that there is nothing in their system which forces them to do so. For that reason Lenin's promise of the death of the state machine in Communism was self-deception; for that reason they have built up a totalitarian state here, contrasted with which Hitler's system seemed little more than the work of a dilettante, a state *comme il faut*, which shrinks from no sacrifice except the sacrifice and limitation of its own power; for that reason the power and theory have become so identical in the rule of the Polit-bureau that Communists can no longer distinguish them. Because of this the inhabitants of Western Europe, who are comforted by the thought that even here when the soup is dished up it is not as hot as it was when first cooked and that even here human values can have their place, have looked for comfort in vain. The Western European is wrong, despite all the concessions which are often made to these values, because he does not suspect and cannot imagine how determined everyone here is *not* to give way to any value, because in his sceptical indifference to all theories he cannot imagine what power theory has over the minds of these men, nor to what extent this theory makes them indifferent to all these standards of values, all traditions for the rights and obligations of others, and how immune it makes them from every appeal to their sympathy or to their conscience. Heine's famous prophecy of the political conse- quences of German philosophy (in the last chapter of *On the History of German Religion and Philosophy*, 1843) does not apply to National Socialism, to which we once applied it, but to the men in the Kremlin."

16 October 1948

An exciting day for me: newspapers from East Berlin bring joyful reports of essays in the periodical *Unterwegs* which is published by a group of my friends in Berlin, and reports of Karl Barth's words about the East-West problem. The pleasure of hearing in this way the voices of my distant friends was marred by the indignation with which some of the men here reacted to them. There was a bitter dispute.

"Your friends haven't understood, then, that Communism is the plague from which the earth will have no respite until it is rooted out!"

"My friends have understood that Communism is not a plague which can be rooted out, but the result of social and spiritual misery. Take away the misery, and you won't have to fear the plague."

"Then you would dispute the fact that today the West had ahead of it the task of freeing men from Soviet power, when you see as well as anyone how they are suffering under this system."

"I certainly would dispute that as forcefully as I can. For that would be war, the most terrible war that has ever been waged. Are not the Communists frequently in the right with their complaints against the West? The Western countries need to be quite different in order to set themselves up as liberators. And how do we know what we would look like at the end of the war which you wish to let loose! We would certainly not have sufficient strength to order the affairs of the ravaged Eastern countries."

"Then must they just write off the people here and leave them to their exploiters?"

"They must see to it that they themselves don't get swallowed up by Communism. And they must prove that they have sufficient strength in themselves to triumph over social and spiritual misery. Thereby they can contradict Communist propaganda which always represents them as irreparably rotten. That is the only service which today they can render the unhappy people who are groaning under Stalin's yoke. We must leave the future to decide what tomorrow will look like and whether tomorrow there will be any chance of putting things in order here. Anyway God has still some say in the ordering of world events."

"Then we must put our hands in our laps and trust in God!"

"Now you are talking in an un-Christian manner, you who wanted to take up 'Christian politics'. Nothing else will please you but a war! Christian politics in my opinion means getting a grip on the tasks which God sets before us and not running away from them to attend to problems the solution to which He has definitely kept to Himself."

We parted thoughtfully; I went for a walk round the camp and noticed a few children playing beyond the fence on the bank of the lake, while their mothers sat chatting happily together. These children would be the victims of the war with which our thoughts have been toying when asking ourselves how this powerful terror-regime could be changed. I did not answer lightly before; I have often fought against the same temptation when I was seized with horror at the system. But I know that crusades are always hypocrisy and that war can never liberate.

20 October 1948

I am still interested in watching the reactions of former Nazis. It was not to be expected that they would remain united.

The collapse of the Third Reich, and the unmasking of its horrors and of the deplorable record of its leaders, did not incline them towards the new system of values which was ready and waiting, but led them into a chaos of contradictory conclusions and promises of conflicting ideologies. In their conversation they do not often talk about the past—and yet it is essential that the clearing up of their ideas should begin by considering the past. Today I had a long talk about this with Toni K., a sympathetic Austrian member of the S.S. and a former soldier. Suddenly he stopped in the middle of a detailed political analysis of the problems of the *Anschluss* and said, "But this is all rubbish! I don't know why I insist upon it so obstinately. All the political business was just a result. I was a Roman Catholic, and my belief in what the Church preached was turned sour by our parish priest, by the Church, by my studies and by myself, because I wanted to live without any ties—oh, I don't know! Anyway, there was a vacuum, there was nothing for me to live for, and into this vacuum flowed all the ideas about Nationalism. Now I will tell you at last, as I have meant to do for some time, what it was that drove out those idols. Not the fall of Nazism, but a strange experience I had at that time."

He then told me how, with some of his S.S. comrades while retreating near Vienna, he had run into a detachment of Cossacks, and before they knew where they were, they had been taken prisoner. The Cossacks' triumph at catching the S.S. men was great; they tied their hands behind their backs with wire, drove them along muddy field paths, beating them all the time, and announced that they would be shot ceremonially. Utterly exhausted, they had to wait on a main road for a lorry, and lay down in soft mud. He had wished for nothing better than death and was determined that if he were not shot soon he would kill himself in some way or other. Half consciously he had tried to move his frozen, aching hands, and felt something hard in the mud. Thinking it was a stone he held on to it. The lorry came, they were forced into it and put in a cellar at Baden, near Vienna, where their hands were untied. Then he remembered the object in his hand and before throwing it away, looked at it in the dim light of the cellar window. It was a little medallion, with a crucifix on one side and a figure of Our Lady of Lourdes on the other. "There was my sign. I could not believe that it was just chance. Here it is. I knew all at once that hitherto I had looked at life the wrong way round, and it was not to be thrown away now. I knew that help was at hand, and since then I have changed a great deal." We spent a good evening as we talked of how far this sign took us past the Lady of Lourdes.

23 December 1948

The distrustful and the pessimists have been right again; next week another year will have passed, and we are still here. Anyone who, a year ago, gave voice to his distrust was threatened with detention: "The Soviet Union is well known for carrying out international agreements to the letter; anyone who thinks it capable of anything else, is acting in a manner hostile to the Soviet Union"—that was what our Polit-officer declared. Later the announcements were more modest: "in principle" all P.O.W.s should be repatriated this year. Who then "in principle" will not be going? This was asked anxiously. After the West German currency reform in June, the encouragingly high numbers of men sent home dropped suddenly. How then could they get the three hundred thousand men, who according to our reckoning were still in Russia, home before the end of the year? We optimists consoled everyone by saying that they could do it in a month if they wanted to. Then in the P.O.W. newspaper in October there appeared an article by General Barusoglebski, who was on the military staff of the P.O.W. administration, an article which was so characteristic of the way in which they announce the breaking of promises in this part of the world, that I did not know whether to laugh or cry. Under the harmless heading "Nationalism versus Internationalism", he first of all uttered the doctrine that the progressive man must think along international lines, and yet be a good patriot; the patriotism of the Germans, however, must today be shown in their friendly feelings towards the Soviet Union; this friendship was only genuine if it was a hundred per cent. true, and offered with no "ifs" and "buts". And then came the snag: a German patriot was thus one who, on New Year's Eve 1948, if he was still in his P.O.W. camp, would raise his glass of tea in a toast to the Soviet Union, whose government had had its good reasons for not fully carrying out its programme of repatriation this year; the enemy of the Soviet Union was one who was ready to drink this toast only on condition that he was home by New Year's Eve.

Now we know, and the excitement in the camp was tremendous. Their audacity had, however, not yet reached its peak with this article. A few weeks later, there appeared in the P.O.W. newspaper a resolution of the anti-Fascist school in which the blame for the breakdown of the Moscow agreement was laid on the Western powers, and which welcomed the longer duration of our captivity as an opportunity for further reconciliation and getting to know the Soviet Union better. Everyone who grumbled would be condemned as an enemy of the Soviet Union. This was written by men (of course, on the orders of their Soviet instructors) who had avoided life in a labour camp and who already had the order for their repatriation signed and sealed in their pockets. It was also thought that the Polit-officers in every camp wrote and signed these resolutions. Here the "club" had taken charge and ordered a camp-meeting to be held, at which the Russian camp leaders were to give the prisoners their reasons for breaking the promise of repatriation, since otherwise political work in the camp would no longer be possible. "We shall not declare, you shall declare," said the Polit-officer, "you will hand in this resolution or else be unmasked as deceivers and enemies of the Soviet Union." For some weeks I had been curious to see how they would inform us of this fact, and avoid any harmful effects on their political propaganda. In my curiosity I had, however, once again been thinking democratically, i.e. I had presupposed that the regime and its functionaries would regard those with whom it dealt as partners and treat them as such, and that it would have to justify itself to them and give explanations. They were obviously only astonished and displeased that we still made a fuss, since their own people had long since been prevented from doing so. Because the self-abasement which they expected of us comes naturally to them, they did not hesitate to demand audaciously that we who had been so bitterly deceived should also thank them and show confidence in them; because in reality their propaganda aims not at convincing, but at breaking down resistance and at making puppets with no wills of their own, they were not worried at no longer having any effect; they knew that in a few weeks, when all the excitement had died down, the fearful ones and the calculating ones would come back to the fold, and that henceforth, in their sphere of influence, at any rate outwardly, there would be no more movements but those desired by them; they are quite indifferent as to what we really think, for they believe that what they force the masses to do outwardly will eventually sink in, and that the average man always ends up by believing, contrary to his original convictions, what he is forced to repeat continually parrot-fashion. They will not succeed with us any more, if we really are going home next year, as they have promised. What do they expect from nations who cannot see any end to their subjection?

The camp did not hand in the resolution demanded of them, the club did not even dare to press the camp to agree; instead the camp inmates declared to the club that in view of this bitter disappointment they wanted nothing organised for them at Christmas but services. There is to be a musical evening on Dec. 26th, but I do not suppose that many will go. Tomorrow we shall have a combined service for Christmas Eve; the Roman Catholic army chaplin K. will conduct the service and I shall preach the sermon, which amid scorn and depression and the new uncertainty must point to the Light of Him Who alone can order the hour of home-coming for each one of us.

III

THE LAST
YEAR

I

IN THE
LABOUR CAMP
AGAIN

For a year now I have been working here in the wood-yard, one of a small brigade of six men who have lived peace-ably together in spite of all differences. It is the hardest work the camp can offer, and is therefore done voluntarily only by us six, helped now and again by others sent here as a punishment. In summer and winter, in heat and frost, in snow and rain, we stand beside the vast mountain of tree-trunks and work daily with our hammers and wedges till there is enough firewood for the kitchen, the bakery, the laundry, the hospital and the Russian guard-houses. The only thing that matters is that we do the job, how we do it is our own affair—so we are our own masters in our working-hours and in the speed at which we work, and live our own lives up there in our little hut, sun-burnt, muscular figures, admired as the "strongest men in the camp", and courted because in our hands lies the fuel and the warmth of all the huts. The kitchen and the bakery care for us with extra soup and extra bread, so that we keep up our strength, and we are willing to continue this healthy work, insured against hunger, until the end of our captivity. Then one day came the turning point for me. At midday today, as I was struggling with the roots of a great fir-tree, young H. who occasionally acts as runner and brings orders from the com-mandant, came up and called out, "Helmut, stop! You have been chopping wood the longest of all, you are going on a

221

transport!" I knew then what it must feel like to be struck by lightning: in a split second time, present and future, is cut into two halves which bear no resemblance at all to each other. Transport: that could mean either the best or the worst. At once I put the question, "Where to?" and when he answered by shrugging his shoulders, I continued with all the questions which seek to gain some indication of the goal and the nature of this transport: Who else is going? When do we start? For how many days have rations been drawn? Did the officers drop any hints? Do we get new clothes? Nothing definite could be concluded from the answers. Three others are going with me, and the group is strangely assorted; an upright and straightforward major in the anti-aircraft defence who is in the camp and seems to have a clean bill, a blatant anti-Fascist, a not very forthcoming person, and a man from the Schill Unit (an adventurous detachment of the *Wehrmacht* which was formed towards the end of the war to go on daring special missions)— he has already tried to commit suicide and to escape several times. One begins to reckon: the anti-Fascist, that may be a good sign: the Schill man, that is suspicious, but perhaps they are tired of him and want to get rid of him; the major— perhaps they are just sending him as a "blind" to throw dust in our eyes (a favourite trick of the N.K.V.D.: if they are particularly interested in a man, if they want to take him for special interrogation or to a punishment camp or anywhere else, then they like to take a few uninteresting people along too, so that neither the suspect, nor anyone else, can guess who is the object of their attention and what their plans are). The inmates of the camp, disturbed by the sensational news, eagerly joined in our calculations and tried to take an optimistic view of the matter! After all, it's March 1949! They can't just make us disappear! That the anti-Fascist is going too, is a good sign; they must be sending you home! Give the homeland our love! Make a note of our addresses!

The farewell is painful and moving. In these twenty-two months I have grown very close to some of them. For many of them I see a gloomier home-coming than my own. Unforgettable are the last embraces, the last handshakes with best friends. Then for hours we sit in the guard-room. For no tangible reason, the barometer of hope falls. Finally, I feel in my bones that it is not a transport for home. Where then? Why was I brought here in 1947? Why am I being transferred to another camp? Are they going to put pressure on me again to try and make me more tractable? Or are they taking revenge because I've been so intractable up till now? It could only be a labour camp—and this prospect made me realise what luck I have had to live in this camp, and how much easier it was being imprisoned here because it was easier to be human. Now it would start all over again; the hunger, the slavery, the exhaustion, the loneliness, the lack of books, the lack of spiritual inspiration and discussion, the rough life, every morning the day ahead seeming like a hill one has to climb, though at the end of one's strength—and for how long? Obviously for quite a long time, or else they would not send us away just now. All four of us stare about us in melancholy, the same thoughts are going through our heads; now and again one of us makes an attempt at a joke or at a word of comfort: with the Russians you never knew what their aims were, you had to reckon on the most unexpected and illogical things, perhaps after all we would be taken to the homeward-bound transport. We shake our heads and make sandwiches from the provisions with which we have been issued, to last four days.

In the late afternoon we are led outside the camp where a transport lorry is waiting. When it drives off the much-feared N.K.V.D. commissar who was to work on my case comes out of the camp. I look at him, and think of the friendly way in which he used to receive me several months ago, of the threats during my recent interviews, the spies he put on me, and I know that I have him to thank for this change in fortune. He walks behind us and watches us, we stare at each other fixedly for some time, until we turn the corner, and within me grows the feeling that I am invulnerable: this slim man, born in Berlin of Russian parents, educated in the Western manner, well read in Hermann Hesse and Thomas Mann, is the prisoner, and I am free and would not change with him for all the world. Yet at the same time I see what I still owe him. I have had discussions with him, have refused his demands, have upheld my own opinions, have countered his threats with obstinate silence, but I was only defending myself against him and returned his pressure. But had I striven to convert his soul? Did I in my prayers only ask to be made strong against him and not to let fear and cowardice master me? Was he not my neighbour whom I ought to have loved? Was not his soul entrusted to me during the times when I was in his room with him? Ought not his soul to have heard through me words which it needed so badly? Had I not regarded it as hopeless to seek for his soul, and had I not believed in his derision and hardness more than in the power of God's word? What lay ahead of me I did not know, but I could hardly say that in the past I had fulfilled my trust very well. I wished that the lorry would turn round and that I could have another interview in that room to which I had always gone, when summoned, with a lump in my throat, so that I could do what I had left undone and then go wherever they were taking me more calmly. But the drive continued, and after a quarter of an hour we stopped in front of the nearby labour camp, where we picked up twelve other Plennis.

The usual enquiries followed our greetings: what did we know and who were we? The answers only confirmed our fears. There could be no question of going home. More unfavourable still were the personalities of our new companions: S.S. men, members of the Schill Unit, an expert on the Balkans, all undesirables in Russian eyes. We took stock of each other and had to admit that our conclusions did not promise anything very wonderful. A couple of quite young men were among them, with that blank expression which many of the most recent generation of Plennis had acquired, and there was also one very young member of the S.S., an anxious and sad look on his school-boyish face.

The lorry drove on into Moscow. Night was falling and we could not recognise any of the chief sights, we drove a long way through the city out to that dreary part which the visitor to Moscow is not shown, stopped at various military checkpoints, were sent on from one to the other, and finally landed up alongside a large railway goods yard. By the light of a few dim lanterns we saw sooty snow, a low hut with peeling paint-work in front of the dark fence, and behind, stretching for a considerable distance, the faint lights of the signals. At the door of the hut there was a lot of palaver, with papers and passes being continually waved and lists and official stamps compared with each other, then at last they agreed that we really belonged here; an officer gave a command and a troop of N.K.V.D. men with dogs rushed out of the hut, surrounded our lorry and ordered us to get out. Weapons of all kinds, without any safety catches, were pointed at us, the dogs, pulling at their leads, closed in around us, and escorted us over the snow-covered railway line. One of our number, who had already had long experience with such transports and had been dragged around the most varied camps and prisons in the Soviet Union ex-claimed, "Heaven help us if we are put in a G.P.U. carriage! For goodness' sake hang on to your belongings, for in five minutes you may be stripped of everything!" After stumbling over the rails for a long time, driven on by the usual cries of *Davai*, we came to a train, with no lights, standing in a dark siding, and when the beam of light from one of the lanterns fell on the carriage, the man in front cried, "Ugh, a G.P.U. carriage!" While the mouths of many pistols stared at us from all sides, we clambered up to the entrance, and leaving behind us the cold night air, were struck by a nauseating wave of heat. The carriage was over-heated and the air was heavy with the smell of many perspiring bodies. It was constructed like one of the carriages of a German express train, with a corridor, out of which led the compartments, the walls made of solid iron, and the doors having nothing but small square peep-holes in them, heavily barred. We were driven along the corridor, but had enough time to glance in at the compartments and to see the faces of the inmates which were pressed to the bars. They were filled with civilian prisoners, children, old men, men and women, squashed together like sardines, many of them naked, staring at us newcomers with wide-open eyes, like animals. We looked in as though we were looking in at the gates of Hell, and waited until a compartment was unlocked for us. Once we

were in, the first feeling was one of relief that we had a compartment to ourselves. A second glance made us ask how we could
all fit in here. It was as narrow as a small broom-cupboard; on
one side were three tiers of wooden shelves, each of which
would accommodate two people if they lay head to foot; six of
us were thus provided for, while the other three crouched on
the ground, and we promised that we would all take turns to
do this. Nine of us were here, and the other seven were in the
next compartment; they called out to us that there was an
eighth man with them, who had been there already and was
also a Plenni. He was, as we learnt later, an unusual person
who was travelling in this carriage, provided with a wireless
set and with extra provisions, and was presumably carrying out
special duties of a secret nature for the N.K.V.D. Our luggage
—surprisingly enough we had not been searched—had been
taken away from us, but we were promised that we should get
it again at the end of the journey.

Long after midnight, the train moved off. Enquiries as to
our destination, by means of which we tried to worm some
facts out of our guards, were never answered. Otherwise the
behaviour of these men was very correct. In front of every
compartment stood an N.K.V.D. soldier with a loaded weapon
who conducted us, when we desired it, to the lavatory, which
was comparatively clean according to the normal standards here-
abouts. He also brought us water and handed us in our meals.
We were given the provisions we had brought with us according to instructions, and there were no complaints or ill-treatment. An old campaigner responded to the situation straight
away by going to sleep, and so for hours we sat in dismal
silence, which gradually sent us to sleep, and I was awakened
by the first words of my companions. We began to sound each
other, with that caution usual in men who have had a good deal
to do with N.K.V.D. and who therefore choose their words
carefully. Such conversations sound strangely fragmentary.
The talker suddenly breaks off, one notices that he has omitted
something or is afraid he has said too much. Any more
penetrating questions are often answered with silence and
strange looks. Only by easy stages did our tongues become

looser, and fateful adventures, which in all probability no generation of Germans since the Thirty Years' War has experienced, are recounted as though they were everyday happenings. One man had led the glider-detachment at Mussolini's rescue, another had spent all his life wandering around the Balkans as a member of a Macedonian terrorist organisation, a third had tried to organise the "Were-wolf", a fourth had worked on Russian ships in East Prussia, in the harbours of the Baltic, under a false name until he was recognised to be a German, a sixth had worked with the Russian secret police and with the Secret Service and had thereby got himself into several ticklish situations—and then there was the youngster with the school-boyish face, who knew as little as the honest Westphalian farmer, the major and I, why we were such "undesirables"; perhaps they were only being used as a "blind" after all, perhaps there was a reason for their presence, just as I suspected that there was a reason for mine too.

With the well-developed instinct of one who had been a soldier for nine years, I had manœuvred to get a place where there was a little light falling through the grille, so that I could read, and throughout the journey I read the Epistle to the Philippians, slowly and with increasing thought and deep meditation, as though I had never read it before. By peering through the grille and through the window behind it and by watching the shadows of the telegraph poles, we had gradually made out that we were travelling eastward. From the fact that we had been given provisions for four days we calculated that our destination was just inside Siberia, and that it was probably somewhere in the Urals. One or two could give reports of punishment camps in that region: things were bad there but one could exist—though for how long, with the kind of food provided there, was doubtful. Nobody dared to think any more about home and repatriation. Head and heart had had plenty of practice in suppressing such thoughts. Anyone travelling eastward in 1949 under such conditions as ours, had to put away such thoughts for many years, perhaps for ever. Thus, with this prospect in view, I read the words of the Apostle, who also had nothing but the coming of Christ to look forward to, and yet whose heart had not been hardened, but was so full of joy that he was able to pass on this joy and courageousness to his friends. This reading brought with it such unforgettable riches, and the words yielded up their innermost meaning in such a way that I imagined I was sitting beside the Apostle himself in his cell, which was probably not much better than mine, and that he was speaking quietly to me, closer than he had ever been before. Then my thoughts turned to the future. The punishment camp had lost its terrors. But who was waiting for me there? To whom was I being sent? Who needed me there? Whom would I have need of? What community, known only to God, would welcome me? Now and again I recited a poem to a companion who had an ear for poetry and the last lines of Carossa's *Old Fountain* came to me like a comforting promise—

many a man is on his way to Thee.

For three days we travelled through the never-ending monotony of the Russian countryside, with its forlorn villages, unattractive towns all alike, the steppes and scrubby woodland. When we heard the name Kazan at a big station, we knew definitely in which direction we were going. We had rapidly attained that degree of intimacy with each other which is possible only among one's fellow-countrymen and especially prisoners; many a tale, many a kind word, had drawn us together and revived drooping spirits. Now, on the fourth day, we were travelling through the foot-hills of the Urals, and shortly before we arrived at Sverdlovsk we were given our luggage, and ordered to get ready to leave the train. Here everything was done with far less commotion than in Moscow. While the Sakljutshonnyis poured out of their compartments and we looked on in pity at a twelve-year-old boy and a few kindly women who were among them, we had to sit in the snow, following the usual instructions of the N.K.V.D., who thereby made the task of guarding us easier, waiting for a transport lorry. From every side there came more columns of Sakljutshonnyis, grey and miserable, of every age and sex, driven along like cattle by well-fed guards, ordered to sit down, and then driven on farther. Thus we got some idea of the N.K.V.D.'s vast army of slaves, of the countless numbers of people in this unhappy country which is revealing its slavery everywhere in the grim columns of people seen all over the place, and especially in the Urals and Siberia—a sight which does not arouse revolt and indignation in the hearts of those who see them, but only makes them look the other way in horror.

In the cold clear light of the evening our lorry drove away from the grand-looking station through the centre of the town, where old-fashioned houses dating from the time of the Tsars alternated with the large, half-classical, half-cubist dwellings and offices of modern times; most of them were badly built, and in these people were expected to live. Then out into the mean suburbs stretching for miles, then through the settlements on the outskirts with the great factories, finally stopping outside the high wooden fence tipped with barbed wire of a P.O.W. camp, where we waited for an hour while the guards decided whether or not we had come to the right place. It was just after seven o'clock, and the camp's work brigades were returning from work. Looking down from our lorry we saw them marching up with the tired stumbling gait of the Plenni, dressed, as we were, in worn clothes, long brown columns of men, staring glumly at the ground, not even glancing at us, incapable of showing any curiosity or interest, their faces covered in grey dust, hardly distinguishable one from the other. This was the youth and manhood of Germany four years after the end of the war, and we were soon to join their ranks, marching in this army of grey and hopeless creatures without faces. Silently they stood waiting outside the gate, were counted, and then tramped silently in. Some of the camp "aristocracy", who could move about freely, came towards us and for the first time questions flew to and fro. We learned that here nothing had been said about repatriation, and they learned that we had come from Moscow—news that spread quickly through the camp and only served to increase the hopelessness; for if they were sending someone from Moscow here now, then one could only reckon on a distant date for returning home.

29 March 1949

We spent only one night in that camp at Sverdlovsk and had learnt that we were to go on to the "regime-camp" at Asbestos. Prisoners in the Soviet Union had nothing good to say about the "hell of Asbestos", as its name implied; earlier I had heard that many people died there during the famine years. What we had heard about it now was more encouraging: everything was well-ordered, there were opportunities for earning better pay, and better work to do than mining, which occupied most of the other camps in this region; there were large clean huts with a great many single rooms, plenty of concerts and plays performed by the excellent culture group. But it was still a regime-camp—and that meant a bad look-out for those who went there. Why? Because the prospects of returning home were infinitely smaller there than at an ordinary camp. Regime-camps are not exactly punishment camps, but are distinguished from other camps by the fact that all the inmates have been sent there on special, and usually unfavourable, grounds: there, men are assembled together against whom the N.K.V.D. has a particular grudge, either as individuals because they were suspected of escape or sabotage or because they had expressed Fascist opinions or because they held some post in the Nazi party, or because they formerly belonged to some particular military detachment. So one met there mainly members of S.S. divisions, the divisions *Grossdeutschland*, *Feldherrnhalle* and *Brandenburg* which (quite unjustly) they suspected of being particularly Nazi, and also tank and infantry divisions which for some reason or other had got a bad name for themselves among the Russians. The effect of that on life in the camp was that one must reckon on being one of the last to leave for home —if one ever left at all—that one was more closely guarded, that there were more frequent interrogations, and that in these camps there was none of that limited "self-government" by the so-called "Anti-Fascist Committee" that had been in force in the ordinary camps since the spring of 1948, so that the German camp leaders and the club could here enforce a regime of terror and favouritism, unchecked by any sort of control whatever. (In Asbestos, as we were to find out, this was kept

in check by the excellent German camp leader, a butcher from
the Magdeburg district, who through his courageous intervention and his complete integrity and care had won for himself
the undivided admiration of Germans and Russians alike, and
to whom many men owed their lives and good health.) The
catering and the earnings were no worse in the regime-camps
than elsewhere.

In the Sverdlovsk camp we had already observed that since
1947 conditions in labour camps had altered considerably.
Professor Janzen was right in his prophecies. The murderous
conditions existing in the years just after the end of the war had
disappeared, the welfare regulations in force were carried out
correctly, the bugs had gone, the hospital was a model, the
sanitary arrangements were mostly faultless. There were rarely
any deliberate encroachments by Russian officials, flogging or
personal exploitation. The regulations about hours of work,
the safeguarding of health, and provision of winter clothing
were observed to the letter. What had the greatest effect, however, were the new regulations about pay which had come into
force after the currency reform of December 1948. While
earlier on only a few particularly valuable specialists had
earned money, and the others were enticed to work better by
promises of thicker soup, a hundred grammes of bread and
other extras, we could now all earn money. The achievements
of each brigade were arranged every month between the
contractors and the camp: the camp received 450 roubles per
working man; that was so to speak the price we had to pay for
board and lodging; of anything which was earned over and
above that sum, each man received up to 250 roubles; if still
more was earned, that again fell to the camp. Again there were
a few highly paid specialists working on their own whose whole
earnings excluding the 450 roubles were either paid direct to
them or credited to their account until they were sent home,
so that some of them received several thousand roubles when
they were discharged, which they had to spend in Russia—not
an easy thing to do. Those were the regulations on paper, but
in practice everything did not work out so smoothly. However,
money was coming into the camp, and hunger was not so

widespread. This would not have been so, had not the general standard of living of the Soviet population risen noticeably since the currency reform. All wares that were not basic essentials were of course terribly expensive; but ordinary food-stuffs, especially bread, were now much cheaper. The rouble had the spending power of 0·1 of a mark in 1938. A pound of black soggy bread now cost 3 roubles, a pound of margarine 9 roubles; anyone of us who earned from seventy to a hundred roubles in a month could add to his diet so that at least he did not lose weight when working, as was the case when the meagre "norm-catering" was in force.

It is a bad thing to be a "new boy" in a camp. Everywhere you get what is left over. The administration puts you in a bad brigade at a bad place of work where nobody else wants to go; you have nobody beside you to help you make your way; you never get your money until the month after, because the accounts are always done later, and so for the first month you have to live on bare rations. You may have to do this for even longer, for the brigade is bad just because there is little prospect of earning more than the 450 roubles deducted by the camp at this bad place of work. We were lucky and joined the brigade working in the "career". What is that?

Asbestos is a town lying on the Asiatic side of the Urals, which got its name from the fact that near it is the largest source of asbestos in the world. It is an unattractive industrial settlement, stretching for miles, in which many P.O.W.s have worked and died since the end of the war. Anyone who uses an asbestos-mat on the gas-stove at home should ponder the fact that the material was probably dug up by a German Plenni. Asbestos is found in long seams in the cracks in sandstone; if the seam is broad, then the asbestos is found as tightly packed glass-like threads up to an inch and half in length; if the seam is narrow, then the short threads, when scraped off, disintegrate into a fine dust which is pressed into mats, while the good quality asbestos, for which a high price is paid, can be woven into suits. The digging is done in open-cast mines, where the sandstone is blasted apart; then the enormous blocks are broken up with heavy iron hammers, and the veins of asbestos are scraped and hammered out. The places where this work is done are called by the strange name of "careers", and the work there was very highly coveted by the P.O.W.s in spite of its strenuousness and although in summer and winter one was exposed to the elements, for the simple reason that one could earn plenty of money there. It was of course all a matter of luck; one could get a "career" where the broad strips of asbestos shone like gold amid the blue of the sandstone, whereas somewhere else, with all one's efforts, one could only manage to fill half a bucket. Before the German P.O.W.s came, the "norm" for the best places was from five to eight buckets; when we arrived in 1949, there were places where, on account of the thickness of the seams, the norm had been fixed at up to twenty-five buckets. Here, as everywhere in the Soviet Union, the arrival of these P.O.W.s, driven by hunger and by promises of extra food and also by an inborn and fanatical love of work, caused great displeasure among the Russian population because the norms were raised so high, a state of affairs which would no doubt give the Soviet Union cause for rejoicing.

Now, picture to yourself a vast number of our companions who had been taken prisoner during the first two years after Russia entered the war and who had worked day after day (excluding the Wychadnois), for six years, at these "careers", most of them never doing any other work, but spending day after day of these long years in the drab grey stony wilderness of the mining district, seeing nothing but their walls of sandstone; they knew all the necessary tricks, stood in high favour with their masters, always exceeded their norm and earned good wages, they had plenty of self-confidence and their arms bulged with muscle—yet could that make up for the dullness and emptiness of these years? If one of them, like my Silesian friend Franz for instance, whom I soon got to know well, retained any mental awareness, that was most astonishing. When I met him—we found each other by that same strange instinct with which rare fish in the mighty ocean find companions of the same species—it was as though he had been a prisoner only a few weeks, so vivid were his recollections of all he had learnt before going into the army straight from school, and so deeply had he meditated

233

on and thought over all the impressions of these monotonous years. He was indeed the one exception among all the men of his age group; for this deadening of the intellect took place in the younger men with more potent effect than in the older ones, because the former brought too little with them to nourish the mind and to enable them to draw the right conclusions from their experiences; so, having fewer defences, they fell into empty cynicism and a thoughtless egoistic way of life. Again and again when observing them and trying to influence them one cursed the Hitler Youth education which had given them nothing but empty phrases as their armour for these hard years.

Anyone who, like us, had come from such a "gentleman's camp" as the one at Krasnogorsk, where everyone addressed the other as *Sie*, where there was an intellectual life, courteous talk, and a sense of physical well-being, into a labour camp such as this, was first and foremost depressed by the blank expressions on the faces of all the men, as the result of their strenuous work, by the monotony with which the conversation turned on nothing but work, percentages and food, and also by the bad-tempered and off-hand manner in which everybody treated everybody else. Life at Krasnogorsk had some faint resemblance to life at home, because there we had the health and strength to brighten our lives with small pleasures. Joylessness was spread over the labour camps like a leaden blanket. Newcomers like ourselves felt this more than those who had grown accustomed to it. After the first few days we noticed that even under this grey blanket human life was tough enough to survive, and was more easily endured than in the former years; here too we found men with whom conversation was not limited to the burdens of the day, here too souls were alive behind the blank faces, here small pleasures were not unknown, here too there was laughter, music, poetry, philosophy. Above all there was prayer here too.

The first time we marched to the "career" I was walking beside the conductor of the camp orchestra, a small weedy professional musician who had been given an easier job to do out there, and he told me about the activities of the culture-group. I was electrified when he told me casually that there was a copy of Kant's *Critique of Pure Reason* in the camp. It is amazing what such news can mean; the effect upon me was as of the elixir of life; I had always believed that all this was not a waste of time for the soul—but now the prospect of being able to concentrate on Kant as I had never been able to at home made me realise that it was not a waste of time either, as far as the intellect was concerned. That copy of Kant, however, was not to be found, and had probably fallen into the hands of a commissar as an undesirable source of the poison of idealism, but there was still a good deal of literature apart from the "classics of Marxism", so that I could continue my studies undeterred, to the surprise of my comrades. The works of Lessing, Schiller's historical writings, Zola, and above all Goethe were inspiring companions during that season when the Siberian summer was approaching slowly.

More important still, on my second evening in Asbestos one of the old inmates of the camp came up to me and asked if it were true that I was a pastor. When I said "yes", he sat down beside me, obviously very pleased, and invited me warmly to join their small Bible-study group, which met once a week. I looked at him as though he were an angel, in the same way as Robinson Crusoe must have welcomed another human being, and forgot the noise of the crowds in the hut. He was an East Prussian, the son of a farmer, whose family was devoted to the village community, and was an enthusiastic member of the E.C. (Youth Movement for Decisive Christianity). In his broad East Prussian dialect he told me how for some time now a small group had been meeting to study the Bible and would welcome the presence of a clergyman at these meetings. Anyone in a foreign country who feels that he is a cast-away, that he is "miserable" [1] in the original sense of the word, feels at home as soon as he finds there a few fellow-countrymen who speak his language and have fellowship together, and from whom he can get help and advice. One might be disappointed in one's fellow-countrymen in the earthly realm, but I was sure that among such fellow-countrymen as I met here I would

---

[1] miserable=German "elend", which originally meant "in a strange land", "outlawed". (*Translator*.)

find nothing but helpfulness and generosity, however human they might be. Those who gathered round the Bible were my fellow-countrymen in a higher sense and lived the same life, and the same life here in the camp as I did. Thus, during this evening, everything that had weighed down on me since my sudden departure from Krasnogorsk was lifted, and I knew that here I was not alone, that I had companionship as well as work to do.

Like those of the ordinary members of the working class, the thoughts of the prisoner, who lives a proletarian kind of life, have a natural affinity with the Marxist "historical material-ism", and such material questions as "What shall we eat?" and "Wherewithal shall we be clothed?", cannot be ignored as they are by bourgeois idealism. (This is distinguishable from the Sermon on the Mount in that the latter makes light of these questions, not simply because spiritual problems are more important but because we must trust in God to provide for the needs of His children.) The new friends which I made during these first few days had their significant part to play in assuring a happy material existence. Long weeks of a hard fight for a livelihood lay before us. We had been carting and breaking up blocks of stone in the "career" for several days, when on the orders of the Russian camp administrators we Muscovites were formed into a special group, together with a few others accused of various crimes (thieves, men suspected of trying to escape, "Fascists" and so on), and were sent to a particularly well-guarded place to work, with the instructions "hard work and no pay!" At this spot, the officers in the camp had begun, under dreadful conditions and with little possibility of earning anything, to build a settlement of log-huts. Within the regime-camp, we now formed the "regime-group", made up of those accused of particularly serious crimes, and could gather from this fact what had been said in the reports about us that had been sent here from Moscow. "They are trying to kill us", was the depressing conclusion reached by us in our distrust, and since we had heard about those instructions we could hardly expect anything else. If we stood up to the rigours of the following months better than we had expected that first morning, then in my case at any rate this was due to the "good friends and loyal neighbours", whom I found so soon, the Bible-study group, the musical circle, the doctors, not to mention Franz, the young Roman Catholic from Silesia, who was as pleased as I was to find a partner for long literary discussions in the evenings. The others made friends in the same way, friends who "supported" them. We all benefited from living in a camp which earned good wages.

In the small sphere of such a camp—the camp at Asbestos, now the only one remaining out of the eighteen camps formerly in that region, had a population of some 1700 prisoners—one could study the possibilities of solving the social problem in human society, in so far as the problem was a material one and a question of food and clothing. Its solution could be thought of in a more vivid community spirit: all for one and one for all! That was what the "Utopian Socialists" meant, and it was what those of us meant who wanted to solve the problem from the point of view of Christian love; part of this Utopian belief is still retained in Marxism today, a part of that confidence in the proletarian's sense of solidarity even after it has seized power. (This "confidence", as has been demonstrated since, is a folly equally as great as that of which Marx accused the Utopians; for the proletarian official who has "arrived" has no longer any sense of belonging to those who helped him to power!) The "social question" in the P.O.W. camps could have been solved by just such a community spirit, if the Russians had not prevented it, by sharing out equally what was earned by the community as a whole, on the basis of the sense of comradeship which we had all possessed when taken prisoner. What might be considered as Utopian for society as a whole, could have been carried out in the smaller sphere of our camp, and it would have saved many men from going to pieces.

After this way had been closed to us, the only possibilities left were those adopted by society in general. These were reduced to the two questions of how much capital there was and how it was handled—that is, if as a layman I have understood correctly the lessons in sociology which life in the camp taught us. Our capital, of course, was derived from production results. This was the vital beginning, but was not the decisive factor. The question was, how much capital could be spent on living conditions. As long as the camp administration put only a small part of our earnings at our disposal for the tiny amounts of extra food, it acted in the same way as the Soviet Government, which reinvested the greater part of the capital it made in building up the armaments industry; the social problem cannot be solved under those conditions, and the life of the people becomes a continual battle for the bare necessities. If, however, a larger part of this capital is put back into circulation, then the standard of living of the masses is raised, even when the distribution of earnings is unjust and unequal, even when the community spirit of the higher-income groups, of the "capitalists", is as undeveloped as it had become in the camps by reason of the anti-social ideas suggested to us and impressed upon us by the Russians. This was caused by the fact that a considerable number of men in the camps earned good wages; in our camp, for example, many brigades were on "full-pay", i.e. they were paid 250 roubles monthly—and thus so much of this money worked its way downwards on to those who earned little or nothing at all that hunger, if not kept completely at bay, was at least not as rampant as before. This was brought about, not because of any community spirit, not because the "capitalists" were ashamed of their wealth and began to share it out—most of them had not the slightest intention of doing this!—but because they were now so well fed that the others could cash in on their "sweet tooth" and their comfort. Anyone who earned 250 roubles could spread butter on his bread, have roast potatoes and bake cakes; the thin soup in the *Stolovaya* (dining-room) was no longer to his taste, nor did he feel any desire to scrub his room or to do any jobs in the camp after working hours; he found plenty of hungry men in the camp who would do odd jobs for him for some thin soup and a piece of bread. If all the instances of community spirit were taken into account as well, that is, those times when the "capitalists" were moved by friendship or pity to make large and frequent gifts to those not so well off, then the social problem was solved as far as could be desired, allowing for the un-Utopian and petty ideas which are so prevalent in this world: the result was, we no longer suffered from hunger and from being outcast as we had before. During those first months, when the great strike in France led us to compare the position of the working class in France with that of the working class in England and Scandinavia, a friend of mine who had a working knowledge of social economy said: "It may be that in France the ruling class has too little sense of social responsibility; but the chief reason for that is probably that they have not got enough money. Not until there is sufficient money available can the social ethics of men with enterprise be put into practice. Since the brigades working in the 'careers' have been able to put butter on their bread and buy chocolates, you others have more soup and more dry bread. It is the same all the world over!"

These observations caused me to become critical of my habitual anti-capitalist opinions. Two questions were puzzling me: why in its early stages the British Labour Movement took a different course from the one Marx had hoped for, and why today the Communist demagogy, contrary to Marx's prophecy, did not win its followers from among the people of the foremost capitalist countries but from among the people of those countries where the capitalist system was not highly developed. I arrived at a totally unexpected answer to these questions. The social problem in its material form, set by the misery of great numbers of people, has its source, not in "capitalism", that is, industrial production organised under private ownership, but in undeveloped capitalism, and it cannot be solved by bringing about the downfall of capitalism by means of a revolution, but rather by developing it further and by making it more democratic. A highly developed capitalist system, in which also the organisations of the people can bring pressure to bear on the ruling class, does away with all the misery to which it gave rise while still undeveloped, instead of increasing this misery, as Marx wrongly believed it would. This is possible—and here the problem applies to more than just the conditions of life in our camps—only in so far as the people have sufficient freedom to influence the ruling class, which is now more prepared to act

in the interests of society, both by exerting pressure themselves
and through the force of public opinion. This may seem to be
rather an amateurish explanation, but what I observed in the
camp made me cease to hold those unfavourable views of
capitalism which seemed so natural to the rest of my generation.

These observations did in fact make me take an unfavourable
view of those aspects of "socialism" which suggested that a
socialist society could become an objective in which goodness
seemed to be inherent as an end in itself. My socialist friends will,
I hope, forgive me for this comparison which has forced itself
upon my notice and which I cannot reject: was the society in
such a P.O.W. camp not a socialist society in miniature? There
was no private ownership of means of production. What each
one of us possessed for his private use was the money left to
him out of his earnings after the necessary sums had been
deducted for the general upkeep of the camp. There was no
unemployment, no dole, no justification for laziness. There
was a complete system of social insurance: we did not have to
worry about work or wages, about medical care or about how
we should live if we were ill. Everything that was our due was
laid down by law and we existed because we were given what
was due to us. The dangers which beset the individual when he
has to venture alone into the battle for existence, as indeed he
has to in middle-class society, were all removed. We were
looked after in every respect—and for the benefit of this comparison we can overlook the fact that what we were given was
little enough in all conscience. What did not come into it, and
what could not have come into it even if we had not been
P.O.W.s, was what we as socialists had expected from socialism
beyond this assurance of our existence: what did not come into
the picture was the removal of man's dependence on the power
of other men, the disappearance of class distinctions and the
genesis of a new social ethic. The power of the law had not
taken the place of the power of the few; but rather it was still
the few who determined where I went to work, how my
earnings were reckoned up, whether I came out on top or sank
to the bottom. And it was certainly not true that the workers,
especially those who did heavy work, were on the top step of

the social ladder; this step was occupied by the officials, the
overseers, the bureaucrats. There definitely were class distinctions: it was considered a "come down" socially if a man who
had been in an office or in a hospital or who was a group
leader, was sent "to work" because of some transgression. Each
class could easily be distinguished from the others by the
clothes, the physical well being, the friendliness and the way of
life of its members. This led to a visible class-consciousness
among the upper levels of society, which was toned down only
by the fact that we were all prisoners together. Yet in the
socialist society self-interest by no means gives way to community spirit; the individual is sufficiently conscious of his own
interests that he makes sure of his position and his advantages,
and wishes only to be distinct from the lower classes. He is
particularly careful to see that he gets what is his due, and, as
is only too obvious all over the Soviet Union, he busily continues to fend for himself behind a hypocritical fog of empty
socialist bombast.

One might raise the objection that I am thinking of everything from the point of view of the reality of a "betrayed
socialism" in the Soviet Union, which served as a model for
the socialism in our camp; but I was never able to get away
from the question of whether all this is not one of the inevitable
characteristics of a society governed on socialist lines. (I could
mention plenty more examples, above all the inability to feel
any responsibility for one's own life and work, the concealed
lack of interest in one's work since it is no longer necessary to
guarantee one's existence, the lack of any initiative to order
the course of one's life, the unquestioning obedience to
prescribed rules, in short all the characteristics of men condemned to camp life.) I know that such a socialisation of life,
in this age of over-population and of industrial production, is
being continually carried out in non-socialist countries, and
that it would be sentimental to cling to a way of life which
offered personal freedom, and which was possible only at
times when industries were under private ownership. But
what I have observed of the pattern of such a camp life has
stripped socialism of its glamour, it has shown clearly that

socialism as such can guarantee neither equality nor liberty nor fraternity, and has revealed its limits and dangers which were overlooked during the "first fine careless rapture" of the socialist idealists. These observations point to the fact that a socialist society can endanger equality (that is, in the eyes of the law), liberty (that is, independence from the power and the wills of other people) and fraternity (that is, community spirit and sympathy), and can make them impossible just as much as, according to the socialist theorists, a bourgeois society could do so. They lead me to decry the claims of socialism to be an ideal which is an end in itself, an unquestionably exalted form of society, and to show it up for what it is: namely a doubtful system of social legislation, having its own dangers which have to be met, and which can create and guarantee human happiness and satisfy human needs just as little as any other system. As long as socialism as an ideal had the power to fascinate, its disciples could believe that it would either help Christianity to reach its fulfilment (according to Saint-Simon and Weitling) or else render it superfluous, and therefore they chose it for their religion. We ought to reject the remnants of Utopian philosophy, and also ourselves to be taught by the Gospel, which tells us that the world is old and is approaching its end, and that we ought to stop expecting ideal results from our undertakings. The social problem can be ideally solved neither in a highly developed capitalist society nor in a socialist society; it can be solved only relatively, and every solution will bring with it fresh cases of injustice and opportunities for evil-doing, and at best alleviate to some extent, but not remove altogether, the burdens and misery of man's existence.

We did not dislike our new place of work. On the contrary, later on I much preferred it to the work at the "career". It lay outside the town on the edge of a vast stretch of woodland; the weather that summer was pleasantly warm. We dug out foundations, trimmed beams and set them up, laid the supports of the roof, and were pleased at seeing a house growing up; finally we even earned a little money. It would take me too long to describe what kind of stratagems, bribes and calculations were necessary to provide sufficient wages so that each member of a brigade should have 100 roubles left for himself. Normally, if the brigade was working at a bad site, a man had little prospect of earning more than the 450 roubles which had to go into the camp treasury, because of the high norms, the low wages paid by the firms (for even here there was no fixed scale and therefore rates of pay differed widely), and the poor working conditions. Suffice it to say that we succeeded, and so the good things in the camp shop were no longer unattainable. Taking it all in all, and contrary to my expectations, these months spent in Asbestos were made more enjoyable by energetic and varied work, as well as by firm friendships, and were only spoiled by the noticeable deterioration in postal communication with Germany, about which we had been complaining since the autumn of 1948. They were also troubled by the uncertainty of our repatriation, though our hopes were beginning to rise again. They were raised even higher when, at the beginning of August, something astonishing occurred, namely that with two other members of our "criminal transport" from Moscow I was transferred to a "brigade with civilian escort". That was one of those turning points in my life brought about by the inexplicable decisions of some Soviet official. Until yesterday I was still a dangerous man, conducted to work closely guarded by soldiers, who were often accompanied by dogs as well, and working only in places that were enclosed; today I am to have a civilian escort. That is the least strict method of guarding us, and was in fact merely a token: in the morning, going to work, we were met by an old civilian, armed with an antique rifle. He took us to work, then lay down to sleep, or else we sent him to do some shopping for us in the nearby stores; then in the evening he escorted us back again. To anyone who was put in such a brigade, this was a sure sign that there was no longer anything against him and that the door leading to the homeward road was opening once more. In our case this was confirmed by the fact that in the middle of August the whole brigade, except a young S.S. man and me, were sent home on the first transport.

My own prospects have at least not become worse. For at

the end of the month, I was sent to join a special group going to take the place of an "outside duty" brigade which had been sent home, at a distant M.T.S. (Motor tractor station); so it was most likely that we too should be sent home soon. Together with a sergeant and a private, we were housed for six weeks in a little farmhouse close to the M.T.S., where we were engaged in working on some half-finished buildings. Our lodging was surrounded by barbed wire, which was broken down in several places and which was also nothing but a token. In reality we enjoyed complete freedom, by which some profited to the extent of having affairs with the girls in the village, as they had done during the war years, and these men often spent the night out. It felt very strange when for the first time during our stay in Barkhenovo I was able to spend one evening going for a long walk; stretching as far as the horizon lay the fields of a collective farm, with their meagre crops, on both sides wooded hills framed the landscape, which was cut through the centre by the sharp line of the Trans-Siberian railway; in a hollow lay the village, built in the Slavonic style with long, straggling streets, the small houses cowering humbly on the ground, with their thatched roofs the same colour as the countryside. While on that first walk I was painfully aware of the contrast between this freedom, which reminded me so much of walks at home, and this landscape which was so unlike anything at home; my longing for the hills and dales, the rivers and towns of the Central European countryside made me look with real reluctance at this monotonous, gently undulating land here, and I thought that if I were condemned to live in this country I should never be happy again. Yet the more often I went for these evening walks, the more I came to feel the attraction of this land: it was possible to be happy here, one could feel at home in this country which was indeed home to those who lived here. Yet one would alter completely and grow to be like these people: short of stature, unassuming, hardly noticeable in this vast area, letting themselves be carried along rather than living actively, leading a shadowy, monotonous existence, without all the restlessness and urge for change found in the West, patient and tractable, amenable and acquiescent.

They feel no desire to govern and order their own lives, they have no creative urge, they accept things as they are.

When I returned from my walks to the M.T.S. with its garages and tractors, they seemed to me to be a symbol of the struggle which was going on: on the one side stood the industrial era and its representatives, infiltrating from the West, and also the Soviets with their plans for the enslaving and fettering of nature; on the other side stood the country and its inhabitants, who are at the mercy of the Soviets because in their patience and passivity they are so much weaker than the more active Western nations, and who yet, tough and obstinate, draw back from the encroachments on their liberty and always follow their own way of life, taking such attacks in their stride and yet remaining just as strong. The strength of the Russian peasant, and of the Siberian, too, lies in his patience and capacity for suffering. The conversations I had with the villagers, sitting in front of their huts with them in the evenings, showed this in a moving way. They taught their children the old, wistful songs, built their houses in exactly the same way as their ancestors, offered their visitors a glass of milk and a cucumber sandwich with genuine friendliness and their customary hospitality; they walked eight miles every Sunday to the only church in the neighbourhood (we are using the tiles of the church in the next village to construct the walls of the M.T.S.) and hated the system of collective farming, the officials of which lived beside them like members of a foreign race.

Here, we are living in the freshness of summer. Since the potato harvest has been gathered in the problem of our food has been eased; for now we can collect up the potatoes left lying in great heaps in the fields (even the girls who dig them up have a norm for their work, which is calculated according to the area, and so they leave so many lying there that a whole camp could be satisfied with them), a sackful every evening, and later, the secretary of the collective farm engaged us to load fruit at the station during our free time, so that our kitchen is not short of supplies. In all this we are urged on by the hope of returning home soon; we no longer work so hard since our discovery that the accountant of the M.T.S. was cheating us so much that we could not count on getting any pay, and this had taken away our initial zest for work. I shall recount in the last chapter why the hopes of the majority of being sent home were fulfilled, but not mine or those of one or two others, and why I spent the last two months of the year in that camp at Sverdlovsk that I had seen before.

2

THE
LIFE OF SOVIET
CITIZENS

DURING the twenty-two months I spent at Krasnogorsk, I had hardly ever left the camp enclosure; the guards were the only Russians I ever came across. Now, during the last year of captivity I could meet civilians almost every day and learn something of their lives. Unfortunately my knowledge of the language did not go beyond the usual jargon that the Plenni acquires for everyday use. In Krasnogorsk I had had the opportunity of getting better acquainted with this difficult language with grammars and good teachers; but there I was hoping to go home soon, and wanting to spend all the available time studying the Marxist theory, which seemed more necessary. When I at last realised how long I was going to spend in this country, I had lost all enthusiasm for learning Russian. Now I regretted this, but could not make it up. So I had little opportunity of penetrating the thoughts of the people I met, and cannot presume to enlarge on the accounts of those who know Russia better. Those of our number who, as drivers and specialist workers, could move more freely had a better command of the Russian language and gained a much clearer picture of life in the U.S.S.R. I envied them, and asked them many questions. Here I can tell you of only the few special experiences which must figure in an account of a prisoner's life in Russia.

We were not prisoners in a land which was open to the rest of the world, but in a land which had always been a mysterious and shadowy region and which, for decades now, had hidden itself behind an iron curtain: we were involuntary witnesses to a way of life which the rest of the world had seen only distorted by propaganda which either praised it or condemned it. We were in a land about which the world was told every day that the history of man had taken a new turning, and that this was the first country where socialism had come true, its birth in 1917 signifying the birth of a new mankind. It was our duty to judge for ourselves and to return to our own country which was standing at a turning point in its history, and give our testimony as to whether the road on which the Soviet Union had set out could be recommended or not. This was a difficult task, since every day we had to exercise control over ourselves in order not to become a prey to propaganda or to resentment, not to rush into generalisations, and not to forget that the P.O.W. sees everything in a perspective which is most unfavourable for the purpose of getting a fair picture of another country and nation; for the P.O.W. sees only a small slice of the real life of that country, and the administrative personnel in the camp gave an unfavourable picture of the select few rather than a favourable picture of the average citizen.

The task was made more difficult for us by the Soviet itself. Every day we were told that it was our duty to get an un-prejudiced view of life in the Soviet Union in order to tell those at home about it—but they only meant that we were to be blind and deaf towards what we saw and heard for ourselves, and to accept the picture as portrayed by propaganda. They would have liked best of all to erect an iron curtain round the camp, and, as it was, our opportunities of meeting the civilian population were as limited as possible. They could not prevent it entirely since our work threw us together, but I am sure that during the First World War the German P.O.W.s were able to move around much more freely. Where this was possible, as in Barkhenovo, it was due to the negligence of our guards rather than to a relaxing of the regulations. "If we really have to spend several years here, then it will be very pleasant, we shall soon be running around free and can get ourselves billeted on civilians!"—that was what we imagined during the first few months. Instead of that we were still stuck behind barbed wire after five years of captivity, and even if at times they relaxed their vigilance, we were soon behind the bars again and even more strictly isolated. What was the real reason for this? With simulated friendliness we asked the Polit-instructors, "Why don't you send us out, why don't you let us wander round the town in the evenings and get to know the 'new life' which the Soviet citizen is enjoying?" They always answered with embarrassment, afraid of being spied on, "There are some of you who are not yet friends of the Soviet Union, and even those of you who are will one day be interrogated by the Americans at home; therefore we have to keep the Soviet defence measures a secret." That was certainly not the only reason. They were undoubtedly even more afraid of the infiltration of Fascist poison, since they still regarded us as the carriers of that poison—not unjustly, since by "Fascist" they meant any way of thinking that was not Communist. The chief reason, however, was probably that they wanted to prevent any possible communication between Germans and Russians: the Russians might have learned how distorted was the picture of the world as drawn by the Soviet Press, and the Germans might have found out what the Russians really think and how they live.

If one of us took out his photographs, a group of civilians immediately clustered round him; the women looked in wonder at the clothes, the jewellery, the children's shoes, while the men were amazed when we told them how many roubles the motor-bike in the picture would cost, and they wanted to know whether the little house in the foreground was really inhabited only by one family. Then one of them mentioned what the Red Army soldiers who had been in Germany had told them—and then suddenly grew silent, because they remembered that they were on dangerous ground. Only if they happened to be quite alone with one of us did they give rein to their feelings. These Red Army men, who had got to know the central European area because of the war and the occupation, were another source of dangerous information which the Soviet Union was finding it difficult to dam up. All those who had been P.O.W.s, or who had done forced labour in Germany, were considered, in spite of the rough treatment that they had

usually undergone, to be infected with Fascism, and had to
endure a long term of imprisonment before they were allowed
to go back to their homes. In the saw-mill near our forest
camp were working brigades of girls and women who had been
in Germany. They sought every opportunity of talking to us
about Germany, and told us how they had been warned and
threatened with the prolonging of their punishment if they
told their fellow-countrymen anything praiseworthy about that
country. The same stern warning was given to each member
of the Red Army who came home on leave or who was
demobilised. That the German working classes lived in the
same style as a high-ranking *natshalnik* in Russia was due to the
fact that the Germans had plundered all the other nations and
that these working classes, by becoming the working aristocracy,
had betrayed the proletariat in all the world—so they were told.
If such a man on leave saw us, he would make his way to us
cautiously and as soon as he was alone with us, would start to
enthuse—only to fall silent again if others joined our group.
So the effect of such knowledge was limited, and the Russian
people were left with the comforting ideas which their government wished them to hold, namely that although they were
badly off, the masses of other nations were still worse off and,
as the strikes proved, were leading their unhappy, monotonous
lives in hunger and misery under the terrible oppression of the
land-owners and capitalists. I often had the impression that
they no longer had the ability to conceive of any other way of
life. If we told them what happened when there was a strike,
what a court of arbitration was, what happened when one
travelled abroad, or how a law court worked (though here we
often had to make an exception of the conditions during the
Hitler regime), then they shook their heads, not understanding,
listened incredulously, and soon grew tired, like people who
are told of far off things which do not concern them.

The German P.O.W., however, was continually seeing fresh
signs which seemed to prove that even National Socialism was
better than Communism. Not until I came here did I realise
what a small number of people really suffered under the Hitler
regime and were conscience-stricken at all by its horrors. For

many, the good things offered by the economic boom were offset by the burdensome lack of liberty and of security before the law. Thus they measured the Soviet Union only by the standard of its living conditions, and that sufficed. They rarely found any deeper reasons for rejecting this regime. At all events they bade farewell to Soviet territory with a definite refusal, and were immune to all propaganda. It can be estimated that ninety-five per cent. left the Soviet Union completely proof against Communism, and that of the remaining five per cent. the majority were either opportunists or else victims struggling helplessly in the net, but certainly not convinced Communists. When one considers that Lenin, during the years of the civil war, declared that an important factor in the next stage of world revolution, that is, the causing of a revolution in Germany and in the rest of Europe, was the return of hundreds of thousands of German P.O.W.s infected with the Bolshevik bacillus, then one can judge what political importance there is in the fact that this time the German P.O.W.s returned cured of all sympathy for the Soviet system. One could rejoice unequivocally at this fact if they were all equally cured of all sympathy for Hitlerism. That I dare not state this just as unequivocally is due to the fact that the fault lay in the Russian methods of curing the men of Fascism during their captivity.

If we met together to exchange our impressions of the Russian people, the accounts of most men of discernment were often interrupted by spontaneous declarations of affection for these people. When we remember that these declarations came from prisoners for whom the time spent among the Russians meant also some sad and cruel memories, it is obvious that they are a testimony which could not be finer nor more expressive. As well as these declarations there were many expressions of utter perplexity. "Their minds don't work in the same way as ours! Don't trouble, you will never understand the Russians"—these were phrases that met us as soon as we tried to think out the meaning behind the puzzling measures ordered by some Soviet officials. They were an expression of the resignation with which the Germans came to terms with contradictory impressions and actions which made a mockery of any reasonable explanation.

The striking lack of balance in the make-up of the eastern European races, the co-existence of brutality and gentleness, of rough indifference and warm sympathy in the actions of one person, the sudden swing from giving kicks to offering a friendly cigarette which each one of us experienced—here was the reason for it. But the other, to which we often paid too little attention, was the very existence of the people under the terrible and incalculable power of state control, which made them fear the consequences of even the most insignificant action, consequences of which we had not the slightest suspicion, and which made this fear become second nature to them. Thus it was impossible to generalise, and the longer I thought about it, the more I learnt to avoid drawing general conclusions from isolated incidents. I am telling you what follows, with the proviso that you should not generalise to the extent that an otherwise sensible friend of mine did when he said one day, "They are men who have strayed far from the ten commandments; they steal and commit adultery and murder, and sooner or later they will bring about their own destruction." The facts which he had observed and which he used to illustrate this statement, were all well known to me; but I could have quoted many more facts which contradicted his statement. In Russia no statement is true unless the contrary view is given as well.

The German prisoners were particularly prone to generalise when they talked about the thievishness of the Russians, and often quoted that well-known phrase of Gorki's (see p. 84). The facts did, indeed, seem to point to the truth of this, for a terrible lot of stealing went on everywhere, but it was worth while to examine the facts carefully, here as everywhere, before pronouncing a final judgment. During the war I had witnessed the strict honesty of the inhabitants of the Ukraine, and we had all grown accustomed to leaving our things about and not locking them up; then when we had retreated over the Dniester into Bessarabia, we were robbed right and left by the people there. The Ukraine, of course, is exceptional; if one judged the whole of the Soviet Union by the people and the conditions in that one province, one would gain much too favourable a picture of the whole country. Yet have the Russians really less respect for other people's property than the Ukrainians? When we looked more closely into our own experiences and those of our friends we learned to draw distinctions and we were able to understand. Anyone who has lived through the post-war years in Germany will have realised, as we did in our camps, how want is able to break down a man's strict sense of ownership, even though he was not brought up to steal. The improvements in living conditions have put things right again for most people there, and would do so here in Russia, too.

It is not the laxness of their principles, nor the lack of respect for other people's property inculcated by socialism, which drives men to steal, but dire necessity. Anyone who is not a well-paid official or skilled worker can hardly hope to survive even in normal times without doing a little "organising", let alone in war-time or during the post-war period. The trouble is twofold: the privations suffered by individuals, and the lack of supplies for industry. It is because the individual is so hard put to it to find enough food for himself and his family that it was not safe to leave things about; for this reason the wares in Russian food-shops can never be put on open counters as they are at home; for this reason, too, stealing became more and more widespread in every district after the war, as in no other country. During those years one could not travel in a train without seeing the miserable beggar-like figures of those maimed in the war slinking through the carriages, while the newspapers told in colourful language how such a state of affairs occurred only in capitalist countries and how wonderfully the grateful Soviet Fatherland cared for its heroes. Since materials for the factories are in such short supply because the demands of the Five Year Plan had led to a general lack of co-ordination in industry, and since the central planning authority was unable to cope satisfactorily with such a vast economic system, even the managers of the factories had to resort to cheating, bullying and "organising" in order to keep the factories going. The first inkling we had of all this was when our camp commandant ordered us to steal so that new work-shops could be set up in the camp. So in Ramasukha we used to go out at night to pinch planks from the saw-mill to

build new huts; the camp officers "kept cave", we were shot
at by the sentries (every work-shop and building site is guarded
day and night by armed sentries, the buildings are all enclosed
with high fences, with watch-towers at strategic points) and
when the raid had been successfully carried out we were
rewarded with extra soup. The same reward was given for a
box of nails, a roll of wire for the lighting, for tiles, or for tin.
In most of the camps which I got to know the whole electric
light system, the materials for decorating the huts and for
furnishing the club rooms, and so on, had all been taken from
nearby factories. This did not go on only in P.O.W. camps,
where the excuse was that they were particularly poorly sup-
plied, but also among the various factories themselves. One
night while we were at Ramasukha, a group of men from our
camp were roused from sleep and ordered to report to the
manager of a combine in the forest. He made them get on to a
lorry and drove with them to the nearest railway station. There,
while the manager kept watch and warned them to be careful,
they loaded the lorry with rails for a field railway, which were
stacked on the station platform; they then took them to the
forest, where a line was to be laid connecting the place where
the trees were felled with the motor road. This picture would
not be complete if I did not mention the fact that a few days
later that felling site was abandoned and so the railway was
never laid at all. When I passed that way six months later, the
pile of rails was still there, sinking slowly into the marshy
ground. Thus one factory steals from another, and if chaos
does not result from these goings-on, then it must be due to
the fact that since these methods are practised by everyone the
goods are circulated somehow and thus the balance is restored.
There is, of course, a heavy penalty for such actions. Thefts of
"public property", i.e. the property of the industries, are much
more severely punished than thefts of private property. In 1947
these penalties were made even more severe, so that the minimum was seven years' hard labour, and many of our friends
were condemned to this because, driven by hunger, they had
stolen a couple of pounds of potatoes from the camp stores.
However, because so many people are engaged in these dealings

they provide cover for each other; anyone who falls does so because he is in someone else's way.

The first thing that struck me so forcibly about the people of the Ukraine, and which I observed later in all parts of Russia, was their strong individuality. That Nazi propaganda should have represented them as sub-human, merely in order to prepare the German soldiers to fight pitilessly, was one of its greatest crimes. They are not only "men like us" but they come of farming stock, living in a region still almost entirely given over to farming, and are deeply sensitive people with strong passions, a lively intellect and amazing tact. These qualities were particularly obvious to anyone who came into contact with peasants, craftsmen, or the remnants of the middle classes.

The other deep impression was made, from the very first, by their unbelievably good health, physical as well as mental. This was more noticeable in the women than in the men, who were often not so strong and had not such forceful personalities. You ought to have seen a group of Russian girls, working in bitterly cold weather, unloading heavy sacks of cement from a lorry, and then driving off joking and singing, while we Germans watched them, shaking our heads: "They don't get much more to eat than we do!" A young Ukrainian woman who in 1944 went back over the Dniester because of a love affair with a German officer, looked scornfully at our fellow-countrymen, lying in Akerman, exhausted by the retreat. Proudly slapping her strong thighs, she called to me, "With these I ran from Kharkov to the Dniester and I run to the end of the world. German soldiers too weak for war!" Often these people seem to be the very raw material of nature, uneducated and yet unspoilt, free to love and to hate, still possessing sheer animal strength—if they had not been so, they could never have survived all that has happened to them in the course of history, particularly during the last three decades.

All this, however, has not been without consequences. We often shook our heads at the thoughtless and callous way in which they treat each other, although they have frequently shown us great sympathy. In a neighbouring camp at Asbestos a group of our friends were on their way up to the pithead of a copper mine after working their shift. A Russian woman in the shift going to relieve them had been knocked down by a small motor-van and was lying there with a broken thigh bone; they carried her up to the top and laid her down on the ground because they had to fall in for roll-call. They stood there for half an hour, while hundreds of Russians rushed past, not one of them even glancing at the woman who lay there groaning. When the prisoners suggested to the sentry that they should carry the woman to an ambulance, he swore at them and said that that must be left to those whose job it was.

In Beschiza our engineers were working at a large administrative centre. It was in the spring of 1947, during the famine which followed on the great drought. Owing to a shortage of materials, there were in the town thousands of unemployed who received practically no assistance, since according to the Stalin Constitution a man who does not work must not eat. Every day the engineers told me of the beggars who besieged the building, among them a young man who had been coming every day for a week to ask for work, who was as thin as a skeleton and who looked more like a corpse every day. He would sit for hours on the ground at the entrance to the offices —and not once did any of the well-fed civil servants give him as much as a piece of bread.

During that time I was working on the roof of the public baths which were being rebuilt, and where the ground floor was already in use. One morning, when I was grumbling about our food to the two women attendants who were sawing wood beside me, they asked me exactly how much I had eaten the day before. "Much, much!" they said when I told them, for they had eaten their last meal yesterday morning, a meal of "Borshtsh and Kartoshki"; for their evening meal they had a few potatoes left, and that was the end of their allowance till the day after tomorrow. Did the manager, who killed a pig yesterday, not give them anything? A manager never gives his employees anything, they said. And would their trade union not see to it that they received the rest of what was due to them a little sooner, since anyway they ought to have had it long ago? That seemed an utterly ridiculous question to ask, and they looked at me as though I were crazy. Anyone who is starving just starves, they said, shrugging their shoulders, it was no different anywhere else.

Once, while I was in the forest camp, the girl who ran the local day-nursery rode a short distance with me in my lorry. She was a delicate, charming creature, whom I had often seen playing with the children in the playground which we had built for them. She wanted to know exactly what German nurse-maids did during the holidays, and only after a short time did I find out why she wanted to know. In summer, most of the children were sent to look after the cattle and to help with the harvest, so that the nursery was closed, and the burgomaster would not give her a ration card unless she went to work in the forest. I looked at her and realised that one week in the forest would be the death of her. She knew that, too, but otherwise she would starve. Could she not get food from the farmers? Even if they could spare her some from their meagre harvest the burgomaster would not allow it. I could, however, see the burgomaster's point of view; he has been ordered to provide a certain amount of wood for the combine, and the wood-cutters, whom he had brought from Briansk the year before, had with great foresight found employment elsewhere, because they were horrified by the present wages and conditions of work in the forest. Now the burgomaster was busy rounding up as many people as he could find who were capable of working, and the next day the girl moved out to the empty, damp mud-houses in which they were all to live like animals for weeks; she would use up all her feeble strength trying to haul tree-trunks around, and would never fulfil her norm.

One Sunday morning in the forest camp one of our brigades was fetched out and piled on to a lorry. When they returned in the evening the men told us that they had been driven to the best house in the next village, where lived an unusually well-dressed family with several children. They had to take down this house, while the family stood by, bewailing their fate. Finally, when the house had been completely demolished, all the usable materials were taken away and their furniture and other household effects were left lying in the open. The burgomaster's explanation: this house had been burnt down by mistake during the German occupation, and the Germans had rebuilt it as quarters for their officers, and finally handed it over to this family. Because they had accepted it, they were collaborators and did not deserve a house at all.

During that same summer (it was at the time of the great drought and the farmers were all looking forward anxiously to the winter), I was driving to the forest one day when I saw Russian drivers taking their lorries backwards and forwards across the fields of millet which the peasants had sown in the forest in the spaces where we had cut down trees. Since the war they had taken advantage of the lax administration of the collective farm system, and had sown more land than law allowed in order to cater for their own needs. Now the Supreme Soviet had issued a decree which forced them to obey the old regulations, and so their millet had to be sacrificed, although it was the only crop which had survived the dry summer and which could have saved them from starvation.

All this demonstrates the absolute power of a state which no longer needs to fear any rebellion or any public opinion, because it has taught the people by means of the most cruel oppression how dearly they would have to pay for any rebellion. I have often asked myself whether the silent submissiveness with which everything was endured was merely the result of this teaching or whether it was already one of the nation's characteristics. In Barkhenovo we sometimes managed to buy white bread on Sundays, though it was not easy to obtain. For it could be bought only once a week, on Sunday mornings, and we were not the only ones who wanted some to brighten up their Sunday. In the village stores (the Soviet *magazin* is somewhat similar to our co-operative stores), in which one felt all the benefit of the Stalinist education in cleanliness but which had only a modest supply of wares, there were three shop-assistants: one for the bread, another for the food-stuffs, and the third for everything else. When there was a crowd trying to buy white bread on a Sunday, the first girl had to serve a queue of people which stretched right out into the street, while the other two just looked on; if a consignment of pastries arrived, the whole village stormed the shop, not storming it literally, of course, but besieging it in another long queue, and so the second girl had to work feverishly. When we had seen this happen several times, we began to grumble from our places in the queue and suggested that the other girls might at least give the overworked one a hand by serving the other things not so often required, for instance black bread on Sundays or cigarettes on the day the pastries came. The effect of this protest on the crowd which had hitherto been moving up in silence was as though someone had, in broad daylight, urged them to overthrow Stalin: the shoppers and the assistants were equally horrified, there was no question of support for our sensible suggestion, everyone remained dumb, the proprietor appeared and declared in a long, impassioned speech that we had no right to criticise the organisation of the Soviet State—and everthing stayed as it always had been.

In the autumn of 1946, while carrying out the task of fetching food for the forest camp from the central stores, we found ourselves, well after midnight, in the waiting room of a small station where we had to change. The hall was packed, just as in our German stations during the war; people lay packed together like sardines, not only beside each other but on top of one another as well, and it was a miracle that we were able to squeeze in at all. While I was lying with my head on the back of a loudly snoring Mushik and my legs on the buttocks of an old woman, trying to get to sleep, I saw the door, which opened inwards, being forced open and in the crack appeared ten men who began to squeeze their way in. It was obvious that they would not find a spare inch anywhere, but with growing astonishment I saw that they wanted more than just to find room for themselves: in the corner farthest from the door was the booking office, and they wanted to force their way to it. Anywhere else in Europe this hopeless attempt would have been greeted by loud protests, but here nobody moved. Pushing and shoving, climbing over the bodies lying on the floor and squeezing their way between the people standing up, feeling their strength and knowing just what they wanted, these men did in fact manage to get to the booking-office in a quarter of an hour, without having been met by so much as a curse.

This scene seemed to me to typify the essential nature and the destiny of these people: when they come up against the will of anyone with a stronger personality, who knows just what he wants, they accept it as their destiny and submit to it calmly and patiently. In the history of this nation, as of any other nation, there have been rebellious spirits, and in this country perhaps more than in any other there have been many martyrs for the sake of freedom; yet its fundamental attitude is not one of rebelliousness but of submissiveness and patient silence.

However, what else can they do? What the average German citizen felt to be oppression in the time of Hitler (namely, "that we no longer have freedom of speech") was paradise compared with the risks that accompanied "speech" under a system of government where one could no longer escape from politics, where every complaint uttered against an official or against any discomfort was immediately suspected of being an expression of political revolt. The realm of politics is the realm of the unforgivable. Many of our number had been in the same prisons as the worst criminals. They all affirmed that these criminals spoke openly about their misdeeds but never expressed any political dissatisfaction and never answered any of the political questions which the Germans asked, and above all they never associated with the political prisoners even if they were in the same cell. They would rather be convicted of robbery with violence than of Trotskyism or of counter-revolutionary activities. Outside the prisons they did speak more openly but never among themselves, only to us. I once had to confer with the *natshalnik* of a factory about settling the wages for our brigade. When the book-keeper, who had been present, left the room, all of a sudden he burst out swearing, with that inexhaustible and varied wealth of oaths, unfit for publication, which are at the command of all Russians (though the older men say that this has only been so since the Revolution); first of all I thought that all this applied to me, then I began to understand that by "rogues" and "bandits" he meant other men, in fact the whole system from the bottom to the top, though those right at the top were of course unnamed. Such outbursts on the part of an official are rare, although the farmers and workmen all told us exactly what they thought of everything. Then came the question: why had we lost the war and did I think the Americans would come soon. Then he cursed the collective farms, and the Jews. I once asked a peasant-woman in Briansk why they were so against the collective farms. "Do you love captivity?" she asked, and when I laughingly said, "No," she replied laconically, "Nu vot!" ("Well, then!—")

In the Soviet Union anti-Semitism has been anything but overcome, as propaganda pamphlets are constantly asserting, in fact it is strangely virulent. Here as everywhere the Jew is a scapegoat always to be had cheaply. It is no help to the Jews that their synagogues are oppressed to the same extent as the churches, nor that the autonomous state which the Jews were allowed to found in a poor district of Siberia is neither autonomous nor Jewish. In Zarentum the younger generation, all out for emancipation, found a sympathetic confederate in the revolutionary movement; when the middle-class intelligentsia had been liquidated by revolution and civil war, the Jewish intellectuals surged into the vacuum and today are still all too visibly seated in all the coveted and feared positions on those lower steps of hierarchy which can be seen clearly by the man in the street. Thus Russian anti-Semitism survived into the new era and may break out again even more horribly.

It is impossible to estimate accurately the numbers of those who reject and those who accept the Soviet system. What is certain, however, is that dissatisfaction is very widespread, and it is equally certain that there are no opportunities for any organised opposition, and that therefore no other political ideas can give form and content to this dissatisfaction. So things have to stay as they are, and only in sighs can one express one's feelings; the older men cannot agree among themselves whether things had been better under the Tsars or under Lenin, but they are all agreed that under Stalin things are "plokho" (very bad). It is certain, too, that there are a not inconsiderable number of people who are convinced supporters of the system. How far these convictions are genuine or how far they are born of opportunism or of fear, is a question which can mean something only in the Western world, for it presupposes freedom. When we ask an official of a totalitarian regime questions about whether his convictions are genuine or not, we are starting from a premise which is not even given. It presupposes the possibility of free decision and independent opinions which never existed. His decision in favour of Communism is just as free and genuine as our decision not to jump in front of a moving express train: if he wishes to live he has no other alternative. Freedom of decision only comes to him when he has experienced Christianity. Such experiences are frequent, though probably less so among the higher officials than among the ordinary Party and Comsomol members. That young lieutenant in the forest camp, who used to come to see me and, after stressing his own unbelief, would ask me, fixing me with a penetrating gaze, whether I really and truly believed in God, was perhaps well on the way. When one of our number, a merchant from Hanover, foolishly attempted to escape and was caught again after a few hours and taken to this lieutenant, he asked the man whether he believed in God. The man answered truthfully, as was only to be expected from the average German sergeant-major, that he didn't. "A pity," said the lieutenant thoughtfully, "otherwise you would be able to thank Him for the fact that I am the Deshurni [the officer on duty]; for anyone else would have had you flogged unmercifully."

One cannot put any greater value on the convictions of many of the younger generation than one could on the enthusiasm of many Hitler Youth leaders. "Youth has no convictions, but only enthusiasm"—I remembered this *bon mot* of Sauerbruch's, dating from the time of the Third Reich, when I was talking to some students on the Metro during my first visit to Moscow. They could speak English and German, and at once began to question me eagerly about my opinions on America. They had read Theodore Dreiser and Sinclair Lewis, and held extravagant ideas about American production and living conditions, but without being at all envious: one day life in the Soviet Union would be like that, but now it was more important to retain a simple way of life. "The Americans live for themselves, but we live for socialism", said one of them. This sounds a proud and enviable sentiment; but it is one thing when a young member of the Comsomol expresses such sentiments today, and quite another when they were expressed by a member of that militant generation which spoke in the earliest examples of Soviet literature and which was then liquidated during the great purges in the 'thirties. When one reads the reports of meetings in *Komsomolskaya Pravda* (the daily paper of the Union of Young Communists), and the monotonous, nonsensical resolutions in the Comsomol wall-newspapers, when one hears their songs and sees their club rooms, then one realises that it is all just the same as the Hitler Youth. They are young men who have been robbed of every opportunity of living their own lives and of having their own opinions, who have no room in their lives for opposition, nor for questioning or finding out for themselves, young men whose idealism is, from the first, official, compulsory and empty. They can for a time bring to this idealism enthusiasm and warmth because of their need for faith and sacrifice; but it cannot grow mature, it cannot develop, and therefore it can only turn into hypocrisy and cynicism. Anyone who was able to read Ilja Ehrenburg's novel *The Second Day*, will have found in it a clear though unintentional illustration of this. Inner emptiness—that is the fate of youth under the totalitarian system.

The hardship, which gave rise to this dissatisfaction, was often so surprising that we sometimes wondered whether it had not been created deliberately, not by saboteurs but by the government itself. At the time when the great drought in the summer of 1946 was causing such distress in vast areas of Central Russia and the northern Ukraine, in other parts of Russia the harvest was so good that the people there could certainly have helped. Yet hardly any help was given; at the same time large quantities of Russian grain were exported, and also added to the reserves hoarded in case of war. For a few weeks during the summer of 1949 there was no bread in the whole district round Asbestos; it was alleged that the district had used up its allocation too quickly and would have to wait until the beginning of the next ration period for further supplies. We had just received our first pay-packet and were bitterly disappointed at being able to spend it only on chocolates, instead of on something more solid to appease our hunger. Outside in the town long, long queues stood silently in front of the stores, to get what little bread there was available. Not a voice was raised in protest. We asked ourselves how this situation could be possible after the record harvest in 1948, and our mistrust had become so violent that we did not need to ponder over the matter but knew for certain that such shortages were contrived deliberately so that the people should know who was their master and should continue to feel insecure and therefore dependent on that master.

However, similar difficult situations arose, even without the help of deliberate action. Anyone who has worked in the Soviet Union in industry or on the land, can understand why the Germans, who could never be told too much about such affairs, used to sum it up by saying, "The Russians will never get anywhere, because what they build with their hands they knock down again with their backsides!" I have already described the piles of potatoes which were left lying on the fields belonging to the collective farm in Barkhenovo. At the same time, one member of our working party, a farmer from Brandenburg, told how a few years before he had helped with the harvesting in a collective farm for the first time. A whole group of farmers had been chosen for the job. On the first morning they were each allotted their area of the field to be cleared of potatoes. They dug them up carefully, as they had been accustomed to doing at home, and in the evening it transpired that they had not finished clearing their allotted areas. The activist who was leading the group told them, "You have not fulfilled your norm and therefore you will get less bread and no milk today." They told him that they had been working very hard and that to clear the field completely would take more than a day—such was their opinion as experts. He answered, "I am not saying that you should not work carefully but that you must fulfil your norm, otherwise your rations will be reduced; but if you can exceed your target, then you will get extra milk and bacon!"

"Well," said our informant cheerfully, "next day there were no reductions in our rations, on the day after that we got bacon, and so on till we had finished, and everyone was satisfied. But nobody showed the slightest interest in the fact that our piles of potatoes never grew any larger than they had been in the first day, and you need not ask how many potatoes were ploughed in again—our hearts bled at the sight." What was the sense of it all? The farm manager could keep to his original target, received sufficient potatoes to fulfil the quota demanded of him—and the field had just not yielded any more. Now and then there appears in the local papers an article, which exposes the fact what poor harvests there had been; some poor man is made the scape-goat, but otherwise nothing is changed, because the managers, in the grip of the Plan, have no other alternative, and because critics are allowed to speak only of the consequences and dare not approach the roots of the evils, namely the Five Year Plan and the superstitious belief of the Communists that a central planning authority is not only possible but is also the salvation of their country. This is so above all because nobody is really interested in making any changes. The only person who would be interested in doing so is someone who felt a responsibility towards everything, who grieved over the wastage of such vast quantities of material, and who was willing to undertake to arouse those in positions of responsibility by his reproaches and suggestions. However, anyone who, because of this feeling of responsibility, is concerned as much about things in general as he is about his own private affairs, soon gets broken on the wheel of the Soviet system. By this action he is doing just what is demanded of him daily by the official state education—and what in fact his experiences day by day counsel him not to do, if he wishes to avoid being ruined. Anyone who allows himself to feel such responsibility instead of leaving everything to his superiors, soon gets on the wrong side of the law, makes himself enemies, is allowed to come a cropper over one of the inevitable risks attached to his undertaking, and before he realises it he is blamed for the very evils which he was seeking to do away with.

If five prisoners sat talking, and this subject happened to crop up, there would follow an endless succession of fantastic stories. At first one would take them to be nothing but exaggeration or malicious slander, and one's own experiences would be regarded as exceptions or as the concomitants of such new and daring experiments as Communism makes from time to time. Gradually, however, one became aware of the fact that here was a manifestation of the very nature of the system, which could be seen anywhere at any time, and that this enormous wastage of material, the use of the wrong materials, and the production of shoddy goods were not the consequences of the exercise of bold initiative but rather of the complete suppression of initiative. Two of my own experiences will serve as examples of this.

In January 1947 thirty of us took several weeks to dig through some rising ground, so that a railway line could be laid in the grounds of a locomotive factory. The sandy ground was frozen as hard as cement to a depth of over six feet and we broke it up, piece by piece, with wedges and sledge-hammers, with the result that one after another were made unfit by the heavy work. Three men could have done the same job in a few days when the thaw came. In April I once passed that spot, and the line was still not laid. Why then all this waste of labour? Because, according to the Plan, the laying of the rails had been prescribed for the first three months of the year, without anyone in the planning office having known anything about the hilly ground, and because the chief engineer had not dared to alter the plans laid down by the authorities.

In Asbestos a specialist worker was once put in the detention cell because he could no longer refrain from raising objections to this wastage. As a much-esteemed skilled worker, he was in charge of a brigade of turners, composed of both Germans and Russians. He was ordered to make several thousand large nuts; for material he was given old iron rods which were lying in the factory yard. The nuts were then to go to another factory to have the thread cut. He tried out a rod, and was convinced that they were made of steel that was so hard that the thread could not possibly be cut in it. The manager of the factory, when told of this, insisted that the order should be carried out. The German refused to obey this order: to make useless nuts would be deliberate wastage and sabotage, of which he did not wish to become guilty. The manager then reported him to the camp authorities, who summoned him that evening to a ceremonial interrogation before the commandant, the N.K.V.D. commissar, and the labour overseer. His explanation and his protest that he had acted only from a sense of duty were of no avail; the responsibility was the manager's, not his, they declared, and locked him in the detention cell for the night because of his disobedience. Next day he dutifully turned his nuts, the manager could deliver them according to plan; in the other factory, at the first attempt to cut the thread, some of the taps broke, and then the nuts were lying in the yard as scrap iron once again and the manager had to find a way of fulfilling his part of the plan.

It would be very foolish to think that with industry in such a state nothing in the way of reconstruction could be achieved. Where a country with such a large population and such vast quantities of raw material puts these at the disposal of the Government, and when they are employed with such a lack of consideration, then in spite of bad management such imposing results and such an industrial boom as has occurred in the Soviet Union, can be achieved. The world will never know how many unprofitable dealings, how much waste and how many sacrifices went into the achieving of these results—and still go into it—and these disproportionate costs and these sacrifices were borne not by those responsible for them, but by the Russian people in various ways. First of all, they suffer by being poor, because the fruits of their labours, even after thirty years of planned economy, have not yet brought them as many advantages as they might. They suffer, too, because in the distribution of these fruits distinctions are made, so that the differences in financial circumstances are similar to those in the Western countries. Finally, they suffer because they have to increase their output in order to counter-balance the worst conditions. For this purpose there is the so called *subbotnik*. This word really means "Saturday work", and derives from the fact that during the civil war Lenin once called on the people of Moscow to repair voluntarily a stretch of railway line which was essential in order to keep the supply line open. Nowadays, when there is work to be done that is not catered for by the Plan, the people are called upon for the *subbotnik*, and one can imagine how voluntary it is! In the great saw-mill at Sverdlovsk, the large yard in front of the mill was covered with gigantic piles of chips, to which we added daily when cutting planks. In a private business the work of stacking the pieces would have had to be done by the men in the mill. The manager cut down his expenses, however, by making the prisoners remove and and stack the pieces on a free Sunday. A meeting was held beforehand, at which this *subbotnik* was praised as being their voluntary, and of course unpaid, contribution towards the triumph of Communism. As they went to work, we saw from their expressions how enthusiastic they were over this lost Sunday!

The "antagonism of class interests", which Marxism portrayed as inherent in the capitalist economic system and thought to overcome through the socialisation of the means of production, is apparent from this example: the bonus awarded for reducing the running costs is paid, not to the factory nor to the worker, but to the manager; therefore his self-interest cost those who worked in the saw-mill their free Sunday. This conflict of interests has very obviously not been overcome any-where, and is distinguished from the similar conflict in the capitalist countries only by the fact that the Soviet worker has lost the right to have his interests protected, a right which had been fought for and won during the hundred years since the birth of the modern Labour movement. It is the totalitarian state which gives him work; he has impressed upon him daily the fact that their interests are identical. The personal experi-ences of the workers, however, go to show that they are offered to the state as sacrificial victims and cannot defend themselves against this. The exaggerated idealism which is demanded of them, while, with their strength draining away and with miserable houses and poor wages, they are expected to make the victory of socialism and classless society possible for the benefit of their children or grandchildren, would be bearable if it were demanded from and achieved by all alike. But since Stalin, recognising how egoistic man is, introduced in 1929 the grading of wages and salaries and higher pay for the higher officials, there is no longer any equality of sacrifice. The man on top is enjoying the profits now, the man underneath has only the comfort of knowing that his children will profit later on— if he still believes this. The man on top can now lead a life which to the under-dog is nothing but a promise in the distant future. The latter must believe that the proverb about the well-fed man who does not understand the hungry man is no longer true, but rather that those at the top of the ladder who are now well fed are anxious for nothing but that he should achieve this satisfaction too; he must believe that those who are now enjoying plenty still feel a sense of solidarity with those who now have to go without. While such tremendous faith and idealism are demanded of him, he learns daily how pitilessly he is sacrificed and how he has been deprived of every means of forcing those at the top to consider his needs, as they did in earlier capitalist days. His trade unions are in reality nothing but organs of the state, and thus of those who are at the top; strikes and assertions of dissatisfaction are counter-revolutionary.

During my first weeks in Russia, an old German Communist, filled with horror, showed me the ground plans of some small wooden houses, which his brigade were just building for demobilised Red Army men; they were small square huts of the most modest proportions, with one room and one window. They were hen houses, not human dwellings, and he could not understand how a proletarian government could build such wretched houses for the families of workmen. A few days before I left Russia, I took a lorry to fetch some stones from a sandstone quarry, where, in the dim light of oil lamps in a cave that was just the height of a man, dozens of men and women were working, hewing out the stone amid clouds of dust which clogged the lungs, their faces pale and haggard; a picture of slave labour such as might have been seen in a quarry in ancient times. At home our health authorities and workers' tribunals would have opposed it, but here the state, the great capitalist, was using these methods in order to economise.

⯈ In the evening of that same day I heard a group of Germans in the camp talking about some P.O.W.s, who had voluntarily pledged themselves to stay as civilian workers. Amazed, I asked whether this news was reliable, since I had never met anyone yet who wanted to stay. The man who had told me this, a miner from the Ruhr, dealt with me scornfully: "Not here of course," he said, "but in France. Who on earth would want to stay in this workers' paradise!" I travelled home with this workman's bitter mockery ringing in my ears and with the picture of that quarry and many other such incidents before my eyes. Once upon a time the Communist party seemed to be the most determined representative of the interests of the proletariat. The worker who still believes this does not know what Stalinism has done for the Party, or else he does not want to know because he is bitter and in need of something to which to pin his faith. Where, in capitalist countries, it still appears to be fighting for the welfare of the working classes, in reality this is only an excuse for the battle for power. Those in Russia who want to come to power do not serve the interests of the working class but merely make use of them, and then only until they achieve power.

Today the Soviet citizen lives his life in the shadow of this power, cut off from the rest of the world, cut off from every prospect of liberation, for which he can hardly hope since it would only be possible if there were a war and if his country were thereby laid waste; cut off, too, from every opportunity of imagining any other kind of life, a life which only the older generation, now dying out, could remember dimly. He can seek to find freedom from this power only while under its domination, and does so in many ways, according to the strength of his desire. Eagerly he reads Russian classics and those of other countries which are available. Soviet statisticians are fond of pointing out how much foreign literature is read in

the Soviet Union, but conceal the fact that it is popular because
it affords relief from the monotony of modern Soviet literature.
He sings and makes music, and throws himself into amateur
dramatics with an enthusiasm born of his natural talent. In
various small towns I have seen theatrical companies made up
of amateurs who moved about the stage unselfconsciously and
mimed excellently, as though they were professionals; I would
now understand those amazing early films of Pudovkin and
Eisenstein, made during the golden age of the Soviet film, for
which the actors were taken from the streets of the city. When
they used to gather in front of their houses in the evening and
sing in harmony the many songs from their treasury of music,
as well as more modern ones, we Germans were filled with envy
and sorrow because we realised that our own nation has lost
its community songs and has now nothing but army songs and
dance music.

Above all, however, he still has his Church. Opinions differ
as to the number of Soviet citizens who are still church-goers,
and I was anxious to see all I could in order to form my own
opinion. It is well known that they had to pay a high price for
toleration—in the Russian Orthodox Church as well as in
other Churches, of which the largest was the Baptist Church—
by having to renounce all political influence and by having to put over Party political propaganda in their official
proclamations. It is not for us to judge, however many questions
may occur to us. It is certain, however, that beneath this curtain
the Church still lives its own life and is substantially unchanged,
in spite of outward compliance. I had no experience of any
underground communities, and I do not know whether and to
what extent any such communities are in existence. During the
war German soldiers were all struck by the customary shrines
in farm-houses; these are also to be found in town houses,
though they are rare. It is said that during the time of the
Tsars there were seventy churches in Sverdlovsk; today only
one is in use and is always full to overflowing. If I talked about
religion to the older people they were always grateful, and when
I showed the children the few Biblical pictures I had with me
and told them stories about them, the whole family would

gather round, in spite of my difficulties with the language, and would help me out.

The younger generation was often perplexed and could not understand; that anyone should believe in God was a proof of the most amazing backwardness. In one farm-house I once saw a very beautiful old wooden icon with the twelve apostles on it. I would have liked to have had it and I was referred to the grandmother, who, however, indignantly refused to part with it. I talked to her for a long time, told her who I was and that I would always reverence the icon, but she was so attached to it that I finally gave up trying. When I left, their seven-year-old daughter ran after me and offered to steal the icon for me. My refusal gave me the opportunity to have a long talk with her; she, and several boys who joined us, told me all that they knew about the stars, to prove that God couldn't be above the stars, and the idea that He was here with us was quite new to them. What can one say in half an hour when one has to battle with the language? When I ended by saying that grandmother and I knew why we were here on this earth and that they did not know, nobody spoke up for socialism; they looked at each other and one broke the silence by saying, "Nobody knows why!"

Only when I was in the Ukraine during the war did I go to Orthodox and Baptist services, but never while I was a prisoner; but according to all accounts the congregations are much the same as they always were, consisting mainly of women and old people, though there were quite a few young people. The relationship of both old and young to the Church seems to be much the same as in our average parishes at home. Church-going is by no means confined to the older generation, but when young people here become Church members, that implies considerably more than when young people do so in Germany. Here they are not attracted to it because of enthusiastic work done among them, but they join as a result of an independent decision after much profound thought. A Comsomol-member has to overcome even greater obstacles, and runs a greater risk by going to services than does an ordinary Party-member. Every youngster lays himself open to the pitiless torment and scorn of his contemporaries. The feeling of inward emptiness, the doubts about the official philosophy of life, and about the final authority of science which it proclaims, the longing for another faith that made more sense—all these had to become insurmountable before one dared to expose oneself thus. It is very probable that, now that the excitement of belief in science and of militant atheism has grown less, and that atheism is no longer the expression of a bold sense of freedom, but of the official religion, these doubts and longings are much more widespread among the alert young people of today than they were before the war. Anyone who feels these things must grope his way forward in secrecy and quite alone; many will lay down their arms and comply wearily with the official regulations before they have found the answer. They have been preserved from the chaos and confusion in spiritual life in the West, but are instead confronted with the monotony of a materialistic philosophy which seeks in vain to give itself depth by means of dialectics; as soon as this philosophy arouses doubts and can no longer satisfy one's beliefs (for in Stalinism questioning is doubting, and is treated as such) then the alternatives are more clearly visible than they are in the West—and the New Testament becomes an exciting and much coveted book. That may have been the experience of those Comsomol-members whom one of my friends met in a prison in Novosibirsk, sentenced because they had handed round the New Testament to other members of their group; it may have been the experience, too, of that Moscow student who excitedly lectured his friends on what he had found in Dostoievsky (cf. the excellent account of this in *Russian Experiences* (*Erlebtes Russland*) by E. Jucker, pp. 250ff.).

Among the many experiences of people saved by their faith, the most impressive was my meeting with the German settlers in the Urals in 1949. Those who live in the Urals—apart from the native population—hardly ever do so voluntarily. Even outside the many Sakljutshonnyi-camps most of the local inhabitants have no freedom, being either people sent there for a punishment or natives of other countries deported to that district, who had little freedom to move about. In the autumn of 1941 the German inhabitants of the "Autonomous Volga-German Soviet Republic" and of German colonies in Southern Russia were all deported eastwards because they were unreliable, and their republics were dissolved. Families were split up, the men were sent either into the army or to Siberia and the women and children to the Urals; later the same thing happened to the Tartar tribes from southern Russia and the Caucasus, who had been too friendly with the Germans during the German occupation of those regions. So we often worked with Tartar women, while the German colonists were not allowed to come near us. Nevertheless we soon began to correspond secretly and thus we learnt of the heroism of these women. Even at that time they were allowed to move freely only within a very small area, and were under the strict supervision of special commissars. Yet they met regularly for worship, taught their children passages from the Bible and hymns, and were more than grateful for the copies of the New Testament and other religious books which we managed to send them. In December 1949 I met a group of their husbands in Sverdlovsk, who had come from Siberia to visit their families—for the first time in eight years, and only for a fortnight! Their stories of what had happened to them would have drawn tears from a stone. When I told them that their wives had taught the children to pray, one of them sighed with relief: now he knew at least that they would recognise each other again "in the Spirit", as he said solemnly.

3

THE CAMP
COMMUNITY

WHEN I was at Asbestos I was told once that, taking advantage of the new Church laws of 1942, some of the inhabitants prepared a petition, asking to be allowed to build a church and to be granted some land for this purpose; but because they had not collected the three hundred signatures on the petition demanded by the law, it was not granted. The man who told me this was a peace-loving old fellow who would not harm a fly, who had once been deported to Siberia as a Kulak and was now earning a meagre wage under the tyrannical woman engineer, who begrudged us even the salt in our soup. He was working at our building site, and I asked him whether there were not more people in Asbestos who were interested in building a church. He scratched his grey head; yes, they were interested, but to sign such a petition was just one of those things. It was allowed, though? Oh, yes, but to sign the petition was just one of those things!

The Church is tolerated, but grudgingly; thus it is really not tolerated, at any rate only just. The P.O.W. felt this just as much as the Soviet citizen did; during the latter years, in spite of other improvements in conditions, it was felt more in some camps than in others. So later on I would no longer have subscribed to the views which I expressed at that conference, when we welcomed the Eastern German Trade Union delegation, having since learnt what conditions in most camps really were like.

In the forest camp we asked for permission to hold services

immediately after our arrival. The commandant gave it at once;
religion, he declared, was an opiate, but according to the
Stalin Constitution the practising of religion in the Soviet
Union was allowed, and that went for the P.O.W. camps too.
Next Sunday the majority of the inmates of the camp gathered
round the foundations of a new hut that was being built: the
Gospel for the day was Matthew 6. 25–34, the words of Jesus
about taking no thought for the morrow. What did it mean for
us? To whom did the words apply? They were spoken to the
disciples of old—could they be applied to all men, even to
these here? To seek first of all the Kingdom of God, to look
towards it and long for it, then everything would be added to
us, food, clothing, freedom, the return home! Who would dare
to preach those words as a solemn message and as genuine
advice to these depressed and hungry men who as yet knew
little of the Christian faith?

It was a simple matter to use this text, which directs our
thoughts to our heavenly Father, who knows all that we have
need of, to provide easy comfort for a devotional hour which
made us forget our surroundings for a while; but yet the text
claimed to be good counsel which we could hold on to even in
the face of all that surrounded us, good counsel as practical as all
the advice which the old prisoners gave us about all that we had
to do here in order not to fall foul of the authorities. Taken in
that way it was unbelievable, and while I let the text speak for
itself in the simplest way, I felt how, in the hearts of my comrades, the realities that lay about us rose up to contradict it, and
it was no longer my own certainty but the New Testament
itself which took over the responsibility for this unbelievable
message and counsel, which were summed up in one phrase:
Ye are not alone. We often remembered this text when reality
itself, and the words of our fellow-prisoners, told us that we
were not alone, in times of hunger and bitter disappointment
and when we stood by the graves of so many during the
following winter. The second service raised the text for the
day high above the camp like a lantern: "For in my wrath I
smote thee, but in my favour have I had mercy on thee" (Isa.
60. 10), and so confidently did I make it shine like a light in the

276

darkness, that some took it literally and thought that I had heard a rumour of approaching liberation.

Every Sunday after that we could meet freely, but the circle grew smaller than it had been at first. Exhaustion and privation made for dullness and hopelessness rather than for close attention, the effort to get off one's bunk became too great, and my own weakness often lessened the force of my words. In the winter the camp Polit-officer organised a new "Anti-Fascist Club", through which the dictatorship of a minority was established. Their first action was to demand the cessation of Sunday services. After years of socialist reconstruction the Soviet people had grown sufficiently mature to be able to tolerate religion, but not the German nation. Not until they threatened to disturb the services did the commandant yield and forbid them. Thus they had given proof of the correctness of their opinions, and the fact that from then on their political work in the camp was met by a wall of silence would have worried them only if their opinions had been a matter of conviction and not merely calculated. The worst of it was that I myself could not summon up the strength to say to each individual and to small groups what I was not allowed to say openly. I had plenty of conversations, but I could not manage to form a group of men with brotherly feelings, which could be a constant source of help to us and the secret spiritual focal point of the camp. Only the stories I told in the evening could help to fill the gap.

When I arrived at the factory-camp at Beschiza at Christmas in 1946, I saw what it meant to work constantly and tirelessly. Among the prisoners were three Evangelical pastors and a Roman Catholic theological student. In one of these men, however, the fire of love towards the Lord and towards the men whom He seeks burnt especially ardently. He showed us the real meaning of tirelessness, and really became our spiritual leader. He was an Evangelical assistant pastor of the Confessional Church in Berlin; he was the personification of what had been the real meaning of the fight for the Church in recent years: not defence, not active fighting, but a revival within the Church. Thus while he was a prisoner he carried on the witness to which he had pledged himself during the years of peace. The camp held ten companies, and in each of these he had brought together a little group of men which met once a week for Bible study and for prayer. He was supported by a small group of loyal helpers, who met every morning before going to work, to be told the day's text and to pray together, and his most intimate friends assembled again in the evening to join in prayer. Only someone who has himself been in a labour camp could measure the amount of renunciation, sacrifice and energy demanded of the man who undertook all this work. Anselm was not as robust as I was; when he was at last graded unfit, we were horrified to see how haggard he looked. He was a member of a particularly poor brigade which had to drag out of the nearby river all the logs which had been floated down it. This was wet and exhausting work and the men rarely achieved their percentage, so that they usually had the worst food. Yet in spite of his own weariness he spent evening after evening visiting all the companies and looking after the special groups; in all this it was not only important for him to be there but he also had to be so lively, so alert, that he could always give something to the others. He had first of all to rouse those whom weariness had drawn to their bunks, and then to penetrate the wall of their exhaustion, never in favourable conditions but always amid the restlessness of the crowded huts where there was hardly ever a corner to be found where they could be free and undisturbed. Thus he always had first of all to prepare a road along which he could bring the Word to these men. Without his efforts, the beginnings that were made would have been drowned in the weariness which the Devil uses as a weapon in order to cut men off from all that keeps them alive spiritually. The flame which burned in him and gave him such endurance made it possible for him to help many people, and gave him a reputation in the camp, which inspired confidence as nothing else could.

Everyone who confided in him felt that the Word which he served was a power which gave men strength to live, and not merely an idea which demanded men's allegiance. Like a guardian angel, Anselm fought for the souls of all who joined his groups, helped up those who fell, and never let them fall again. We lived so close together that we could see each other's weaknesses. It was quite impossible for the words we preached to fly over people's heads and not to reach the earth where our poor bodies were struggling; preaching meant at once the care of souls, and theology was nothing but practical spiritual experience such as we had of the Bible teachings, in the midst of the realities of camp life. The terrible distance which so often lies between the sermon and the earth, between the preacher and the congregation at home, was not in evidence here. The Gospel is immediately transformed into a commandment, and a commandment could come only from the Gospel. One member of a group once tried to do what so many did, namely to cheat when food was being served in order to get a double portion of soup, or else he took part in "organising" in the food stores, or tried to get a better position in the camp by means of bribery. Each time he suffered for it, either by being accused and punished, or by becoming neglected and impoverished, or less receptive towards the Word, or by being frequently admonished to turn from his evil ways; the man who has Jesus as his Lord and Guardian cannot do with impunity what others are able to do.

Many real and unexpected experiences revealed that our little community obeyed laws different from those of the world, and that it derived its life from the Word only as long as it trusted in it completely. This distinction is made clear mainly in very small details. The explanation of the many miserable transport trains full of men unfit for work, which the Soviets were sending back to Germany at that time, was given confidently by these men, who said that many of those travellers had made themselves ill in order to be sent home. This was only true of a few, but for many of those who were unfit because of overwork and lack of food, there was no small temptation to do their little bit in order to stay unfit. By selling one's bread ration and by smoking Makhorka tobacco one could prevent oneself from regaining strength during rest periods. There were many discussions as to whether one ought to do this. Our group decided that the Word which was the source of our life forbade such behaviour, and that anyone who did such a thing raised a barrier between himself and that Word, made it empty, took away its meaning and became unreceptive. So it seemed a senseless thing to do. In May 1947 I became unfit and after my medical examination was placed on the list of those men to be sent home by the next transport. This did not materialise for a long time and meanwhile I recovered. There was a danger that I should have to be examined again before the transport left. My friends warned me, "You're getting too fat! Don't eat any more bread or you will be crossed off the list!" It would probably be a matter of only another week, and it seemed a sensible idea. I wavered, and spoke to Anselm, wondering whether in this case I ought not to give way to reason. He looked at me sadly and said, "But Helmut, surely we agreed to allow ourselves to be guided." Everything was clear to me then, and it became apparent later that God had other plans for me.

Neither here, nor in the neighbouring camps, were services held in public. We did not trouble to ask permission to hold them since we did not want to draw attention to our secret work. But in such a camp, where there are secret agents everywhere, it could not remain hidden, and the anti-Fascist club, here tolerant enough to do nothing off their own bat to stop it, was afraid that the Polit-Commissar would get to hear of it and then blame the club for not being alert in "guarding against revolutionary activities". For that reason the members urged us to ask for official permission. Before we did so, shortly before I left the camp, Anselm was summoned and in a friendly interview was forbidden to work with his groups but was given permission to hold public services, which were then very well attended.

This illustrates how differently the instructions of the Stalin Constitution, allowing religious services to be held by the clergy of both confessions, were carried out by the lower authorities—that is, when they were not determined to sabotage them. The conditions in the camp at Krasnogorsk were probably the most favourable in the whole Soviet Union. The camp lay so to speak on the "great highroad", and all the orders favourable to the prisoners were carried out punctiliously, even generously. For each confession there was a recognised camp chaplain, who, in the days before I became one, was exempt from working. He could call on his fellow-clergymen to represent him, and the sermons were never censored. Thus a small but loyal community gathered in the camp for regular Sunday worship. That this congregation remained relatively small—except for the Christmas services— was no doubt due to the fact that in the camp were a dispro- portionally large number of educated Germans, and to the exceptionately favourable living conditions. They had plenty of other intellectual interests; the restraints of modern rationalistic thought prevent so-called educated men from expecting to get any rule of life from the Christian services; the fear of having a minus sign in the political records was also strong, and if men do not have to work as hard for their living as they did in the labour camps then they, and especially the "educated men", stick unmoved to their foolish prejudices or else they just fall back into their old ways. That was why, when conditions in the labour camps gradually improved, fewer men came to the services; on Sundays there were cinema shows and concerts in the camp, sports and chess tournaments, and if formerly many were unwilling to attend services because they were worn out, then latterly the relative comfort of the Sunday in the camp constituted an even greater hindrance. During the first times of crisis, in the shock of defeat, of their own uncertain fate and that of their relations, men had been shaken out of the primitive or complicated philosophies by means of which they had sought to orient themselves in the labyrinth of problems and to find a meaning in life; what had satisfied them up till now seemed to be folly; searching, questioning, they thought they would try listening to the Christian message. What was to blame for the fact that they often grew tired of listening, that searching did not end in finding, is known only to the Holy Ghost and is hidden in the depths of man's soul, even though there are some obvious reasons, such as the inadequacy of the preacher. As a result of this, the years of imprisonment were wasted for many men. It led to increased opportunity and desire to fill up the days and kill time in an enjoyable way, and the urge to understand the meaning of life, and to give it an eternal meaning, decreased. A man who did not become entangled in these developments and who persevered with listening to the Word, found that for him a window was always open towards Heaven, through which a fresh breeze could waft, so different from the stifling atmosphere in the camp; for him no day was wasted because every day he met his Lord and held converse with His Word, because he felt a responsibility for those men to whom this Word sent him, because he was thus always engaged in some task and was daily having new experiences. For him these years were not wasted but were full of riches.

Anyone who came from a flourishing Christian community at home, and who still cherished any illusions about the Christian character of our nation, had these taken from him during his captivity. The realisation of the extent to which our nation had become de-Christianised, which first came to him during the war years, now became still clearer and more definite. Even after the downfall of the Nazi authorities with their agitation against Christianity, and after the disintegration of so many philosophies which had kept the civil population from taking the Christian message seriously, it was apparent that among the prisoners, who obviously had nothing but this message to help them to fill the emptiness of their lives, there were only a few who grasped at it with a calm and determined desire, and still fewer who had been active members of a Christian community. "Christians are few and far between"—the truth of this saying of Luther's became painfully evident to us during our captivity.

At the same time one could not overlook the fact that while as a national institution the Church had far fewer active members than a serious-minded man would have expected, on the other hand it had a far greater influence than our scepticism would credit. A claim to be the last stronghold of Christian teaching, to fall away from which would aggravate the spiritual sickness of the nation, upholds the traditional position of the Church in the life of the people, and promotes the spread of religious instruction and of Christian education and ethics, however mediocre these may be. We have no cause to console ourselves with this thought or to set too much store by it; but we must realise that thereby the Church is given opportunity to exercise responsibility, and that men are showing their readiness to be appealed to, and also that we shall have to make it our business to see that this readiness is not abused. It was instructive to see how often fellow-prisoners, of whom one would not have expected it, said that the cause of the obvious lack of morals in Soviet life, the sexual depravity of the younger generation, the widespread incidence of thieving, inconsiderateness and untruthfulness lay in the fact that this was "a nation without God". (I have said already that this all-too-ready generalisation was untrue.) Their longing to hear the bells of their own parish churches, and their determination to go to church as soon as they reached home were often expressed in a very moving way. Without overrating this, I should, however, not like to ignore it, in so far as it was an expression of a dim understanding of the significance of the Church for the world, and made clear what the Church's tasks were, as long as it existed as a national Church.

As far as I was concerned, my own experiences were much more favourable than was usual in the camps. The Soviet official can tell instinctively which of the orders issued by higher authorities were meant seriously, and had therefore to be carried out to the letter, and which not. In most of the camps there was no religious freedom to speak of. The plea for permission to hold services was often refused point blank, or else the parson who had asked for it was transferred to another camp; often—with or without explanation—to a punishment camp, or else permission was given, but with such malicious conditions attached to it that it amounted to a refusal. Above all, the sermons had to be handed in in writing, the Polit-commissar corrected them with scornful mockery and malevolent distrust, kept on making alterations, and would allow them to be preached only in this censored form. Thus it was virtually impossible to preach the gospel and in most cases one gave up the struggle. Naturally all this applied particularly to the regime-camps; the experiences which the men in Asbestos had had before I arrived were so discouraging that I did not dare to attempt to get this permission. The message could thus only be passed on secretly.

I have already told you how I came to join the Bible-study circle in Asbestos. It became our spiritual home, especially during the last year with all its troubles, of which I speak later, and in many respects was most instructive. We were a very varied community. When we were all assembled together, as happened once towards the end of my stay there—usually we met in separate groups at different times, in a corner of a hut, among the piles of tree-stumps in the wood-yard, or in some other unobtrusive spot—then the company was as colourful as an oecumenical conference. The original members of the group might be described as Pietists of varying shades; those who belonged to the Established Church were drawn from the Rhenish Pietists, the Evangelical Christians and the Y.M.C.A.— one man came from Fritz von der Ropps' sect, another from a Swabian family of missionaries. There were also two Baptists, a Darbyist, and a doctor who had been converted by the Krawelitz Community, also another man who could not deny that he belonged to the Pentecostal Mission. As the circle grew, the members included several more from the Established Church, a few Roman Catholics, Greek Uniate, a Sweden-borgian, and one who had leanings towards Christian Science.

This was the consequence of one of the most important differences between the life of a civilian and the life of a soldier, particularly a P.O.W. In civilian life everyone can choose his own set of friends and therefore lives in a closed circle. One lives within the walls of this circle into which one has been drawn by similarity of interests or of outlook. What one knows about the others has been determined by prejudice or ignorance; it is impossible to become really intimate. Living as a member of a camp community, a man could not select his companions and yet many intimate friendships were struck up. Thus day by day members of the different strata of society, which normally never came into contact with each other, mingled freely with each other, as did the members of all the various branches of the One Christian Church. Fervent

Methodists who were the sworn enemies of the Roman Church, discovered to their surprise the sincerity of the Roman Catholics' devotion to Christ as well as the earnestness possible in saying the rosary; the Roman Catholic, for the first time in his life, frequently gained insight into the power of an individual life devoted wholly to the Saviour and into the riches won from living converse with the Bible. The differences which had hitherto been so obvious were now no longer important. Anyone who, feeling lonely even in the midst of such a crowd, discovered a friend immersed in a little black book, did not now worry whether it was the Psalms he was reading or the *Volks-Schott*, but was immediately pleased to find someone who shared his beliefs. Thus we were united unexpectedly and irresistibly by our own common worship of the same Lord—an act which had previously been partially or completely forgotten in all the arguments over the differences—before we could turn it all into theological theory. But how could such a mixed crowd live side by side for ever if the sense of unity was to be founded not only on the emotions but also on meetings and acting together?

Because I was a theologian and happened to be on the spot, they had confidently entrusted the leadership to me, although to a thorough-going Pietist the fact of being a professional theologian was not exactly a guarantee of spiritual qualities. They all came to hear one thing, and this one thing had to be talked about. We talked about it whenever we talked about the Bible, which was the bond that united us all. In these unusual circumstances the Bible came to occupy for us exactly the same position as it did for the men of the Reformation; in spite of all the differences that existed among us, we realised that, although we did not discuss the Bible so very frequently, only by constant reference to it could we strengthen, inspire and instruct each other; in this way a Roman Catholic could tell a Baptist, as a minister of the Established Church could a Darbyist, what we needed in order to live. Thus all the amazing things, which the Reformers had dared to assert about the Bible, were proved to be true: that it is not a dead book, but one that is always alive, that it is in fact not really a book at all, but words spoken by ever-present, living voices; that of itself it has the power to make itself plain; that it speaks clearly and distinctly, and that it alone is wholly sufficient to bring men to Christ; that it has the power to draw men together and to overcome the many differences between the widely varying ways of thought and experience. We contented ourselves with this experience and did not try to argue it out polemically. Of necessity we did not set out to convince each other of the rightness of our own views, nor did we attempt to convert others to our own particular brand of faith. In other camps there were conversions to and from Roman Catholicism—our only concern here was that we should all be daily turned to Christ. This negative aim, namely, trying to convert men from the beliefs with which they had grown up, was not allowed to exist alongside the other more positive aim, which had such great practical value in helping us to endure, and to find a meaning in these difficult times. We had to leave each other in peace and cling to whatever convictions divided us particularly. These differences were not hushed up anxiously, but we were forbidden to argue about them during our meetings. They were often discussed in individual conversation, but usually this was done more with the object of making clear to the other the tasks which lay ahead of us, namely to carry the effect of these experiences in our varied community into the sphere of our own Confession, at home as well as here. We had many profitable discussions with the Free Church men, during which they triumphantly pounced on Karl Barth's doubts on the subject of infant baptism.

Thus the communal celebration of the Lord's Supper presented no problems. Whenever this was possible during those years, we were immeasurably strengthened by it. If we had waited until we agreed in our interpretations of this Sacrament, then we should have been traitors to the word of Christ which we studied together in Holy Scripture. On the other hand we usually talked about it together beforehand and told each other how we understood it, and we would read and join in meditating on the New Testament story of the Last Supper. But then we forgot our differences when we went together to the Lord's Table and besought Him to give us just what He wished to give us through this mystery which caused so much dissension.

In Beschiza it was Anselm's initiative which had drawn the groups together. In other camps, too, it was from the clergy that the initial inspiration had come. In Asbestos, however, the circle had been formed although there were no clergymen in the camp. It was no mere chance that here, and elsewhere where there were no ministers of religion, the men who formed the nucleus of the circle were either men of Pietist upbringing or members of the Confessional Church. It seems that the average Christian in the Established Church, even though at home he had been an active member, as also the Roman Catholic, took advantage of these Christian gatherings but did not feel the urge to create them himself, when they were non-existent. Such men contented themselves with living out their faith alone. A Christian who has come from the so-called "Community" or from the Free Churches has had such a powerful experience of Christian community life at home that he will seek it everywhere and cannot live without it. Zinzendorf's statement: "I tolerate no Christianity without a community", is firmly branded on their minds. I learned to appreciate this motive force in the Pietist heritage all the more since, owing to the war and to their captivity, many of them had lost that irritating arrogance of the "converted". In comparing the Evangelical and Roman Catholic members of our circle we could observe that the Catholics have brought with them, as the result of the teaching of their Church, a greater store of "material for contemplation", particularly with the figures of the Saints, whose deeds and words served as models for their own lives; they were also well equipped with set prayers and helpful advice as strong armour in hard times and when faced with difficult decisions. It is also, however, not unjust to say that the active Evangelical Christian is distinguished from the loyal Catholic mainly by his much more personal relationship with Christ Himself, by the depth of his understanding of the Bible, and thus by his personal experience of sin and grace.

In conversations between friends, one frequently heard them expressing the good resolution that they would never during their life-time forget these terrible years. "How humble we will be! We'll never grumble about what we are given to eat and will never despise a piece of dry bread!" I was glad to hear these resolutions, and yet I was rather sceptical about whether it would be possible to carry them out. Only a man who is thankful can be humble, and only the man who is thankful will never forget. But a man is thankful only when there is someone to whom he can express his thanks. To the man who was aware of it from the beginning, or who had learnt to become aware of it there, these years of captivity were not years which gave him the sense of being abandoned; but rather they were a time when he felt the presence of a guiding hand, when he felt that he was cared for even in the most trifling matters, although to the prisoner they certainly did not seem trifling. It is difficult to give illustrations of this, for there are many things which are not outwardly apparent; for example, the way in which external events provide the answer to some spiritual problem, the little bit of help which has just brought me through a difficult time and which was the answer to my prayer, or the unfavourable transfer to a brigade which was just what I needed at a time of crisis in my spiritual life, or even the working of a higher purpose—all these can be recognised only by the man who experiences them.

The same thing is true of the connection between the extent of the help given to men during those years in Russia, or the sudden transition from deep depression to carefree joyfulness so often experienced when we suddenly thought of a line of a hymn or a verse from the Bible, and the prayers which were offered to God for us at home. When after several anxious weeks one man was released from the detention cell, which I shall describe in the next chapter, where he had been questioned, he said, "I think they must have been praying very hard for me at home!"

"Because you have just been released?"

"No, because in there I was not afraid."

Because our life is not determined by blind chance, nor by

the mere law of cause and effect, because we are given personal guidance and are cared for by the Eternal Lord who loves us and suffers for our sakes, therefore we have someone to whom we can offer our thanks. This gratitude alone can keep our memories alive, and only those who are grateful will not forget what they have experienced.

4

HOME AGAIN

WE spent Christmas 1949 sitting in the transport train which
was carrying us westwards, and we trembled before every
obstacle which still threatened us and against which our hopes
might be dashed. Once I said laughingly, "This journey is like
a game we used to play as children. There was a race-course
marked out on a board; we threw dice, and according to the
number thrown we either had to move the counters back or
else could move them on quickly—and so on, backwards and
forwards, till we reached 'home'. I am sure that all the set-backs
which the Russians have thought out for our benefit have
never occurred to the manufacturer of such race games!"

Even in 1946, when a new and unusually definite rumour
about our return flew round, and was later "scotched", we
used to console ourselves with the fact that in any case we had
"been there the longest time", and that the time which lay
before us could not be as long as the time we had already spent
in captivity. Since the beginning of 1949 the certainty of our
repatriation had been proclaimed officially, and even after the
shock of our transfer to Asbestos certainty returned with the
summer. But now an unforseen development had put a damper
on our hopes. If previously we had often said, "Anyone who
has never been in Russia doesn't know what being a prisoner in
Russia means," we now said, "Anyone who hasn't experienced
this last year in Russia has no idea what captivity in Russia is
like." This last year brought with it the possibility that everyone who was still in the hands of the Russians might be condemned as a war-criminal, and this possibility was not a distant
one, but was as close to us as to the probable tenth man in a

regiment in which, because of mutiny, every tenth man was to be shot.

The broad mass of P.O.W.s had not been affected by the following up of war crimes which had gone on hitherto. In the P.O.W. newspaper we read that several members of the Wehrmacht, from the rank of general down to private, had been hanged; we were ordered to give information about any war-crimes which we had witnessed; we discussed all the horrible things that had taken place and the right of the victors to avenge them—but so far it had been a problem which did not really affect us. In Moscow I had already gained an impression of the thoroughness of Russian methods of detection, and I knew that those who became involved in any business of that sort would have little prospect of being freed again, unless they had the rare opportunity of proving their innocence in some spectacular way. In the regime-camp, too, interrogations were the order of the day, since members of the accused army detachments had been brought there, and it might happen that in one day twelve men were arrested and put into the detention cells. Then the news went around the camp, "It's the turn of the X Division today!" They were pitied for a short time but life went on as usual with all its rigours; people didn't worry over the arrested men any more than they did over the dead, and were only too glad that they themselves did not belong to any of these "accused groups" and therefore had at least the prospect of returning home still unaccused. For it seemed to us that they were still unearthing crimes committed by individuals, and that, in principle anyway, nobody but the man directly responsible for a crime was sought for and condemned.

In the summer of 1949 things suddenly changed. A large hut was cleared out and cleaned; another was cleaned and its windows were shuttered, and a group of thirty-five commissars and interpreters moved in. Interrogations on a large scale began. Every day several dozen men did not go to work, and every evening a number of them were still sitting in the locked hut or detention cell. Incurable optimists like myself were always of the opinion that it was merely a matter of a final combing-out so that when everyone was set free, no war criminal could slip through the net. Only gradually did we realise from the accounts of those who were interrogated and of those set free from detention what all this really meant: namely, that they were not trying to find war criminals, but to brand as many men as possible as criminals. In Germany, so much has become known about this meanwhile, that I can and must deal briefly with this subject.

Anyone who lived through those months gained deep insight into justice under a totalitarian system, a picture unexpected only to one who, like me, found it so hard to accept the reality of his own experience that in theory humane principles could be carried out in such a way that they were degraded into a complete disregard for mankind, and that theory was unable to act as a brake. Here all this was so hard to grasp because, in spite of everything that we had so far been told about the brutality and total indifference of Soviet justice, we could still see a reason for it, a reason which was readily produced by the Communists who defended it. The preservation of this first socialist country, which was surrounded by other hostile powers, demanded ruthless measures against all those who opposed it, and the fact that they were aiming at the future happiness of mankind justified this present rigorous action. Even though one must contest this idea vigorously, it was at least a sensible reason which to all appearances overcame the contradiction between theoretical humanity and practical inhumanity, but no such grounds were apparent for the mass-condemnation of German (and Japanese) P.O.W.s. We puzzled over it a great deal and none of our ideas about their motives would hold water: it was not that they were interested in manpower (the numbers were not big enough, since only about seventy to a hundred thousand Germans were concerned), nor in the retaining of people who in the event of another war might be important to their opponents (since among the condemned there were not only General Headquarters staff, and those who could speak Russian, but ordinary German soldiers), nor in the satisfying of the desire for vengeance on the part of their own nation, since five years after the war was too late to do this and the Russian people had not been told about it any-way. The most likely theory was that it was a terrorist measure to frighten Germans and soldiers of other armies which might be enemies of the future, who might in this way be warned of what would be in store for them. Whatever the reasons may have been, in the summer of 1949 this was done all over the Soviet Union and we had those thirty-five commissars in our camp until the autumn. Many depositions were taken which seemed to be of use to the prosecutors, and in the autumn judgments were pronounced. Just as we were breathing freely again, a fresh wave of interrogations began on December 7th, directed against those who had survived previous ones, which, as in Asbestos for example, were rushed through by seventy commissars—and once again there were many victims. At the end of January 1950 interrogations and condemnations suddenly came to an end and a large number of those who had been accused, and even many who had been condemned, were released and sent home by the last transport trains. That shows clearly enough that all this was directed by those at the top, and that the second spate of interrogations took place because during the first lot they had not fulfilled their quota of con-demnations. Here then was a system of justice which was commanded by those at the top to impose a certain number of sentences. If a Soviet judge, who according to orders had con-demned a Kulak, a Trotskyist, or someone or other who had uttered a careless remark, was able to soothe his conscience—if it made itself felt—by believing that he was dealing with a class-enemy or a counter-revolutionary, then he was able to carry out his instructions with regard to the unhappy P.O.W. only if he did not question or wonder at these orders—unless he set his mind at rest by believing that at bottom all German P.O.W.s were worthy of the same sentence as "Fascist infiltrators".

A German Communist, who today justifies this crime com-mitted by Stalinism, and against his better judgment calls the P.O.W.s still held in Russia war-criminals, cannot now salve his conscience, but has to hide his disgrace under a veil of cynicism. The only strange thing was that they still continued to look for excuses for their condemnations. If they had numbered the men off, and killed off every fifth man, then the effect as far as justice was concerned would be the same. Obviously they wanted to preserve an appearance of justice, and so people were interrogated, locked-up, flogged, questioned again, until a statement had been signed. Why then did these prisoners sign these confessions and not question everything in them, since they knew what such confessions would mean for them? The answer is simple; often nothing was confessed, but often only seemingly harmless things had been admitted and as soon as the statement had been signed, that was sufficient. With many, the office they had held was enough: they were S.S. officers, members of the Schill Unit or other special detachments, commandants or guards in P.O.W. camps, members of the defence forces—these facts alone signed their death warrants. Others, apparently, were only asked about their officers; if they admitted that these officers had given orders to burn a house, to reap a field of corn as fodder for their horses, or to blow up a bridge, then came questions about their own part in the affair, and before they knew that they were accusing themselves, they had fallen into the trap. A grotesque enlarging of the conception of a "war crime", made the slightest action of self-interest, such as grazing a horse in a Russian meadow, into a crime. Serious war crimes could hardly be discovered by this method; those who were guilty of them had already either been executed or else had been more careful than those who had declared their innocence. Now the fruits of years of spying were becoming apparent: quite harmless or carelessly narrated experiences had been reported and now served as a bait. Once, earlier on, I had told my work-mates how during the war I was in a burning house in the Ukraine, and had killed rabbits in their holes with small hand-grenades; now all my brigade anxiously awaited to see if I would be fetched away; nothing happened, but their anxiety was not unreasonable, since similar stories had had fateful results for many people.

Now, too, came the results of the great expiation drive which had been started in the camps of 1945–46. The clubs had ordered everyone to give accounts of war-crimes they had experienced at meetings of the whole camp, and to clear themselves by their confession as well as to incriminate others. Honest remorse over their crimes was expressed by members of the Wehrmacht, and the worst denunciations were given free rein. Now, however, years later, those who had formerly accused others were questioned about their own part in what they had reported, and even if they had only been lookers-on, powerless to do anything, this cost them their lives.

Another strange thing was the difference between the methods of the N.K.V.D. which carried out the preliminary investigations, and ordinary legal procedure. The N.K.V.D. was not too particular in its methods, though I only heard after my return home, from members of other camps, about Gestapo-like torture, while I personally had only observed the "simpler" methods of obtaining information, such as flogging, being locked-up in a freezing-cold cell, and so on—though these were often carried out quite brutally. When the statement was signed and the accused came before the court, he mostly came into an atmosphere of strictly correct behaviour. In one case it happened that the accused swore that the confessions had been forced from them by flogging; the judge immediately tore up the statement, took as evidence what they declared there and then, and pronounced them innocent. In another case, the N.K.V.D. commissar had omitted from the statement, which was written in Russian and could therefore not be checked by the man who signed it, the fact that a bridge had been blown up not during the retreat but during an actual battle; this came to light at the trial and the accused were declared innocent. These were rare exceptions, which were probably due to the character of individual judges; in most cases the trial was rushed through, and the accused—for the counsel for the defence in the Soviet Law-Courts is the most insignificant figure and takes good care not to give an independent judgment —were too helpless and knew too little about legal proceedings to be able to see their chance and take it. In the camp at Sverdlovsk in which I spent my last few weeks two huts were separated from the rest by a particularly high fence, with watch-towers and searchlights as bright as day; all the accused men from the nearby camps were brought there to be dealt with by the Sverdlovsk court-martial, and with their usual grim humour the Germans called this fenced-off part the "Eastern Zone", although it lay on the west side of the camp. During the month of November, 650 German P.O.W.s came before this court, and at most ten were declared innocent. The sentences of the others varied from between seven to twenty or twenty-five years.

This fresh danger lay like a nightmare over the camp. Our life, which had improved outwardly, was completely altered. All at once our return home, which we had believed to be so near at hand, seemed more uncertain than ever. Impotent with rage we saw our friends behind the barred windows of the special hut, our dearest friends disappeared, people whom we knew well and whose innocence we would have been willing to prove by putting our hands into the fire, were condemned to a lingering death in Siberia. Every day somebody might be struck down. When I met friends from other camps in the train going home, men whom I had not seen for months, they seemed to have aged terribly. For anyone who experienced those weeks in Asbestos, the memory of this dreadful time is bound up with the name of Max Z. He was an ordinary work-man from Berlin, an elderly man in his fifties beloved by all for his good nature, who helped in the kitchen at nights. During the war he had been a driver for the commander of a rifle-battalion and now he was being urged repeatedly in interroga-tions to accuse this commander. He had respected him, knew nothing criminal, persisted in speaking the truth in spite of all threats, and was driven to such desperation that one night he tried to kill himself by jumping into a large copper in the kitchen which was full of boiling water. He just had the strength to cover himself with the lid, but then the others noticed him and dragged him out. He was taken to the hospital with horrible burns all over his body. The whole affair was very embarrassing for the Russians and they ordered the sickroom door to be kept locked. Unfortunately, I allowed myself to be deterred from going to see him, and only when a few days had elapsed did I force my way in to see him. He lay naked on the bed, unconscious, covered with huge black marks, the death-rattle in his throat. Although the German and Russian doctors did all they could, his condition was hopeless. I was distressed because I had not come soon enough to find him still conscious, knelt down and said the Lord's Prayer in an effort to reach his soul. Then the orderly who had been looking after him, a P.O.W. not known to me, said behind me, "He won't understand now, but I have often prayed with him and he was helped by it." Anyone who knows how rare it is to find a man who prays among German medical orderlies, will understand that this seemed a miracle to me. (He was an elderly farmer from East Pomerania, whose great piety comforted me for the second time when I had to leave him behind in December, in danger of being condemned; in the spring of 1950 he was repatriated, in one of the last groups.) Max Z. died the next day and the interrogations continued.

During those weeks we discovered a standard by which to measure everything that was said about human life. I resolved that, schooled by these experiences, I would re-read Boethius' *Consolation of Philosophy* when I got home. This is a real witness of self-consolation, not conceived at home in a study but in just such a troubled state of mind as I was in. But what I remembered about it was the resignation, so worthy of respect, of the man who fundamentally has no consolation. The same resignation I saw everywhere around me in varying degrees. Anyone who saw before him a long period in a punishment camp, which he could hardly hope to survive unless he were released before the sentence was completed, has lost everything which gave meaning to his life, even to his survival in captivity. The philosophies which had hitherto seemed all-sufficient—nationalist, naturalistic or idealistic—had collapsed and nothing but leaden resignation was left. What can one say to such people? The standard of values against which their various philosophies had broken down was also the standard by which to measure what we had to say to them, what the imprisoned members of our Bible-study circle said to each other in the interrogation hut, and what we would perhaps have to tell ourselves tomorrow even more urgently than was necessary today. The Cross of Christ witnessed to the fact that the Gospel stood the test even in the darkest hour. But would our preaching of the Gospel stand the test? Once already in my lifetime this criterion by which a preacher must measure his preaching had presented itself to me in an unforgettable way. After the beginning of the war the German Jews were no longer allowed to emigrate and were deported to Poland. When we realised that these deportations meant death—and what a death!—then the only standards for our preaching were set up in the light of whether our message had any value to uphold these people condemned to such a terrible death. The news that came to us from Poland which confirmed that it had sustained them was the strongest armour for keeping us going in our own captivity. We could, and had to, grasp at this in what we had to say to our friends or to ourselves. Now the Gospel proved to be the light which sheds its brightness on even the darkest places, that is, which gives a meaning even to the fearful meaninglessness of such a fate. To anyone who was not reached by this light, there remained only stoical or dull resignation or the grasping at a vague hope, or even at the desperate hope of a war, in which case the P.O.W.s would probably be the most likely victims themselves. The man, however, who was able while in this state to listen to the Gospel with all his heart, found that it promised to reveal to him the full meaning of life. It did so by showing that our time on earth was merely a preparation for eternal life (we realised now how foolish those men were who had seen in this promise nothing but the Christians' attempt to escape from this world!); it promised the perpetual presence of the Word of God, and held out the prospect of practical tasks to perform, by reminding us of those fellow-sufferers, who were in need of help; finally it showed that even a man wasting away his lonely existence in a dungeon, would always, until he drew his dying breath, be given the strength to praise God and in so doing find the meaning in every hour. This promise will be kept, because it is the Gospel of the Cross and of the Resurrection.

These interrogations were one of the first rocks against which our hopes might be dashed. A second one appeared on the horizon shortly afterwards. Almost from the first, the doctors carrying out the health inspections had shown a strange interest in the underside of our left upper arms. Every member of the S.S. had a sign indicating his blood-group tattooed on his arm, and it was these marks that the doctors were looking for in order to discover whether there were any of the S.S. still concealed among us. When this news was passed round many of those to whom it applied tried to get rid of their tattoo marks. For lack of any other means they tried using knives, lighted cigarettes, and so on (later, experts recommended subcutaneous injections of mare's milk to make the marks disappear without leaving any traces). But then everyone who had any kind of scar in that particular place came under the suspicion of having been in the S.S., of having concealed the fact and therefore of still having some evil deeds on their conscience. Everyone who had not a chance wound or a scar left by one of the boils from which we suffered so frequently during our captivity was overjoyed. I was one of these lucky ones. This had been confirmed and noted down innumerable times already. But Soviet lists are a law unto themselves. I can't tell you how many times we had to fill in the forms all about ourselves. At first all this paper warfare seemed to me to have its origins in a superstitious belief in lists; but gradually I realised that on the contrary it arose from a puzzling distrust of lists: if a list has been closed then it can no longer be relied on, and a new list must be made out in all haste. What is noted in the lists is as transitory as if it had been traced in the sand. Therefore they could never refer to what was put down in previous lists, and it was of no avail to me that the untouched, smooth skin of my upper arm had already been noted down many times. For all of a sudden I found that I had a scar.

At the beginning of August 1949 all those at Asbestos with scars were transferred to the camp at Sverdlovsk which I have already mentioned, which had been nicknamed "the camp for scars". From this fact we could deduce that, firstly, for the sake of security they were treating everyone with a scar as though he were an S.S. man, and secondly that they had no intention of releasing the S.S. yet, since otherwise they would not be making such a fuss about these scars. So a man without a smooth upper arm seemed almost as deserving of pity as those who had got into the clutches of the "interrogation-mill". At that time I was working in a saw-mill with a civilian escort; naked to the waist, we hauled tree-trunks and often returned covered with scratches. One evening, just after a "scar transport" had left, I noticed a new scratch on the under side of my upper arm, but consoled myself with the thought that it would heal up as the other scratches on my chest and hands had done—and anyway the N.K.V.D. already had enough information about me to know that I was not in the S.S.! In September, the news was brought to our "outside-duty" group in Barkhenovo, who were certain of being sent home, about how carefully and relentlessly people with scars were being looked for among those who remained to be sent home. I looked anxiously at my arm and found a lovely scar, just the right size and in the right spot. The depression which descended upon me at that moment I could not have wished on my worst enemy! At least there would be a vexatious postponement to give them time to review my particulars—and that was time enough to let me be engulfed by the waves of interrogation which had so far left me alone.

At first, however, everything seemed to be all right. A camp commission, consisting of two officers and a woman doctor, came for the purpose of examining our arms again. (Soviet commissions are a clear indication of how this system had developed into a bureaucracy; there are separate commissions for everything, each one consisting of several people, and their expenses must cost the Soviet tax-payer enormous sums of money!) Naked to the waist and with arms raised, we came one by one into the inspection room. Magnifying glass and surgical spirit revealed the slightest suspicious marks, and anyone with even a white mark on his arm was set apart. There were five unfortunate men who had to return to Asbestos, deeply depressed. When it was my turn, one of the officers, a young Armenian commissar who had worked on the cases of us "Muscovites" in Asbestos, looked at my armpit, and said, "Kharosh" ("Good"), the doctor cast a perfunctory glance at it—and I had passed the test! When I went out, I couldn't grasp it. Had a miracle happened? Had their eyes been "holden"? Or did they just not want to see it? Had special instructions been issued for my release? The question was unanswerable!

My joy did not last long. We were taken to Sverdlovsk from which our train was to leave, and to our horror we had to pass through that "camp of scars" in order to be tested again. When it was my turn, in a trice the worst happened and my scar showed up clearly in the glare of the searchlight which was directed on to my arm, and I was taken on one side and when the others all went through the open gate of the camp to the station, I was lying on a bunk in the deserted hut, staring at the ceiling. When my friends had sorrowfully said goodbye to me, I called out to them, "It's better for me than for one of you, I can stand it better!" and they understood what I meant by that. We all knew the terrible despair which used to take a hold on those left behind in such circumstances and which drove them to the brink of suicide. What must have seemed to them devilish bad luck, I regarded differently. It was too improbable that mere "chance" had given me a wound in that unusual place just during those very weeks and had prevented it from healing properly. I was not to go home yet; I needed to stay here for a bit longer. It had been only too clear to me during the past weeks of spiritual weakness, of sudden temptation through the years, long arguments with the materialistic view of life, and the obsession with hopes of returning home, that further cleansing was needful, if I was to take home with me all that the school of captivity should have taught me. And I had to think again of those whom we, burning with the hope of our own return, had left behind with pity, and yet shrugging our shoulders: those who remained and who now surrounded me in this camp. There were 250 men here with scars and one can imagine the awful feelings with which they had watched the homeward-bound prisoners, since all kinds of dreadful possibilities threatened them again. How could I have hoped so firmly to return home during the previous weeks without wondering whether my presence was not more necessary here?

The next day I received a sign that this was true. A man who had known me earlier on, came and asked me to speak to the man in the next bunk to him, who was in rather a bad way. I found an elderly South German Roman Catholic, whose thigh-bone had become inflamed as a result of a nasty wound; on account of this he had been taken off one home transport list after the other, he was threatened with an amputation, and he was lying there despondently; missal and New Testament no longer had any message for him. Here another little group assembled, as varied as the one in Asbestos. I remember with especial pleasure the summer evenings when I discussed our occasional Sunday Mass with a Franciscan Brother who knew the Bible well, and a Roman Catholic from the Ermland district of East Prussia—at a time when we were on night duty in the kitchen.

After having done various kinds of work, I was at the moment with a brigade doing night shift at the saw-mill. The winter had set in with all the violence usual in the Urals; already we were working in a temperature of 60° below freezing-point. Every night we returned to the camp at 2 a.m. and watched the stormy sky. First of all long blue lines swung to and fro in the beams of the searchlight, then they united to form a whole, the colour changed to light blue and red, until finally the whole of the northern sky was full of magic lights which changed colour incessantly. These were the heralds of Aurora Borealis. "You can be sure that our transport will leave soon," said one man, who like most P.O.W.s was constantly on the look-out for good omens. When we got back to the camp, we found that they had been waiting for us, and we were sent at once to the baths to wash and get new clothes: tomorrow at midday the transport is going and we are all on it! So the rumour was true that they had now decided to release all those with the scars after all.

Now we came to understand what we had observed in those who left on previous transport trains—they had never shown their joy. No one dared to give way to rejoicing and everyone was very reserved in expressing emotion. We knew how many had been crossed off the list at the last moment, many too had been taken off the train at Brest; many of us had already suffered disappointment more than once. One of my friends had been recalled no less than seven times, and had been taken off the train twice. Thus in every heart, joy and fear waged an indeterminate battle. When at noon next day we went to the dining-room for our last meal there, I was summoned to the office. The camp leader was there; "Ah, Gollwitzer, I have to tell you that unfortunately your name has been crossed off the list!" Why? Nobody knew. The same thing happened to another man who had been in the auxiliary police. The Russian camp commandant told us something about there not being enough seats on the train, and that we should be going on the next one. That was obviously a lie of embarrassment. "In the Soviet Union years can pass by between two transport trains," we replied bitterly, and stared at the ceiling of the deserted hut once again, our heads propped up on our arms.

It was the 5th of December. On the 7th, as we quickly learnt, a fresh horde of commissars had arrived in Asbestos for interrogations; it would be our turn again soon. It was clear to me that there was at least some purpose behind all these disappointments, and that something more was in store for me. They would try on the same pressure as they had used for my persuasion in Krasnogorsk, and refusal would bring with it very serious consequences. When at 8 p.m. my brigade leader informed me that the next day I was to go to the Staff H.Q. for interrogation, and that therefore I need not go to work, I knew that I was to undergo a final test. During the night I had tried to think things over. What I had already experienced and seen warned me not to hold out even my little finger, nor to play any cunning tricks with the idea of deceiving my oppressors. Frankness alone was possible, cost what it might, and even if it cost me my return home, then there remained for me meaning and divine help and duties to perform among the condemned, as there had been during the past weeks. Yet an invisible hand was clamped round my throat, stifling me with the thought that death would be a welcome release. In the morning, a friend of mine who belonged to our circle and who was a Christian Scientist, came to see me on his way to work. He had a premonition of what I was about to go through, and opened the Bible at the fourth chapter of the First Epistle of

John, at those verses which are the source of Mary Baker-Eddy's teaching, but which now he could read to me imbued with the power of a divine messenger, "God is love . . . there is no fear in love; but perfect love casteth out fear".

Thus armoured, I was led in the afternoon to the staff H.Q. Six others had been summoned also—but when I was taken into a special room with padded double-doors, I quickly realised that they were only there as a blind and would have to endure several anxious hours. High officials took special pains with me, a white-haired general, with a face which inspired confidence, spoke to me in a fatherly voice, as though he were admonishing his son to choose the right way, and put before me the choice of either becoming one of the condemned or of supporting the "democratic forces" in Germany. They all spoke only in a shame-faced, round-about way. When I first would not understand and then remained adamant, their tone became more unfriendly. Finally they declared that I had sealed my own fate, and a widespread whispered conversation took place in a corner. I sat there in silence, and felt only relief because it was all over; what was still to come could no longer frighten me. Then the woman interpreter came over to me and said, "You will travel home on the next transport train. The General wishes to inform you that you should be grateful to the Soviet Union. You may go."

Downstairs the others were waiting for me; they were puzzled at only having been asked a few perfunctory questions. I could not explain anything, walking dumbly beside them while they expressed their conjectures, saying over to myself some verses from Paul Gerhardt's morning hymn, which suddenly came into my mind:

> *This day, when darkest shadows lay all around my path*
> *Satan sought to win me, but God hath triumphed o'er him.*
> *Thou hast said, "My child, be still, and fear not this deceiver!*
> *Let nothing make thee fearful, for thou shalt see the sun!"*
> *Thy word has been fulfilled, for I can see the light,*
> *I am refreshed and free from care, safe beneath thy wings.*

The next few days brought with them another great pleasure.

We had known for a long time that people at home could now send small parcels to the P.O.W.s in Russia. A few years before, only a few lucky ones had got parcels from abroad, on which they had to pay a high duty, although the Austrians had been getting them for some time. Now the Eastern Zone newspapers had announced that we should get parcels free of duty, and in other camps some had been distributed already. In the headquarters of our camp lay a huge pile of parcels, but the authorities seemed to be waiting until we had all gone so that they could add them to their own stores. This suspicion was not, however, entirely justified. Certainly most of the addressees were no longer there, but at any rate the parcels were given out before the camp was closed. Those who were still left got theirs and I got two at once. The contents of the parcels which could not be delivered were to be distributed among the best brigades. The club members, to whom the task had been entrusted, realised that this Soviet method of distribution, namely, giving more to those who worked hard and leaving nothing for those who did not do so well, would arouse the greatest indignation in the camp. So they decided to by-pass the Soviet instructions. The best worker in each brigade was to be given everything as a formality, but then he was to share it out among the other members of the brigade. Together with a member of the club I was given the task of unpacking the parcels and of sorting the contents out into equal piles for all the brigades. The room in which we were doing this soon looked like a warehouse; with deep emotion we touched the things we had not seen for years, and we saw to our astonishment all that was available in Western Germany, contrary to the information in the newspapers we could get hold of. We enjoyed seeing the astonishment of the Russian camp officers who were wandering around like children, admiring these treasures which they could not look at and handle enough: the packets of chocolate and tobacco, the cartons of cream and cheese, the propelling pencils and the fruit tarts. These were the products of capitalist countries, we told them, but at home they could be bought by the man-in-the-street, as we proved by telling who had sent the parcels. The final distribution led to quite a feast. Our palates savoured these unwonted pleasures; never again will anything taste as sweet as did those precious things we had for so long gone without.

On December 15th the transport train left and the camp was closed. About one hundred and fifty men left; fifty remained behind, of whom some returned home in the spring of 1950. The selecting of these latter was carried out with that indifferent brutality to which we had grown accustomed; some were told at once they were not on the list, others were crossed off again, and when we finally saw the gate of the camp standing wide open as we had so often seen in our dreams, it transpired that in the meantime varying lists had been found, and that some names were not on all of them. So the unfortunate owners of these names had to fall out to the left, called out their home addresses to us and watched us, their faces deathly pale, as we marched out with all the joy in our hearts once again damped down.

Two things occupied our minds during those days, while the train was rolling westwards: the calculation of whether we should be home in time for Christmas, and the observation that even now we could not rejoice wholeheartedly. This was the railway train round which we had woven our thoughts for years; we had often tried to picture how we should feel when we were sitting in it—and now we felt quite differently. After some time, a few people began to sing but only spasmodically. Most of all it was the long halts which strained our nerves; if the train stopped for a long time, as it often did, our hearts sank; conversation ceased and gave way to dull brooding. Finally one of the men in our carriage remembered how, long ago, I used to tell stories, and begged me to do so again; so throughout the journey, as soon as the train stopped, I told one of the many stories in my repertoire. How right we were to be anxious was revealed in Brest and again in the Horn barracks in Frankfurt an der Oder; at both of these towns some men were kept back, and our joy at being able to travel on was mingled with the bitter sorrow at the fate of such good and unforgettable companions.

The train had moved too slowly and had stopped too many

times. On Christmas Eve, instead of being at home, we were still in Brest. I went from carriage to carriage, wherever I had been invited, celebrating Christmas Eve with my friends by singing the well-known carols, by reading the Gospel for Christmas Day and by saying a few words about the past and the future, remembering especially those whom we had had to leave behind. One of these who was released in the spring of 1950 wrote to me, describing how they had spent that evening. "For ten days we had been sitting and lying on our wooden bunks in a dark underground cellar. Every day between thirty and thirty-five men were taken to the tribunal in the town. Not one has been seen again. Every evening between 8.0 p.m. and 11.0 p.m. the Mongolian-looking guard comes in and spells out the names of those next on the list. We have forgotten what the sun looks like and have exhausted all that we can say to each other. 'Today is Christmas Eve,' comes a quiet fearful whisper all of a sudden, we all hear it. Someone rummaged in his pocket and produced a candle which he divided into four, 'Can anyone tell the Christmas story?' 'We ought at least to sing a carol!' We all remained silent, and the silence was terrible. We all felt as though we wanted to scream so as not to hear the guard coming in. But surely he wouldn't come that day, surely there are some human beings here and not just soulless machines. Then the door squeaked and we heard twenty-one names read out. In a few minutes they were ready to go. The door shut. Thirty-nine men were left; we pressed our heads against the wood of the bunks. I tried to pray and fell asleep exhausted."

In Brest, after we had been searched thoroughly, we were transferred to what seemed to us to be small goods-wagons, on to a line with the German gauge. The new train was driven by German railwaymen to whom we were a common sight but who to us were unusual and exciting. During our conversations with them, as with the people in Poland, we were struck by their subdued and uncommunicative manner, their sudden signs and silences, which are the characteristics of life under a tyranny. After we had passed through the deserted, devastated area east of the Oder, we were greeted in the station at

Frankfurt by the familiar notices, placards and coloured lights praising Stalin, the Soviet Union which was the bulwark of peace, and the democratic forces in Germany and all over the world; we had seen them all before in all the camps we had been in. This sight had the effect of creating a tangible barrier among us: those whose homes were in the Eastern Zone grew silent and realised that they had only exchanged a short length of barbed wire fence for a longer one; enviously they looked at us, who were to travel on westwards, and when we said good-bye we felt once more as though we were leaving friends behind in captivity.

The Horn barracks in Frankfurt are occupied by the Red Army, and here our papers were checked and we were handed over to the German authorities who then welcomed us to the dispersal camp at Gronefelde with speeches which we already knew off by heart. Only one speaker made us think, and he made me remember the long period of development which I had gone through myself. He was an old German Communist, who, after long imprisonment in a concentration camp, was an active member of the trade unions in the Eastern Zone; he told us about the reconstruction in the "German Democratic Republic", and soberly, earnestly, without "white-washing", gave an account of the economic imperfections and difficulties in his own words, which were obviously the expression of his own convictions. When we thought of the preceding speakers, with all the propaganda which they had churned out, we saw in this speaker the power of the former militant Marxism, its ideals and its ethics. There was no question, however, as to which of these three men had the most severe disappointments coming to them, which of them were already suffering from disillusionment, which would be broken on the wheel in the event of a conflict: it would certainly not be those tractable propagandists, but rather this honest man who still meant what he said and who did not want to terrorise but to convince us.

While we were going from the barracks to Gronefelde, an old friend said to me, "Now the cold hand is no longer holding us by the scruff of our necks!" "It has indeed let go," I replied, "but may even yet grasp us again!" Thus even on our journey through the Zone our conversations were subdued and cautious. In Frankfurt we dashed up to the first civilians we saw and began to question them, and were then taken aback by their warning gestures: there were spies everywhere and we had better not ask them so many questions. Then children came up to our carriages, begged for bread, and told us the latest Hennecke jokes. Their way of talking was cheeky and outspoken, their jokes bordered on the obscene, and we, though not all that soft-spoken, watched them dubiously and shook our heads; all this was so unlike the wonderful pictures we had made for ourselves of our homeland, people's way of talking seemed so much harder than it was in our memories. What our reason had told us up to now, our hearts began to feel too; this was not the paradise we had dreamed of, but a ruined country and a sick nation were welcoming us home to share their troubles. So we handed the bread ration, which we had been given in Frankfurt, to the children, the station workmen and the thin women in their patched clothes who came to the train over the barriers in the station, and we wondered anxiously how we should find things at home.

After the train had crossed the Bavarian frontier, I said to my friend, "Now the cold hand cannot reach us, the Iron Curtain is between us." Then we were standing in front of the gate of the American dispersal camp at Hof-Moschendorf. The German camp leader welcomed us and gave us our first instructions: we were to give all our particulars in the office, the real ones of course, which meant that those who had up to now been sailing under false colours no longer needed to do so, "For now you are in a world where justice and freedom are supreme!" When he said this, all of a sudden a storm of rejoicing broke out among the hundreds of men; although that warning to give our real names did not apply to many of us (one of my former brigade leaders, a trusted friend of the S.S. who was standing next to me, told me his name, which he had concealed for years), it was a sign that barbed wire had disappeared; our long suppressed joy surged forth, we embraced each other and for the first time we laughed as we marched into the camp. It was New Year's Eve, 1949.

While writing these pages, I experienced the same sensation as I felt when I used to lie on my bunk in the evenings and with closed eyes would think of old times: I saw myself going through the Schwarzer Grund in Dahlem, swimming in Lake Constance, or looking down on to the Lake of Zürich from Bergli; I was exploring a bookshop or attending a conference. "Then" and "there" seemed so vivid, so far removed from the bitterness of the present, that I could have touched the water and the books with my hand, except that a wall of glass formed a barrier, the glass wall of "now". What do all these words mean, "now", "then", "there", "here"? What does it mean when I say that I "was" the man whom I saw swimming and looking so closely at the books, and that I "am" the man whom I see lying here on the bunk in the patched and worn jacket? What kind of glass wall is this, that divides the past from the present, which can yet touch each other within me, since I still am both the "then" and the "now", the former no less than the latter? What is time? What is the meaning of past and present? What does our existence in time mean?

So once again—I am writing at a table in a friendly room, when I look up my gaze falls on many beautiful things, I can stand up and go for a walk, I can plan a journey, I am a free man. At the same time, however, I am back in that hut, I feel the persistent pressure in my breast and the gnawing homesickness, and looking through the window I see the barbed wire and the sentry yawning on the watch-tower. How is it that formerly I was the one and now am the other? What do "was" and "am" really signify? There are others, who have grown dear to me and of whom I think often during the day, for whom today is their "now" just as for me today is "then"; and because for them it is still the present, so it can never really be the past for me—if for them, as we hope, it will some day be the past, then for many others it will still be the present; and how do we know what will become the present for us and whether we shall once more stare through bars and barbed wire out into unobtainable freedom, when the "now" of today has become the "then" of the past! What kind of hieroglyphics are these, which we accept daily with so much certainty as though they were not riddles and secrets, and by means of which we believe that we know all about what we are and what we experience? "For we are but of yesterday, and know nothing", it is written in the Book of Job. These words have a much deeper meaning than we are always willing to admit. God alone knows what time really is, and thus He knows all about our "then" and "now" and "I" in both past and present. Not until we see Him face to face shall we see our life face to face, and no longer think of it as "in a glass darkly", in "signs and symbols". Then the glass wall will fall and we shall see how everything, "then" and "now", falls into place, and what we were in both.

In this life, however, while we still have to bring hiero-glyphics and symbols to our aid and cannot grasp what our existence really is, while we stumble blindly in an enigmatic world of yesterday, today and tomorrow, we are given Bread to sustain us in the midst of all these riddles, and a Light to guide our feet step by step through the riddle. It is worth while seeking for that Light and partaking of that Bread. It is the only thing which is worth while.

5

CHRISTMAS
1945-48

When they had eaten the thin soup every evening, they would sit for a while on their bunks before crawling under the blankets. If one of you had been able to become invisible and walk through the huts, this picture would seem to be the saddest and most characteristic of life in a P.O.W. camp: in the dim light of a few miserable lamps you would see the thin faces of the men who stared motionless in front of them, often with closed eyes, the dreamy figures leaning silently against the posts of the bunks, each one as though standing alone before the sorrow of the whole world. But if you had been able to see inside these men you would have been astonished to learn that these were the happiest moments of their miserable years: outward things vanished, the ugly, smoke-blackened walls, the dirty coats lying on the bunks, disappeared, and in spirit we were at home. We walked along the street, pressed the bell, which we saw clearly before our eyes, the familiar, brown-painted door opened, and we were embraced by those people who were the dearest in all the world; then they led us into the room, the Christmas tree stood there, just as it always did, and we could choose the carol which everyone was to sing. Evening after evening the dream was repeated and nobody grew tired of it, least of all at Christmastime during the worst years of captivity.

They were working days like the others. There was a festive meal according to our standards, only because we had saved some of our meagre ration; whenever we could we had decorated the hut with fir branches, and we had even managed to get hold of a few candles for the little Christmas tree, on which hung a few stars with silver paper stuck on them—it was a mystery where this could have come from in the wilderness! All this was not carried out without some opposition. The Russian camp leader had given his permission, but some of the prisoners objected loudly and even begged me to forgo every reminder of Christmas; "Only by not thinking about it— that's the only way I can endure it; if you celebrate I shan't be able to stand it and I shall hang myself. . . ."

He did not hang himself; not because at the decisive moment he was too cowardly but because he had seen the Christmas Light which shines in the darkness. Not "not to think about it", but rather to think about it with all one's might—that was the lesson that Christmas Eve taught us. But what exactly were we to think about? To immerse oneself in that dream could not of itself bring salvation. Homesickness filled our hearts too bitterly in those days. But when we heard the Christmas Gospel and discussed it, a miraculous light seemed to have been turned on; "God hath not forgotten those who sat in darkness." On earth there was no power that could or would help us. Surrounded by vast forests, we were forgotten and abandoned. We hardly dared to hope that things would ever be different, and yet we could not stop hoping. Was it that someone was thinking of us and knew about us, someone stronger even than Stalin and the N.K.V.D.?

"For behold, I bring you tidings of great joy!" We had written Christmas Greetings on small, smooth pieces of wood —for paper was rare here; at the head of my bunk was one on which a friend had painted the words in John 14. 19, since he had often heard me quote it in my sermons: "Because I live, ye shall live also." We had been deprived of everything that made life worth living, and now here were written words which said that life itself would not be taken from us. Whether repatriation lay in store for us, or a grave in the frozen earth of Russia—and so many of us were to be laid in it that winter—this hard road led to life; that was certain because Christmas had a meaning;

that at least could not be taken from us, and made us breath a sigh of relief.

Earlier on we had scoffed at the familiar Christmas carols and their sugary sentimentality. It cannot be denied that the old Reformation hymns preached the message of Christmas more powerfully than those often-sung carols, *Silent Night* and *O du Fröhliche*. But now I asked them to overlook their prejudices, and I was glad that at least they have survived as the common possession of our nation. Not only because, now all at once, as we sang them, they transformed the ugliness of the barracks and conjured up pictures of home, and drew into the atmosphere of Christmas those who had so bitterly resisted it. Who could have despised this "atmosphere" which was as soothing as a mother's hand to these men whose hearts had been hardened because they had experienced nothing but hardness? But these carols did not only bring "atmosphere", they also contained the great message: "Christ our Saviour is born"—"to a world forlorn Christ was born", "now in this redeeming hour, Jesus Lord, at thy birth". The message was here for us in these huts which next morning, when the magic of the "atmosphere" had worn off, had regained their ugly appearance and out of which we step into the cold winter air on our way to our slave labour, while at home people are going to Christmas services.

23 December 1946

"For us to earth he cometh poor, our redemption to secure." These words kept running through my head with the persistence of a melody during all those long hours when we were sitting locked in a dark cellar, with an uncertain, and possibly a horrible, fate before us. Our former camp had just been closed and twelve of us, separated from the others, had been transported to a new camp. Why had they taken us twelve particularly? We were mostly people who, for one reason or another, were *personae non gratae* to the Russians, and some of us had belonged to a certain detachment of the German Wehrmacht. On our arrival at this camp we were informed that we were to be put in the detention cell and after a few weeks would look

314

as though we could support ourselves on a blade of grass. That was how we spent Christmas. The year before we had gone out to work on Christmas day, full of resentment and showering liberal curses on the Russians who had no respect for our greatest festival. Now, in the darkness, my friend Herbert said to me, "If tomorrow we were able to go out to work with the others, that would be our best Christmas present!" How relative all things are upon earth, how poor we all are in this world! But what is a Christmas present really? Surely it is a token that we remember the gift of the living God who saved us from the hands of death. During the night, to our great surprise and with no further explanation, we were brought up out of the cellar, and then we compared ourselves with the Christmas gift: "I lay in fetters bound, Thou camest to set me free." We had got our longed-for Christmas present. They had changed their minds about us, and we were "allowed" to go out to work with the others on Christmas Eve, to demolish a concrete wall with pick-axes and iron wedges. During the lunch break I sat by the fire with my companions, and using what we had just experienced as an illustration, I explained to them the opening verses of *Vom Himmel hoch* (From Highest Heaven).

24 *December* 1947

The hardest day of all for the P.O.W. to bear was Christmas Day. However, I have been very much moved by some phrases from my mother's last letter, phrases which, as far as I can, I pass on to my friends. "At Christmas all that is difficult in our lives must become not harder but easier: for now we know Him, from Whom all things come and to Whom all things lead, and Who is with us to the end of our days. Without Christmas everything would be unbearably difficult; but at Christmas the heart of the man who hears about Christ becomes not heavier but lighter." Because we had no hymn-books, we followed our custom as for every ordinary service and wrote out plenty of copies of the carols; not one of them sounded as triumphant as the one by Paul Gerhardt, "Come let us worship Christ", . . . "we. who welcome our Salvation, all our sorrows cast away."

315

25 *December* 1948

When on Christmas Eve I went to the hut in which we were holding our service, joined by our Roman Catholic brothers, a young Swabian was leaning against the wall. As I passed, I heard him say pitifully to the man standing beside him: "It's all so meaningless, so senseless!" That was just it; not only our fate but everything in the world was meaningless, and everything in the world, even our fate, would be filled with meaning, the eternal meaning of Christmas, through the "redeeming hour", in which Eternal Life took upon itself the nature of our poverty.

Why did I pass by and leave him there leaning against the wall in despair, instead of inviting him into our service, since he obviously had not got the courage to go by himself? He could probably see no hope for himself in this message, and yet it might have reached out just to this very man; for it concerned him. I have often been able to take action and preach the Word—but on this occasion, limp and weak myself, I passed by on the other side like the priests and the Levite on the road to Jericho. Thinking about it today, I know that herein lies our worst and most frequent failing—that of enjoying the Gospel instead of passing it on, of passing by when a despairing man had lost all faith in the Gospel because he had never really experienced it personally.